ANTHROPOLOGY AND THE NEW GENETICS

The growth of "new genetics" has dramatically increased our understanding of health, diseases and the body. Anthropologists argue that these scientific advances have also had far-reaching social and cultural implications, radically changing our self-understanding and our perception of what it means to be human; that we have become "biomedicalized," fragmented, and commodified – thus redefining our notions of citizenship, social relations, family, and identity. This book shows how anthropology can contribute to and challenge the ways we have come to understand genetic issues. Exploring a range of issues and case studies in human genetic research, it provides an ethnographic "reality-check," arguing that we must look beyond the "gene-centrism" of genetic codes, family trees, and insular populations, to explore their wider cultural, ethical, and philosophical implications. Merging natural and social issues with the real world of medical science, this book will be welcomed by anyone interested in anthropology, sociology, biology, health, and medicine.

Gísli Pálsson is Professor of Anthropology at the University of Iceland, and an Honorary Fellow of the Royal Anthropological Institute. He has published over 100 scholarly articles and twenty books, including *Coastal Economies, Cultural Accounts* (1991), *Nature and Society: Anthropological Perspectives* (1996), *Beyond Boundaries: Understanding, Translation and Anthropological Discourse* (1995), and *Images of Contemporary Iceland* (1996).

NEW DEPARTURES IN ANTHROPOLOGY

New Departures in Anthropology is a book series that focuses on emerging themes in social and cultural anthropology. With original perspectives and syntheses, authors introduce new areas of inquiry in anthropology, explore developments that cross disciplinary boundaries, and weigh in on current debates. Every book illustrates theoretical issues with ethnographic material drawn from current research or classic studies, as well as from literature, memoirs, and other genres of reportage. The aim of the series is to produce books that are accessible enough to be used by college students and instructors, but will also stimulate, provoke, and inform anthropologists at all stages of their careers. Written clearly and concisely, books in the series are designed equally for advanced students and a broader range of readers, inside and outside academic anthropology, who want to be brought up to date on the most exciting developments in the discipline.

Anthropology and the New Genetics

GÍSLI PÁLSSON
University of Iceland

CAMBRIDGE UNIVERSITY PRESS
Cambridge, New York, Melbourne, Madrid, Cape Town, Singapore, São Paulo

Cambridge University Press
The Edinburgh Building, Cambridge CB2 8RU, UK

Published in the United States of America by Cambridge University Press, New York

www.cambridge.org
Information on this title: www.cambridge.org/9780521671743

First published 2007

Printed in the United Kingdom at the University Press, Cambridge

A catalogue record for this publication is available from the British Library

ISBN 978-0-521-85572-3 hardback
ISBN 978-0-521-67174-3 paperback

For my mother, Bára Sigurðardóttir

Contents

Figures and table

Figures

Table

Acknowledgments

Work on this book began during the summer of 2004, following an invitation to the University of Edinburgh under its Northern Scholars Scheme. I thank my hosts Janet Carsten and her colleagues in the Department of Social Anthropology for rich and stimulating discussions on some of the implications of the new genetics. The form of the book owes much to discussions with the editors of the *New Departures in Anthropology* series. I greatly appreciate an early discussion with Jonathan Spencer and the critical reading of the first draft by Olivia Harris and Michael Lambek. Thanks to a part-time position at the University of Oslo from 2002 to 2004, I had the opportunity to engage in sustained dialogue with Norwegian colleagues, notably Signe Howell, Torben Hviid Nielsen, Arne Kalland, Marit Melhus, Aud Talle, Henrik Treimo, and, last but not least, the late Eduardo Archetti. During a lecture trip to Canada in the fall of 2005, at the invitation of the anthropology departments at the universities of Alberta and British Columbia, I had challenging discussions with a number of colleagues about some of the issues presented here. In particular, I would like to thank Mark Nuttall for facilitating my trip and organizing my stay.

I owe a particular debt to Paul Rabinow, one of the pioneers of the subfield of anthropology concerned with the new genetics and its implications, for his hospitality during a sabbatical leave at the University of California at Berkeley in the spring and summer of 2001 when some of the ideas presented here took shape, for his collaboration on issues relating to

Acknowledgments

Icelandic biopolitics, and for his theoretical inspiration. I am also grateful to Kristín E. Harðardóttir, Lecturer in the Department of Anthropology at the University of Iceland. Not only did she co-ordinate in a superbly efficient fashion a research project for which I was responsible, but my work has benefited extensively from her own perceptive observations and analyses. Along with Arnar Árnason and Barbara Prainsack she read the entire manuscript and offered a number of highly useful comments. I thank them all for their observations and effort. Many other colleagues have been of help in one way or another, as collaborators, editors, or commentators, including Anna Birna Almarsdóttir, Nancy Marie Brown, Anne Brydon, Philippe Descola, Paul Durrenberger, Herbert Gottweis, Agnar S. Helgason, Stefan Helmreich, Eric Hirsch, Klaus Hoeyer, Tim Ingold, Linda Hogle, Örn D. Jónsson, Bruno Latour, Susanne Lundin, Benjamin S. Orlove, Hans-Jörg Rheinberger, Ingrid Schneider, Lesley A. Sharp, Halldór Stefánsson, Marilyn Strathern, and Melanie G. Wiber. Research assistant Sigurður Örn Guðbjörnsson traced a number of important references.

Last but not least I acknowledge my debt to both my wife Guðný Guðbjörnsdóttir, whose sober take on the new genetics and ongoing commentaries upon my work helped to keep me on course, and all the practitioners of the new genetics who have shared with me their thoughts and opinions during informal fieldwork and formal interviews. In particular, I appreciate the cooperation of the staff of deCODE genetics – especially Kári Stefánsson, Director, Jeffrey Gulcher, Director of Research, Þorgeir Þorgeirsson, Assistant Director of Research, Unnur Þóra Jökulsdóttir and Eiríkur Sigurðsson, Co-ordinators of Communication, Stefán Einar Stefánsson, Co-ordinator of the osteoarthritis team, and Þórður Kristjánsson, in charge of the company's genealogical database the "Book of Icelanders." Also, I have had useful contact with the staff of Frisk Software, Reykjavík, including Director Friðrik Skúlason and anthropologist Elín Klara Grétarsdóttir Bender.

Acknowledgments

I have reproduced parts of works co-authored with Kristín E. Harðardóttir ("For Whom the Cell Tolls: Debates about Biomedicine," *Current Anthropology*, 2002), Agnar Helgason ("Blonds, Lost and Found: Representations of Genes, Identity, and History," *Developing World Bioethics* 2003), and Paul Rabinow ("Iceland: The Case of a National Human Genome Project," *Anthropology Today*, 1999, and "The Iceland Controversy: Reflections on the Trans-National Market of Civic Virtue," in A. Ong and S. J. Collier (eds.), *Global Assemblages: Technology, Politics, and Ethics as Anthropological Problems*, Blackwell Publishers, 2005). Also, I have drawn upon articles I have previously published: "The Life of Family Trees and the Book of Icelanders," *Medical Anthropology*, 2004, "Decoding Relatedness and Disease: The Icelandic Biogenetic Project," in J.-P. Gaudillére and H.-J. Rheinberger (eds.), *From Molecular Genetics to Genomics: The Mapping Cultures of Twentieth-Century Genetics*, Routledge, 2005, and "Appropriating Family Trees: Genealogies in the Age of Genetics," in F. von Benda-Beckmann, K. Benda-Beckmann, and M. G. Wiber (eds.), *Changing Properties of Property*, Berghahn Books, 2006. The research on which this book is based has been generously supported by several funds and institutions, including the Nordic Committee for Social Science Research (NOS-S), the Icelandic Center for Research, the University of Iceland, and the University of Oslo.

Introduction: "As deep as life itself"

"Aylmer," resumed Georgiana, solemnly, "I know not what may be the cost to both of us to rid me of this fatal birthmark. Perhaps its removal may cause cureless deformity . . ."

"If there be the remotest possibility of it," continued Georgiana, "let the attempt be made at whatever risk . . . You have deep science . . . Cannot you remove this little, little, mark, which I cover with the tips of two small fingers? . . ."

"Noblest, dearest, tenderest wife," cried Aylmer, rapturously, "doubt not my power. . . . I feel myself fully competent to render this dear cheek as faultless as its fellow; and then, most beloved, what will be my triumph when I shall have corrected what Nature left imperfect in her fairest work!"

Nathaniel Hawthorne, The Birthmark, 1843

The great dry fog and deCODE genetics

In 1783, a massive volcanic eruption took place in the Lakagígar area in southeast Iceland. Not only did the ash from the eruption settle on pastures throughout Iceland, it was also carried over great distances, covering the Northern Hemisphere like a large veil. The summer of 1783 was characterized by a phenomenon described by contemporaries as the "great dry fog," in areas as far apart as many countries in Europe, Alaska, Labrador,

Newfoundland, Tunisia, Asia Minor, and possibly China (Demarée and Ogilvie 2001). Icelanders carefully observed the eruption and could hardly fail to see where the ash came from. Meanwhile, continental Europeans remained puzzled, eagerly commenting upon the causes of the fog as well as its implications. For some, it signified the end of the world. In Europe the cause of the great fog remained unknown for months. Scholars and the public at large observed that it correlated with a series of other natural events, including earthquakes, fireballs, climate change, and epidemics, but it was unclear how, if at all, these events were causally related. Later, however, when Danish merchant ships arrived in Copenhagen with the news from Iceland, the larger world learned about the actual nature and origin of the "fog." The local geological events of the Lakagígar had widespread and complex global consequences, climatic and social. Roughly two centuries later, another great dry fog began to spin around Iceland. In 1998, the Icelandic government planned to construct, along with a private company, a national Health Sector Database for the purpose of biomedical research, as part of a larger project combining three kinds of "dry" data (see Gulcher and Stefánsson 2000) – genealogical records since the Middle Ages, medical documents since 1915, and genetic information on modern Icelanders.

Almost overnight, the international press got focused on the story of a tiny nation selling (or giving away) their "Viking" genes to a multinational corporation, deCODE genetics, and its Icelandic subsidiary *Íslensk erfðagreining*. An entourage of observers from all over the world flew in to cover the story – journalists, bioethicists, and scientists of all kinds (see, for instance, Specter 1999, Fortun 2000, Rose 2003). And a whole army of commentators stayed behind, constructing their narrative on the basis of second-hand information, puzzled by this new mysterious fog and upset if not outraged by its potential implications (Chadwick 1999, Lewontin 1999, Greely 2000). This time the news erupted first on Euro-American shores, although Icelandic scholars soon joined the debate (see, for instance, Andersen, Arnason, and Sigurdsson 1999,

Palsson and Thorgeirsson 1999). During the following months and years, a whole series of somewhat similar "biobank" projects were conceived and planned in different parts of the world although they received far less attention. While some of them have collapsed, many others are on course. Winickoff rightly observes that the Icelandic Health Sector Database became an experimental site for geonomics and genomic governance in the sense that it "helped produce the technological, political, and normative terrain of all large-scale genomics initiatives today, not just Iceland's" (2006: 97).

In 1996 deCODE genetics was established by two physicians, the Icelander Kári Stefánsson, a professor at Harvard University, and his collaborator and former student Jeff Gulcher. In company lore, the deCODE idea was conceived over coffee at Starbucks in Boston. The plan was to exploit the relatively homogeneous Icelandic genome and the wealth of local historical records for the purpose of biomedical research. Investors received the idea warmly and soon the company began operations on the outskirts of Reykjavík. While the company operates in Iceland, it was funded by venture-capital funds co-ordinated in the United States. deCODE genetics soon strengthened its financial position through a business arrangement with the pharmaceutical giant Hoffmann-LaRoche. At that time, the company had outlined plans for a national Health Sector Database on Icelanders. The central idea of the database project, and the source of much of the controversy around it, was the assembly of medical records for the entire population. After nine months of national debate, in December 1998 the Icelandic Parliament passed a bill authorizing the construction of the database. The company grew spectacularly during its first six years or so, hiring more and more staff (employing 600 people in 2002). Then came an economic backlash, triggered partly by general trends in biomedicine on the global scene, as a result of which the company was forced to make about one-third of its personnel redundant. In an attempt to make ends meet, the company streamlined its research on patient groups and increasingly moved into drug discovery and development. At the same time, work on the database project slowed down. In 2004, most of the people involved seemed to assume that the project had collapsed, although accounts of the reasons differed. According to some narratives, the "shelving" of the database was due to legal developments (Abbot 2004), but in reality the reasons seem more complex. Despite the apparent collapse of the database project, deCODE genetics has made important advances in genetic research. A recent somewhat generous article in *Time* magazine suggests the "Iceland experiment" has "captured the lead in the genetic revolution" (Lemonick 2006: 50).

The fog persists. Somewhat similar biomedical projects (usually with less comprehensive records but on a far larger scale) have been reported in many other countries, including Australia, Canada, China, Denmark, Estonia, Japan, Newfoundland, Norway, Quebec, Singapore, South Africa, Sweden, Tonga, and the United Kingdom. Despite all the accounts, popular and scholarly, the unfolding events are poorly understood, along with similar events in biomedicine and bioinformatics. Just as the Lakagígar eruption during the *annus mirabilis* of 1783 has potential implications for the understanding of current environmental change – it probably had climatological, oceanographic, and geophysical implications throughout the Northern Hemisphere – the Icelandic Health Sector Database may be seen as an empirical site with potential implications for genomic and medical research elsewhere. Iceland is neither more nor less unique than other database contexts, but it happens to be the site of influential innovations in biomedicine and bioinformatics.

This book seeks, among other things, to ground the debates and developments surrounding the Icelandic database and similar genome projects elsewhere, emphasizing their global connections and the contribution of anthropology to the understanding of contemporary biomedical debates and issues. More generally, the book presents anthropological perspectives on the so-called new genetics, focusing on the development and implications of scientific practices that have enabled the visualizing and mapping of genetic material, in particular the social imaginaries they have both fashioned and been fashioned by. It explores its themes by looking at a diversity of projects associated with research on the human genome, genetic diversity, and biomedicine, emphasizing some of their wider social implications for human relatedness. By necessity, a range of other kinds of ongoing projects that truly deserve no less attention have to be only mentioned in passing or practically ignored. This includes explorations of therepeutic cloning, stem-cell research, new reproductive technologies, and reproductive medicine. Among the projects discussed are biomedical studies of particular patient groups, regional and national biogenetic projects, the human genome projects, and the plan to chart the diversity and history of the species (the Human Genome Diversity Project). All of these projects, and many more, illustrate a growing fascination with the potentials of molecular biology and the complex coupling of biotechnology, informatics, medicine, and the market. And most, if not all, are hotly debated among researchers, a variety of interest groups, and the general public. The key issues discussed here, in fact, have been widely discussed for some years throughout the world. Public interest in them is unlikely to wane, given the growing importance of biotechnology and biomedicine and the social and ethical concerns often associated with the new genetics.

Based on my research for the last decade or so, the book draws upon my reading of pertinent literature in anthropology, the social sciences, science studies, the humanities, and human genetics, domestic and international media material, as well as my ethnographic fieldwork in Iceland. While recognizing the successes of the new genetics and its potential contributions to human well-being and our understanding of the history of the species, it is argued, the larger implications of human genetics and the gene centrism on which it is based need to be thoroughly explored. In order to understand "epigenetic" interactions in the constitution of life – the unity of genes, organism, and environment – students of human development, relatedness, history, and diversity need to move beyond both the dualism of nature and society and the languages of genetic codes, family trees, and insular populations.

The new genetics

A few basic observations on the development and conceptual framework of the new genetics are in order to give the newcomer an absolutely minimal idea of an extremely complex terrain and development. At the same time they serve to provide a background for the following discussion of gene hunting, biogenetic projects, and the study of human genetic variation (for detailed introductions to molecular biology and its manifold uses, see, for instance, Krude 2004, Watson 2004). This is necessary, moreover, to appreciate theoretical attempts to move beyond the simple language and determinism of genetic codes. To underline more complex mutual interactions in the constitution of life, a growing number of scholars representing a variety of disciplines are operating with the notion of epigenetics (Neumann-Held and Rehmann-Sutter 2006). Given such a perspective, development and evolution are co-operative projects rather than the monologues of genetic codes and adaptive pressures. The tension between this theoretical perspective, I suggest, and the successes of reductionist molecular biological methods deserves particular scrutiny.

Biological understanding of the nature of inheritance seems to take a great leap forward every half a century or so. In 1900, three men, Carl Correns, Erich von Tschermak, and Hugo De Vries, rediscovered Mendel's laws of inheritance, thereby paving the way for modern genetics (the term "genetics" was coined by William Bateson in 1906 and three years later the term "gene" was introduced by Wilhelm Johannsen). Then by the middle of the twentieth century, a series of critical insights, experiments, and measurements developed by Francis Crick, Rosalind Franklin, James Watson, and Maurice Wilkins and some others mainly at King's College London and the Cavendish Laboratory in Cambridge led to the discovery

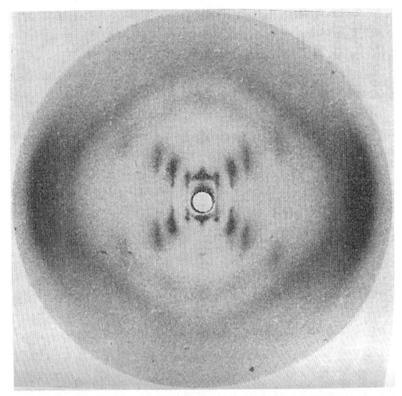

FIGURE 1.1 Rosalind Franklin's Photograph 51 of the B form of DNA

in the spring of 1953 of the double helix of DNA, revealing at last the mechanisms of inheritance, the "secret of life." Key developments were Franklin's calculations and X-ray images, including Photograph 51 of the B form of DNA taken between 1 and 2 March 1952 (see Figure 1.1). Franklin's photograph had a strong impact on its own as it was the clearest picture ever taken of a DNA molecule, with a stark x radiating from the middle and blank spaces between the arms of the x. To some of the key players in the discovery of the structure of DNA it immediately suggested the molecule was a helix (see, for example, Maddox 2002). In Watson's own words (2004: 50): "The X-ray pattern of this B form was a distinct cross . . . DNA had to be a helix!" Gradually, the image has achieved an iconic status along with that of the three-dimensional helix itself (Nelkin and Lindee 1995, Keller 1996, Klug 2004).

Finally, in 2000, the first draft of a map of the human genome was announced. On that occasion, the journal *Nature* triumphantly published a poster, "The geography of our genome" (see Figure 1.2). *Nature* underlined its cartographic language by inviting its readers on a tour into the "universe within" with the following grand statement:

Since ancient times we have drawn charts of the sky, of the world, and of our anatomy. Today, a new chart is added to the collection: The map of our genome. Its purpose is to synthesize the insights and meaning gained from the sequence of the human genome. We invite you on a tour of the geography of the genome, exploring the chromosomes, the sequence, and the differences between individuals and populations. The integration of these exciting new findings ushers in a new era of scientific and medical progress.

Intensive research over the past decades has revealed what practitioners of the new genetics would take as the elementary structures of the universe within and the geography of the genome. Each organism, in their language, possesses a *genome* that contains instructions necessary for constructing and maintaining a living example of that organism. Most genomes, including that of humans, are made of *DNA*, polymeric molecules (deoxyribonucleic acid) made up of chains of subunits called *nucleotides*. The iconic double helix of DNA is built up of four kinds of subunits, the chemical bases of A, G, C, T – adenine, guanine, cytosine, and thymine. The human genome, a copy of which is contained in practically every cell in the adult human body, has two parts: the *nuclear genome* encompassing approximately 3.2 billion nucleotides, divided into 24 linear molecules (chromosomes), and the *mitochondrial genome* (mtDNA), a circular DNA molecule of 16,569 nucleotides. *Genes* are seen as the most important part of the genome thanks to the biological information they contain. In humans, genes are unevenly distributed

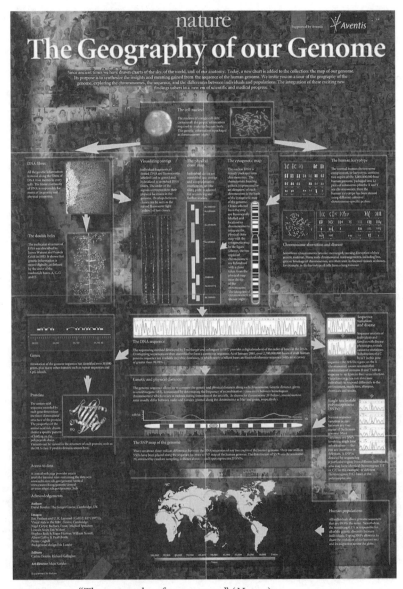

FIGURE 1.2 "The geography of our genome" (*Nature*)

on chromosomes, clustered at particular sites. Most of them encode one or more protein molecules, with RNA (ribonucleic acid, called *messenger* or *mRNA*) operating as an intermediary between genes and their protein products. Only a fraction of the genome (about 2 percent) is reported to encode for proteins; the rest is usually referred to as "junk," although such a terminology is increasingly being qualified.

Now that the structure of the human genome is being established in the wake of the human genome projects and associated advances in sequencing, computing, and bioinformatics (International Human Genome Sequencing Consortium 2004), the genes that it contains and their "functions" and activities are surveyed and studied in detail. This is more complex and ardous, however, than it may sound. The genome projects produced an enormously complex landscape of over 2.6 billion base pairs of sequence and between 30,000 and 40,000 genes, far fewer genes, though, than originally anticipated by the architects of the projects. To provide a sense of the scale of the genomic enterprise, popular and scientific accounts have often referred to geographical distances and numbers of books. The entire sequence in the "genomic alphabet," it is reckoned, would stretch thousands of kilometers and fill thousands of books.

Humans obviously differ from one another as each individual, with the possible exception of "identical" (monozygotic) twins, is biologically unique (for some recent works on twins and identity, see Prainsack and Spector 2006, Davis and Davis 2007). Any two humans, it is generally estimated, differ on average by approximately 0.1 percent of nucleotide sites or one variant per 1,000 DNA bases. Sites in the sequence where people differ at a single DNA base are referred to as single nucleotide polymorphisms or SNPs (pronounced "snips"). The exploration of genetic variation is made easier by the fact that sets of SNPs on the same chromosome are inherited in chunks, as so-called "haplotype blocks" or "DNA neighborhoods." To hunt for genes by exploring the immense expanse of SNPs in the genome would be a daunting task, working from a list of at least 10 million SNPs. Mapping the haplotype blocks provides a highly convenient shortcut. A leader in this field is the International Haplotype Map Project (in short, the "HapMap Project") that has focused on four populations with ancestry from parts of Africa, Asia, and Europe (The International HapMap Consortium 2005). The mapping of SNPs, it is argued, is a platform on which the understanding of what makes some people susceptible to common diseases will be built.

The nuclear family has proved to be a useful unit in the study of monogenic disorders that clearly follow "Mendelian" lines, "running" in families. Many common diseases, however, are "polygenic," skipping generations, and, moreover, the result of complex human–environmental interactions. To understand their complexity and sporadic nature, more information is needed. One avenue is that of "linkage" analysis adopted by deCODE genetics and many other companies and research teams. Here, the road to identifying the underlying cause of pathology draws upon the tendency of genes to be inherited together as a result of physical proximity on a single chromosome. Family-based linkage studies of patient groups will, no doubt, remain important in gene hunting. However, large-scale genetic databases and population-based association studies will probably play an increasing role in the future. Already, the HapMap project, with its database of common variation in the human genome, is changing the scene, paving the way for a new dimension in the exploration of inherited genetic variation, its role in human disease, and the development of appropriate medicine. All of these approaches (and some more) – their combination, scientific basis, relative practical merits, conceptual frameworks, social implications, etc. – have been extensively discussed in the biomedical literature (see, for instance, Brown 2002).

Anthropologists and social scientists of all kinds have actively participated in discussions of the implications of the new genetics. No doubt, in doing so they have helped to flesh out some of the pressing issues of the genome era, observing and analyzing at the same time ongoing developments in different contexts from a broad range of perspectives. For anthropology, however, the new genetics is not only a critical site, it also allows for new opportunities in the exploration of human evolution and history, significantly expanding the discipline's knowledge and databases and raising new questions about who we are. While the exploration of individual differences is both a valid and important academic exercise, it is necessarily more politically and ethically charged than, say, the study of archeological remains and language change. Therefore, studies of human history and variation need to be carried out with extra sensitivity and care. For understanding human differences, as we will see, it is best to relax dichotomies that radically separate science and society (Gannett 2004). To denounce subjectivity is to go back to early notions of mechanical objectivity or, alternatively, to give up empirical work altogether, thereby relegating perennial issues of how we differ from one another and how to understand "race" and evolution to those who think they already know all the answers and the narratives worth telling.

The frequent reference in this book to the "new genetics" demands some discussion and explication. While the term is often used in academic discourse, it probably means different things to different authors. Is it, perhaps, confusing rather than illuminating? Any division of the continuity of history into epochs, ages, or times is necessarily somewhat problematic, however long or short the periods may be, as each period is bound to contain some of the strands of both earlier and later ones, given the continuous flow of time. And, indeed, no periodization is immune to or unaffected by the critical discourse of historiography. Nevertheless, professional historians find it useful to refer to notions such as the Neolithic, the Renaissance, the Middle Ages, High Modernity and, likewise, lay historians and the public frequently find it useful to refer to the time before or after some significant event in their lives – World War II, the Holocaust, 1968, 9/11. For me, the age of the "new genetics" above all arrived with the visualizing and mapping of genetic material, what molecular biologists refer to as the universe within. Given such a definition, the new genetics began with the imagery that sparked, along with a series of other conceptual and technical innovations, the discovery of the double helix. In this view, the new genetics matured or culminated with the drafting of the map of the human genome at the turn of the century. For some people, the new genetics may signify something else, the geneticization of kinship, the hegemony of genetic determinism in contemporary discourse, and genetic testing. I see no good reason why the term should not be defined in several ways, depending on the pragmatic motives of the user and the task at hand. If the vagueness and multiple meaning of the "gene" concept is acceptable, if not essential to the practices and successes of geneticists and molecular biologists (Rheinberger 2000), as central as the concept has been for more than a century of bioscience, why would one want to stabilize or to abandon a term such as the "new genetics"?

Leaving aside the issues of periodization, labels, and boundaries, what, if anything, might be "new" in the era of the new genetics? This, in a sense, is the focus of this book. One important development is that of globalization; genome research and industries, as Thacker emphasizes (2005), are inherently global phenomena. The new genetics, I suggest, with its biological gaze and its social imaginary, is refashioning some of the central ideas of our times, including those of belonging, kinship, property, governance, the good life, individualism, and race. The implications of the new genetics, however, are by no means self-evident. One of the contradictions of the era is that despite the genetic determinism that in many contexts has reinforced earlier discourses on biology as destiny the issue of race has often disappeared. Nor is the making of our times a one-dimensional process. While the prominence of genetics in many fields, including medicine and agriculture, have "geneticized" our worldview, existing ideas and practices have also shaped the new genetics. Extending the Marxian notion about the language of bourgeois economics being the "folk" theory of the political economy in which it was embedded, Sahlins suggested that people "seem unable to escape from . . . perpetual movement, back and forth between the culturalization of nature and the naturalization of culture" (1977: 105). Sahlins's early commentary, I think, on the development of sociobiology and its "New Synthesis" is still pertinent. In particular, as we will see, the concept of "population," a central construct in human genetics and biological anthropology, is necessarily embedded in the pragmatic context in which it is used.

Fieldwork: getting involved

How did I arrive at this work site, the new genetics, deCODE genetics, and human genome research? My interests, in fact, developed from several directions. For years I had been studying various aspects of fishing and the environment. Above all, I had examined the commodification of fishing rights (particularly the *de facto* privatization of fishing stocks in terms of so-called individual transferable quotas), the practice of fisheries science and management, and the nature of fishing skills, including the issues of practical enskilment of fishers and the so-called "skipper effect" I explored through collaboration with E. Paul Durrenberger. These interests associated with the high seas and "the environment" somewhat surprisingly easily translated into a concern with gene "pools" and the human body, with gene hunting and biopolitics. If it had not been for two unrelated developments, however, that translation would probably not have occurred: For one thing, my work on fishing skills took me into the commodification and phenomenology of the body. Before I knew, I was organizing and teaching a course in Reykjavík on the anthropology of the body, a course that proved to be as educational to me as to my undergraduate students. At the same time, Iceland became the site of complex and controversial biomedical events as deCODE genetics battled for its plan to construct the Health Sector Database on Icelanders. I decided to turn my gaze to the new genetics. I began by exploring the specifics of the Icelandic context, but later on my interests were focused on other apparently similar cases, genome projects in general, and the new genetics.

My early take on the issue of the database project partly developed through collaboration with Paul Rabinow. Rabinow and I shared an interest in ongoing developments on the Icelandic scene and together and separately we conducted extensive interviews with some of the key players in the debate about deCODE genetics and the database. Later on, I extended my study to media representation and, together with Kristín Harðardóttir, I systematically explored Icelandic media material (Pálsson and Harðardóttir 2002). At the same time, I embarked on ethnographic fieldwork within deCODE genetics. I sent a memo to the director, Kári Stefánsson, outlining in fairly general terms the themes I wanted to explore and the goals of my research. Stefánsson seemed to appreciate that an anthropologist proposed to witness at close range what was going on, at a time when his company and the database project were being attacked domestically and internationally by a whole army of academics who usually based their analyses on either second-hand accounts or extremely brief field trips. I made it clear that while I would present my eventual writings on the Icelandic scene to company officials prior to publication I would not accept any editorial strings.

After some weeks of deliberations, I was given a magnetic security card, which provided me with access to the company's premises, and the permission to more or less "do what I wanted." From January 2000, I conducted a series of interviews with deCODE staff, following the work process from beginning to end, from research design, blood donations, and patient-group research to DNA analyses, statistical testing, and publishing. After consulting with deCODE officials, I began to focus on a particular research team working on osteoarthritis. For a few months, I would interview the participants, some of them repeatedly, sit in on team meetings, and just "hang around." The chief purpose of such a focus was to try to understand the practical world of gene hunting and how it was shaped by the framework of the company and the international context to which it belonged. My primary research interests at this point had far less to do with controversial issues relating to the database project than the perceptions, practices, and politics of the laboratory.

During and after fieldwork, I attended several interdisciplinary conferences on biotechnology, sometimes presenting my observations and tentative analyses of the concept of the Icelandic Health Sector Database and the anthropological issues I had put my finger on. This proved to be a useful extension of my fieldwork as it brought me into contact with other sites, contexts, and perspectives. After all, the fog that surrounded the deCODE saga only partially unfolded in Iceland. Also, during and after fieldwork I was frequently interviewed by foreign journalists who arrived on the scene to present ongoing events. These interviews often provided me with illuminating insights into how the local scene was perceived in the international context, the questions that emerged, and the ways in which the key issues were framed, defined, and compared with those of other contexts. This time the merchant ships arrived in great number, traveling almost with the speed of light.

Some of the journalists in question approached me through contact with deCODE genetics. No doubt, deCODE staff somehow attended to the messages I was conveying at meetings, during interviews, and in my papers. Company officials must have assumed that it was relatively safe to recommend me as a commentator, possibly even useful for their cause in a raging media battle on images and representation. While I sometimes wandered and worried that my work was being transformed into an (unpaid) public relations job for the company I was exploring, I was both curious to see how information and perspectives traveled back and forth in the global world of the media and eager to present what I saw as more nuanced perspectives on the local scene than were usually available in the media, a "thick" description in anthropological terms. Often the journalists, however, turned out to be more interested in normative and political judgments (about, for instance, informed consent and security targets in relation to the storing and use of personal information on health and genetic characteristics) than reflective accounts of what was happening and why and how events in Iceland both resembled and differed from those taking place elsewhere.[1]

Obviously, my relationship with deCODE genetics was complex. I was very well aware of the fact that my roles *vis-à-vis* the company might be contradictory and that by working "inside" with the osteoarthritis team I risked losing an "objective" sense of what was going on, forgoing my liberty to spell out what I might eventually discover, as well as my rights and responsibilities as a citizen to pass judgment on right and wrong. Such complications, which I take to be essential to fieldwork, were somewhat enhanced by the particular context involved. Iceland, it needs to be emphasized, is quite a small community where people tend to be involved in tight and complex networks of relationships that in larger communities are likely to be spread out and compartmentalized. This is illustrated by my fieldwork situation. Not only was I a native, part of the academic context and the Icelandic community to which it belonged, I also personally knew many of the players in the heated debate on the database issue. Such complexities, it may be argued, easily get messy. While they may get exaggerated in the Icelandic context, particularly in the midst of a polemic debate such as the one on the Health Sector Database, they are quite common to the ethnographic enterprise ever since Malinowski's work in the Trobriand Islands. The fieldwork gaze is never from outer space and "participant observation" necessarily suggests some kind of involvement.

Fieldwork, nevertheless, has changed in terms of method, context, and subject matter. Critical examination of methods and practices, and the crises it provokes at times, have been recurring events within

---

[1] When pressed for my own "position," I suggested it was mixed. On the one hand, I pointed out, at the time the database issue emerged I had signed a public statement, along with ninety-nine other Icelandic academics, warning against the potential impact of the first bill for the Health Sector Database on academic freedom and competition. On the other hand, I had not, unlike most of the critics of deCODE genetics and the database project, requested that information on me be withdrawn from the eventual database.

anthropology (Pálsson and Rabinow 1999). A decade or two after decolonization of the major European powers, anthropology (the "child of colonialism" as it was later dubbed) was subject to intense criticism because of its presumed preoccupation with isolated, timeless tribal societies. Anthropology, some of the critics argued, was a discipline fatefully shaped by the forces of the past and the power of the dominant. Peter Worsley, in a far-sighted article published in 1966 entitled "The end of anthropology?," questioned whether anthropology had any future at all (see Asad 1973: 9). In his reasoning, with the dissolution of the colonial regime and the political independence of "third world" countries, the context of most anthropological field research at the time, the discipline was fated to wither away. Decolonization meant there was no longer an ethnographic object, an Other to be perused by detached and distant observers; there was no longer a fundamental division between the West and "the rest." In short, anthropology had become obsolete. History proved Worsley to be both right and wrong. He was wrong in seeing this condition as inevitably leading to the end of the discipline. Unexpectedly, ethnography and anthropology have been thriving during the last decades in many places. The critique of the Western obsession with the Other and anthropology's "fatal" involvement with the colonial project has given way to a more pragmatic and forward-looking exploration of the conditions for a destabilized and pluralized world anthropology; thus Restrepo and Escobar call for "other anthropologies and anthropology otherwise" (2005). Worsley was right, on the other hand, that the then standard ethnographic practice has become increasingly archaic. If the classical notions of rapport and translation, the products of colonial contexts and dualistic worldviews, have always been suspect, they increasingly sound obsolete in the contemporary world. Many anthropologists are moving from a relationship of collaboration with a particular site to even more ambiguous and complicated positions in multi-sited contexts. This is illustrated by contemporary studies of science and biomedicine, including my own. Marcus's discussion (1998) of the notion of "complicity" is useful for presenting the changing conditions of anthropological practice. His use of complicity is fueled by the tension between the "dark" connotation of the term (of partnership in evil action) and the more positive sense of a "state of being complex and involved." The point is not to refuse to get involved but to be open about one's involvements, thereby facilitating "situated accounts," in Haraway's sense (1988) – amplifying, not undermining, the objectivity of our accounts.

Fieldwork often entails moving from one site to another, engaging in different kinds of relations. Not only does such an approach invite different commitments which often turn out to be both contradictory and ethically ambiguous, it also poses a challenge to traditional notions of representation: "The sense of the object of study being 'here and there' has begun to wreak production havoc on the 'being there' of classic ethnographic authority" (Marcus 1998: 117). Even though the focus on a particular site of fieldwork may remain, now the emphasis is on a different kind of knowledge, for which metaphors of insideness, translation, and cultural boundaries may no longer be appropriate. The basic condition, Marcus suggests, that makes complicity a more appropriate figure than rapport is a particular kind of awareness:

an awareness of existential doubleness on the part of *both* anthropologist and subject; this derives from having a sense of being *here* where major transformations are under way that are tied to things happening simultaneously *elsewhere*, but not having a certainty or authoritative representation of what those connections are. (Marcus 1998: 118)

Rather than seeing the anthropologist as a privileged cosmopolitan outsider who only temporarily indulges in local life, one of the defining characteristics of contemporary fieldwork is the fact that both anthropologist and informant are acutely aware of other contexts, anxious to make sense of how they relate to each other and what they mean (Rabinow 1999: 169–171).

The challenges of anthropology

Three key arguments are common to most of the chapters of the book. One relates to the importance of ethnography in discussions of the implications of the new genetics. It is often argued nowadays that due to the advances of biotechnology, including new biomedical and reproductive technologies, "life is outrunning the pedagogies in which we have been trained" (Fischer 2003: 37), in the sense that traditional standards and moralities no longer seem to work. In this context, anthropology has an important role to play. One of its challenges, I shall argue, following Kleinman (1995), Fischer (2003), and some others, is to provide an ethnographic "reality check" about what is actually going on, against both the politics of mainstream bioethics and the hype of the technicians. Anthropologists have just begun to study some of the issues involved, partly as a result of a general and growing interest in various aspects of the human body. An important task for anthropologists – following recent works on the medicalization of kinship, imagined genetic communities, and the phenomenology of relatedness – is to explore the way in which people experience the new genetics and how it may inform particular notions of identity, relatedness, and citizenship. Recent developments are characterized by, among other things, radical re-evaluation of existing notions of kinship connections and personhood and what it means to be human (Hayles 1999, Carsten 2004). While the body is often represented as a bounded space resistant to invasion and commodification, cultural responses exhibit considerable cultural and historical diversity. The nature and implications of biotechnology and genome projects, therefore, need to be carefully explored. Here, anthropology has a crucial role to play, sensitive as it is to particular sites and everyday experience. What each of us makes of the "facts" of genomics and biomedicine is an empirical question that needs systematic attention.

Secondly, I emphasize the importance of giving theoretical priority to relations and processes rather than to codes and substance. The new genetics has obviously advanced understanding of health, diseases, and human history and differences. These advances – and the practices and perspectives of the researchers involved – are anthropologically interesting in their own right. For one thing, the central assumptions of the new genetics – about the "book of life" and the nature and relative importance of substance, relations, and environment (Kay 2000) – need to be critically examined. Such an examination is already taking place across the broad spectrum of the life sciences and the humanities, including anthropology. In the relational thinking of Oyama (2000 [1985]), Lewontin (1995), Griffiths and Gray (1998), Ingold (2000), Jablonka and Lamb (2005), and some others, genes, organisms, and environment are reciprocally constituted.

Related to this is the issue of how to represent relationships. One of the themes throughout the book is the heavy reliance of the new genetics on metaphors, as if they were the only means available. There seems to be a limited number of alternatives, namely the core metaphors of trees and islands. Other competing metaphors, including the one of rhizomes, seem more difficult to grasp visually. Modern gene talk draws partly upon the genealogical view of the world that emerged in Europe during the Middle Ages, a view that drew upon the metaphor of common "roots" of different groups and nations. With the new genetics, the classical family tree has been transformed into an abstract diagram. The end result of such diagrams is usually to underline deterministic and essentialist classification: ethnic, gendered, national, or racial. Personhood simply emerges with the vertical passing on of substance from one generation to another. On the other hand, traditional notions of human relatedness seem to be undergoing a "lateral" shift, somewhat along the lines of relational thinking, qualifying and undermining the "vertical" determinism of contemporary discourses on genetics and relatedness. Indeed, recently the paradigmatic family tree has been challenged from several directions: a variety of ethnographic accounts of cultural concepts of substance and materiality and widespread practices of adoption and fostering. Quite appropriately, I suggest, the web of kin is increasingly digitally explored on the Worldwide Web where everything is potentially interconnected with everything else. As Hanson observes (2004), the introduction of the automated mode of information management suggests a "new superorganic," an extended notion of agency that takes artificial intelligence into account.

During the last decade or two, advances in molecular genetics have paved the way for increasingly powerful analyses of genealogical relationships. In many labs around the world, genealogical relationships are being explored in an attempt to reconstruct the history of our species, human populations, and fellow primates. No doubt, gene hunting is already making its impact on notions of human diversity, including issues of "race" (Wade 2002, Moore, Kosek, and Pandian 2003). Yet, the implications are by no means obvious. Important questions on the anthropological agenda relate to research practices, in particular the potential implications of human genetic research for the construction of imagined genetic communities, the building of social relations and identities on the basis of assumed, shared biological inheritance. While differences between human populations in terms of DNA seem to be minimal, this does not necessarily undermine ideologies of racial essences and divisions. Likewise, while humans seem to share much of their DNA with other primates and "lower" organisms, a general empathy for living things, biophilia, is not necessarily on the agenda.

Finally, the book underlines the value of resuming the philosophical anthropological project. A comparative perspective, I suggest, is essential for understanding the larger implications of the new genetics. Somewhat surprisingly, many of the Euro-American developments involved provide insights into Melanesian processes and concepts emphasizing fragmented, "dividual" personhood (Strathern 1992), and, likewise, the Melanesian world offers an unexpected commentary on the "West" (Bamford 2004). Anthropology has much to offer on this score not only because its comparative perspective poses a challenge to universalistic thinking but also because it has always, in one way or another, addressed humans as both natural and social beings. With the progressive challenge to dualist thinking in the current age and the conflation of the natural and the social in the real world of biomedicine and bioinformatics, the classic philosophical anthropological project seems more important than ever. The fracturing of anthropology (the dualistic structure of anthropology in Europe and some other contexts and the disintegration of the "four-field" approach typical for North America) will be overcome only when social anthropologists learn more biology and biological anthropologists learn more social anthropology: "Both camps must come to see that in order to understand the knowledge they are producing they must themselves become more fully anthropological in the broadest sense of the term. Such a vision is neither nostalgic nor utopian" (Pálsson and Rabinow 1999: 18).

Michel Foucault attempted to demonstrate in *The Order of Things* that the very figure of "Man" was a historically situated discursive invention less than 200 years old, not a millenial fact that anthropology simply took up as its object of study. Foucault famously concluded his book by wondering if the discursive arrangements involved were to disappear then one could "certainly wager that man would be erased, like a face drawn in sand at the edge of the sea" (1970: 387). Given the Foucauldian metaphor of the drawing and erasure of the face of "Man" on the tidal coast, we may, for our anthropological contemporary, see the sand as population genetics and the sea as the tide of genomics. Does current uncertainty, then, about what constitutes life, a species, the human etc., undermine the relevance of the discipline? Or will the growing anxieties surrounding these matters make anthropology even more vital and central than ever before? Anthropology, I suggest, should, almost by definition, take a central place in thinking through what it means to be human today.

Different chapters of the book develop a series of arguments as the discussion progresses from the laboratory to the global context and their interconnections, from micro to macro and back, underlining the importance of ethnographic studies of what Tsing calls (2005: 3) "the productive friction of global connections." In Chapter 2, I discuss the use of mapping in human genetic research and modern biotechnology, focusing on the context, skills, and flow of laboratory research at deCODE genetics in its exploration of the genetics of common human diseases. That chapter also provides a brief background to the "new genetics," emphasizing both the potentials and limits of gene centrism. Chapter 3 discusses changing conceptions of kinship in the wake of the DNA revolution, focusing on the digitalization and visualization of family histories and their use in biomedical projects and for the searching of "roots." Digital genealogies such as the "Book of Icelanders" constructed by Frisk Software and deCODE genetics, I suggest, can be regarded as machines establishing and generating connections and relationships, advancing the search for the genetic causes of diseases and the governing of the national "body." The use of genealogical databanks and the relevant search engines on the web invite new questions on relatedness, the visual representation and communication of belonging, and the rules of access and ownership.

Moving from the laboratory to larger contexts, Chapter 4 explores the structures and histories of large-scale biomedical collections combining genetic, medical, and genealogical information. A comparison of seven cases reveals different ambitions, rhetoric, scales, and designs. While these national, regional, or ethnic projects differ in several respects – in terms of purpose and property arrangements, for example – they all represent the radical extension of the medical gaze to the human genome, a concern with the monitoring and governance of a population. Chapter 5 discusses public debates about such projects, comparing domestic and international representations of different databases emphasizing the notion of moral landscapes. In addition, this chapter discusses the role of bioethics, emphasizing its global connections and institutionalization through an analysis of debates on the Icelandic case, situating different voices in the debate, including those of biologists, ethicists, and physicians. While bioethical studies have been indispensable, it is important to take a critical look at them. Following Hunt (1999) and some others I suggest it is essential to seek "sociological distance" from bioethical controversies by providing a historical perspective and by employing a comparative approach. This allows for a Foucauldian perspective, emphasizing the ways in which "ethical problems" are constructed and placed on the public agenda rather than taking them as givens.

Chapter 6 extends the horizon beyond both individual laboratories working on particular patient groups and national genome projects to the general exploration of the genome of the species. The discussion emphasizes the "Genome War" associated with the Human Genome Project (HGP), global inequalities, and the property debates surrounding genome projects, examining the kinds of regimes that are emerging with respect to genetic material and information and the extent to which they are informed by the specific properties of the "resources" involved. Rather than focus on establishing what genomic property "is," anthropologists should focus on the ethnographic description and analysis of the "work" the property concept does (see Humphrey and Verdery 2004). Chapter 7 explores the implications of the new genetics for the understanding of human differences and history, in particular the framing of "race," the assumptions and driving forces behind diversity projects as well as the debates and issues they have generated. The new genetics, I argue, has shifted the conceptual ground for discussions of human variation but, on the other hand, the notion of racial difference keeps being reinvented. While the human genome diversity projects got into trouble, partly due to opposition from "indigenous" groups, some have struggled on and, moreover, smaller projects on particular populations are being carried out. These projects, it will be argued, raise important questions about the history of the species, anthropological practice, the notions of "population" and imagined genetic communities. At the same time, they play an increasing role in the exploration of the genetic background of common diseases. Anthropology is likely to be actively involved in this enterprise, keeping in mind its knowledge and understanding of human variation and history.

Finally, the concluding chapter sums up the arguments and analyses developed in previous chapters. At the same time it highlights some related themes in the rethinking of anthropology and related fields in the wake of the new genetics, the metaphors of trees and mapping, the nature–society divide, the duality of the anthropological enterprise (physical-biological and social-cultural), the compartmentalization of the so-called hard sciences, the social sciences, and the humanities, the implications of biogenetic projects for discussions of substance and heritage, and the contribution of anthropology to the understanding of relatedness, genome projects, and, more generally, the genome era.

For long, the human body has been silenced in social thought; either it has been thoroughly marginalized under the constructivist banner of the social sciences and the humanities or it has been subjected to the reductionist gaze of the biological sciences. More recently, the body has been seriously addressed from several perspectives, many of which can be summed up by the term of "embodiment." One may wonder why this is the case and if such a state of affairs is likely to stay. To explain the rapid upsurge in anthropological interest in the body in the 1980s, Martin (1992) drew upon Lévi-Strauss's argument about the fascination with the disappearing primitive; just as the category of the primitive seemed to fade away or prepare for departure, as a result of radical shifts in geopolitics, it seemed to demand anthropological scrutiny and attention. Similarly, Martin suggested, the recent interest in the body signified its disappearance, "a dramatic transition in body percept and practice . . . the end of one kind of body and the beginning of another" (Martin 1992: 121). Could it be that a new kind of body is in the making along with the new genetics, with new kinds of objectifications and subjectivities?

In the genome era, the human body has been progressively reimagined. For one thing, in many contexts people have increasingly identified with their bodies, appreciating the fact that they both have and *are* bodies. A whole range of disciplines and subfields have questioned the Cartesian divide of nature and culture. As Herzfeld remarks, the contribution from medical anthropology is "potentially perhaps the most radical, because this field tackles the Cartesian paradigm *at source – in the body itself*" (2001: 242, emphasis added). The anthropology of the body, in a very real sense, represents anthropology at home, or better still, anthropology *completely* at home. Not only have classic dualisms been challenged, the drafting and mapping of the human genome invite unprecedented fragmenting and commodification of the body. At the heart of debates on human genetic material is the atomization of the body, "raising questions about how increasingly minuscule human parts may still embody persons" (Sharp 2000: 309). For Euro-Americans in the age of genomics and biomedicine, trafficking in body parts, genetic material, and dispersed identities is increasingly a bare fact of life. Thanks to these developments, each of us has, to some extent, been reduced to a perpetual patient, a carrier of potentially faulty genes, a bearer of birthmarks.

Many of the issues discussed in the book indeed evoke the idiom of the birthmark. Like genetic "fingerprints," birthmarks are usually seen to be outside history, given from the start, although they often appear and develop after birth. While in the standard dictionary definition, a "birthmark" is "a mark or stain existing on the body from birth," the term is also used more positively in reference to "beauty spots" or "hallmarks"; birthmarks, in fact, can easily become symbols of pride, individuality, protection, and the sacred, much like tattoos (Gell 1993). The same ambiguity holds for genetic signatures, "good" and "bad." These themes are explored in classical literature and visual arts focusing, in one way or another, on birthmarks. Thus, a birthmark plays a central role in one of the short stories of the Russian writer Mikhail Sholokhov (1975). The key character of the story, Squadron Commander Nikolai, is said to have "a love of horses, boundless valor, and a mole like his father's, on the left leg just above the ankle, as big as a pigeon's egg" (1975: 8). These characteristics he inherited from a soldier who disappeared in a war against the Germans when Nikolai was a young boy. The mole is seen as a good thing. A military commissar comments: "'You're l-l-lucky, you know. They say a mole is a sign of l-l-luck'" (1975: 9). In the ensuing story, however, the mole brings particularly sad news. In the civil war between the Red Army and their opponents, Nikolai and his father unknowingly chose opposite camps and eventually shoot at each other. Nikolai is fatally wounded and his killer observes: "Just above the ankle he saw a mole as big as a pigeon's egg. Slowly, as though afraid to waken the lad, he turned the cold face towards him, soaking his hands in the blood that foamed from the mouth. He stared hard for a moment and only then did he seize the angular shoulders in an awkward embrace. 'Son! . . .' he said dully. 'My Nikolai! . . . My own flesh and blood!'" (1975: 19).

While practically everyone has one or more birthmarks, the reading of such bodily inscriptions varies from one context to another. Among the Australian Aborigines who call themselves *Yapa* or *Warlpiri*, a birthmark is referred to as *kuruwarri*, a complex term also denoting mark, trace, ancestral essence, and freckle. As Biddle points out (2001), *kuruwarri* is much more than an inscription or decoration of the surface of the body, through its constitutive force, *kuruwarri* rejuvenates the species, controlling fertility, regulating social relations, and causing illness:

kuruwaaru are embodied traces and imprints. Indeed, they provide a necessary material intercorporeal means for linking Ancestral bodies to *Yapa* bodies in crucial ways. It is not only in the country itself that Ancestral presence resides, but these presences . . . can enter women's wombs, cause conception and, in turn, leave birthmarks, freckles and other identifying traits of specific kinds of subjectivity upon individuated Warlpiri. . . . (2001: 180)

For some, birthmarks represent both a direct link to the past, the ancestors, and the identity of the unique individual, much like the modern notion of genetic barcodes or fingerprints. The markings of the skin, one may add, are not just metaphors for the signatures explored by the new genetics. Not only was the skin the original arena for microbiology, its workings and contours being revealed to the naked eye by the new optics, also skin markings, "especially when they are associated with disease have the flagrancy of the blatant; they blurt out what the tongue might prefer to keep decently veiled" (Connor 2004: 96).

In many societies, birthmarks are seen to indicate that one person is the reincarnation of another. The ethnographic record refers to a number of claims or cases of striking correspondence between birthmarks on a newborn and a body signal on a deceased person, a wound, scar, or lesion. This applies to several North Amerindian cases (including Huron, Iroquois, and Algonquins) as well as to Sri Lanka, Turkey, Lebanon, Nigeria, Thailand, and Burma. Mills remarks (1994: 213) for an Amerindian context that birthmarks are the most visible evidence of previous life identity:

"they have to have the signs [birthmarks] so we can know them when they come back," an elderly Gitkasan woman said. Striking correspondences between scars, lesions, or wounds as a previous personality and birthmarks on the newborn child are typically considered important evidence that someone has been reborn.

Such cases underline a fairly common "folk" theory of birthmarks that conflates, much like the new genetics as we will see, phenotype and genotype, visible bodily inscriptions and hereditary signatures derived from previous lives. It is not unlikely that claims of rebirth and reincarnation will be increasingly addressed by geneticists and psychologists. Thus, Stevenson emphasizes that while nothing is known about why a person has a birthmark at one location instead of another, one plausible explanation may be that birthmarks "derive from previous lives" (1997: 186). A novel kind of fusion of genetics and religion, a development that we may as well call "paragenetics," is already taking place, echoing, to some extent, medieval European notions of a "hylomorphic" union of body and soul (Rabinow 1996a: 148). On the one hand, religion seems to be co-opting genetics, suggesting that religion has a genetic basis (see Hamer 2004). On the other hand, geneticists have co-opted religious themes, through their extensive use of theological metaphors such as those of the Holy Grail and the Book of Life.

Whether beneficial or harmful, "cold" or "hot," as markers of pride or shame, birthmarks tend to stand for embodied nature against the artificiality of nurture. Thus, birthmarks may be equivalent to the genetic code of modern gene talk. Just as some genes are associated with, say, breast cancer, some birthmarks turn into melanoma. While birthmarks tend to be only skin-deep inscriptions on the surface of the body, they sometimes run much deeper, as Nathaniel Hawthorne suggests in his well-known short story "The Birthmark." In Hawthorne's story, the scientist Aylmer is bothered by a birthmark on the cheek of his wife Georgina, a significant stigma or flaw on her otherwise perfect look. Convinced of the power of his deep science, he decides to remove the birthmark with some kind of medicine. The birthmark disappears, but Georgina loses her life. As Hawthorne speculated (1959: 229), "it may be the stain goes as deep as life itself." Apparently, this was a common theme in Hawthorne's time and context – men preoccupied with perfecting just about everything, including the bodies of their wives and daughters. A birthmark, however, need not be a stain or blemish, and much depends upon the eyes of the beholder. Moreover, in an extended sense, birthmarks may be said to stand for the biomarkers stored in one form or another in biomedical collections focusing on groups or populations or, indeed, humanity. Hawthorne's story can be read in many ways, depending on one's perspective on gender, power, the body, ethnos, nation, and science. And so can many of the narratives on the new genetics. The tropes span the entire theatrical spectrum of tragedy, irony, comedy, and romance. While some underline the harmful if not disastrous effects of molecular advances, possibly a return to racism and eugenics, others emphasize playful self-understanding, hope, optimism, and grand solutions to problems of poverty and disease.

TWO

Birthmarks become landmarks: "Little worlds in themselves"

Now that most of the habitat of the globe has been charted, documented and conquered, humans are increasingly turning their attention and interests to the "remotest corners" of living organisms, in particular the human genome. With the new genetics, "Man the Hunter" and "Woman the Gatherer" have finally turned to hunting and gathering in their own genome. What project could be more anthropological? *Homo viator* navigating waters right at home. Dumit concludes his ethnographic study of another kind of corporeal exploration, brain function imaging or "PET scans" (positron emission tomography) which reportedly represent the human brain at work in different moods, states, and activities, with a similar note on the relevance of technoscientific developments for the self-reflective anthropological project: "we . . . may have entered a space of active negotiation of the basic terms of our categories of the person . . . The use of these images in thinking about ourselves is in its infancy. *We* are at stake in this work. How can we not afford to risk jumping in and studying it?" (2004: 185).

Focusing on the practice and representation of genotyping (the description of the genetic constitution of an individual) and the concepts and strategies employed for the purpose of mining the contours of the body in order to trace the genetics of common human diseases, this chapter explores the mapping exercise of genomics, partly through a discussion of the workings of one of the research teams of deCODE genetics. What exactly takes place in the laboratory and in front of the computer screen? How do team members reason about genes, common diseases, gene hunting, and the articulation of genes and other important elements in the constitution of life? If genetic determinism has serious flaws, why are alternative models of development suppressed? Addressing these questions will both draw attention to some of the key aspects of the new genetics and set the stage for the discussion that follows of genealogies, population studies, genetic databases, and other biomedical projects.

The rendering of genes and genomes in terms of maps necessarily invokes spatial images of contours, islands, and coastlines – images, as we will see, that people also seem to find useful when talking about nations and populations. Zooming in on the genome vastly expands the mapping of the body represented by the anatomical atlas. In the opening words of *The Birth of the Clinic*, originally published a decade after the discovery of the structure of DNA, Foucault seems to anticipate new kinds of biomedical mappings:

For us, the human body defines, by natural right, the space of origin and of distribution of disease; a space whose lines, volumes, surfaces, and routes are laid down, in accordance with a now familiar geometry, by the anatomical atlas. But this order of the solid, visible body is only one way – in all likelihood neither the first, nor the most fundamental – in which one spatializes disease. There have been, and will be, other distributions of illness. (Foucault 1973: 3)

With the expanding gaze of the new genetics, the hereditary signatures of individuals and populations assumed to remain practically unchanged throughout the life course have become the subject of both mapmaking and marketing. Rose and Novas suggest that genome mapping – the "flattening" of the body, in their terms – is essential to the current production of what they, following Catherine Waldby, call "biovalue" (Waldby 2002, Waldby and Mitchell 2006):

Contemporary biomedicine, by rendering the depths of the body visible, intelligible, calculable, and capable of intervention at a molecular level, makes it amenable to the production of economic value. In many ways, what is being accomplished through the life sciences is a kind of "flattening" of the vital processes of the body. This not only enables the "surfaces" to become equivalent with one another at the most basic biological level, but also allows them to be enfolded within processes of capital or social accumulation. (Rose and Novas 2005: 455)

With the completed human genome projects, the translation of genomic knowledge into better diagnostics and treatments becomes a vast terrain for the production of biovalue.

Research on the genetics of common diseases is a case in point. Understanding the reasons for the occurrence of a common disease such as osteoarthritis (OA) is obviously something that has plagued people through the ages. Osteoarthritis is one of the most common human joint diseases, characterized by pain and stiffness, particularly in the hip, knees, hands and thumbs. The frequency and seriousness of OA, which often leads to significant disability and the need for joint replacement, seem to vary by age. According to some estimates, at least 40 million people in the United States alone are affected with OA, with at least 70 percent of those 65 years or older being affected. No doubt the explanations offered for OA are diverse and complex, reflecting context and culture. According to a recent study by Schwarz, the Navajo world emphasizes conduct in the present, namely contact with menstrual blood: "Consultations with Navajo people indicate that menstrual blood is a sign signifying a difference between health and danger, while arthritis [*agiziitsoh*] and rheumatism are signs of sexual distortions arising from knowing or unwitting contact with menstrual blood" (Schwarz 2001: 671). One of the persons Schwarz interviewed suggested that arthritis was both on the increase and somehow gendered: "It was said that you can't sleep with anyone when you are that way. It causes body aches. It has great many implications to the man, like arthritis. Today, people are aching all the time" (2001: 650).

Icelanders, in contrast, have often assumed that OA "simply" comes with drudgery, with accumulated pressure on the joints. Indeed, the Icelandic term for OA, *slitgigt*, refers to a kind of arthritis (*gigt*) that develops as people become "worn down" (*slitið*) during the life course.

Neither the Icelandic thesis on drudgery nor the Navaho notion of impurity seems to directly address the possibility that OA is "in the genes." Could OA at least partly be the result of mutations? With the development of the new genetics it has become feasible to explore the genetics of OA, to "map it," and possibly to find remedies. Several laboratories, clinics, and companies have been involved in such research, among them deCODE genetics.

Decoding disease: osteoarthritis

During my fieldwork with the OA team of deCODE genetics I would usually place myself in the laboratory, the coffee room, and at meetings, observing what went on in the course of DNA analyses, interpretations, and decision-making. In addition, I interviewed all of the members of the OA team. In their study of apprentice blacksmiths, Keller and Keller rightly point out that "it is perhaps essential to acquire competence in the activities that constitute the subject of research if a scholar wishes to test the premises developed therein" (1996: 169). The process of becoming a competent gene hunter, however, is long and arduous, and it was beyond the scope of my relatively brief study to seriously tread this path.

Current research on patient groups by deCODE genetics typically begins with a contract with one or more physicians specializing in a particular disease with a potential genetic basis. Through its contract with Hoffmann-La Roche, deCODE genetics began focusing on research on twelve common diseases, including OA. The founding premise of deCODE was that the company would be uniquely placed to achieve major breakthroughs in identifying the genes involved in the most common diseases. The OA team was one of the more established ones within the company at the time of my fieldwork with several permanent members, mostly biologists and technical laboratory assistants, collaborating closely with statisticians as well as physicians specializing in OA.[1] At the beginning, a contract was signed with clinical collaborators, focusing on two particular phenotypes of the disease, OA of the fingers and hips (the latter is particularly common in Iceland). In due course, the study of OA of the knees was also incorporated.[2] Included in the analysis of OA were 1,143 individuals affected by the disease and 939 of their relatives.

The original vision, or program, of deCODE was spelled out by Stefánsson (director) and Gulcher (vice president, Research and Development) (1998: 523). In their view, the aim of linkage analysis is:

to determine whether there exist pieces of the genome that are passed down through each of several families with multiple patients in a pattern that is consistent with a particular inheritance model and that is unlikely to occur by chance alone. The most important asset of linkage analysis is its ability to screen the entire genome . . . this makes it a hypothesis-independent and cost-effective approach to finding disease genes. (Gulcher, Kong, and Stefánsson 2001: 264)

The methods used by the OA team are discussed more thoroughly in some of their publications (see, for example, Stefánsson *et al.* 2003). When their project started it was assumed that there was some underlying genetic factor, since siblings were known to have a higher risk than others of hip replacement. The common forms of OA, it seemed, appeared to skip generations, suggesting complex patterns of inheritance. Stefán E. Stefánsson, the leader of the team, argued that by using extensive family

---

[1] Later on, at a time of financial difficulties that were partly triggered by debates on the Human Genome Project and a general backlash in biotech industries, the focus shifted elsewhere and the team was dissolved.

[2] Before launching the research, deCODE genetics had to request permission from the Data Protection Commission of Iceland and the National Bioethics Committee of Iceland. One of the conditions for research such as this is that personal data are used in encrypted form. Once the license was settled the road was clear for sampling blood from patients, their relatives, and control groups, for the analysis of DNA.

histories available in Iceland his team was able to show that OA is indeed inherited; the patients are derived from a small number of founders, one or more of whom carried the alleles involved into the community, alleles being the alternative forms of a gene or a DNA sequence at a specific chromosomal location: "There is a founder effect. Simply by going back one generation after another. Patients . . . are significantly different from control groups."

Having established a familial connection, the OA team set out to establish the genetic factors involved. S. E. Stefánsson elaborates on the relative advantage of the deCODE team thanks to the "deep" genealogy of Icelanders, the "Book of Icelanders" that has assembled available genealogical records dating back to the Middle Ages, in some cases back to the time of settlement in the ninth century: "Most other groups are looking at sib pairs. They have less information than we have for linkage analysis as they don't have the genealogies. We only need to know how people are related" (interview). By running their encrypted patient lists against data on Icelandic family histories, the OA team explores in detail "how people are related." Of course, precise diagnoses such as those involving OA or other common diseases several generations back are not available, let alone available for the people of the settlement period in the ninth century and the following saga age. Medical records, now as well as in the past, necessarily invite interpretation and narrative; reducing the patient to text, therefore, is not that straightforward. Obviously, the identification of families with the symptoms of "OA," the critical starting point in work of this kind, is somewhat problematic due to the nature of available sources. S. E. Stefánsson explains: "It's not easy to find well-defined families. One of the problems with past records is that diagnoses often were poor. People didn't know the difference between rheumatoid arthritis and osteoarthritis."

The lack of diagnoses for the generations of the past, however, is a less serious problem than one might think. What matters is knowledge of genetic distance and relationships between those diagnosed. Knowing the links, establishing "meiotic distances" (the number of links separating any two persons in a pedigree) among their group of patients, the researchers seek to confirm and narrow down candidate regions in the gene hunt, i.e., regions with genes whose protein products are assumed to affect the disease. In the words of the leader of the OA team, "we track the recombination of DNA through each generation to further localize the location."

The osteoarthritis team started by genotyping the DNA, using around 1,000 markers dispersed throughout the genome obtained from deCODE's genetic map – markers being DNA sequences from single chromosomal locations. Operating like geographical landmarks or navigational aids in the genome, somewhat like islands in medieval mapping of *terra incognita* (Gillis 2004: 55), markers are a fundamental element of mapping. Figure 2.1, which was drawn by the OA team to explain their work to me, explores genealogical relationships among a group of patients, in this case two pairs of sisters severely affected by osteoarthritis. The aim, of course, is to trace the genes presumably responsible for the fact that osteoarthritis tends to occur in certain families. The numbers in the figure show markers and alleles, for the exploration of common alleles, possibly from one of the grandparents.

Software developed by deCODE genetics ("Allegro") identifies common alleles and calculates the likelihood of genetic linkage between loci (unique chromosomal locations defining the position of individual genes or DNA sequences). The alleles from the genotypes are then used to calculate the sharing of the genetic material between related patients. The results, displayed as lod-scores (z) indicating the likelihood of genetic linkage between loci, guide the team to the regions on the chromosome were they expect to find mutations (a lod-score greater than $+3$ is considered strong evidence of linkage). The findings from the gene hunt were passed on to the company's statisticians who every now and then evaluated how the search was going, and attempted to narrow down in probabilistic terms the genes responsible for the disease.

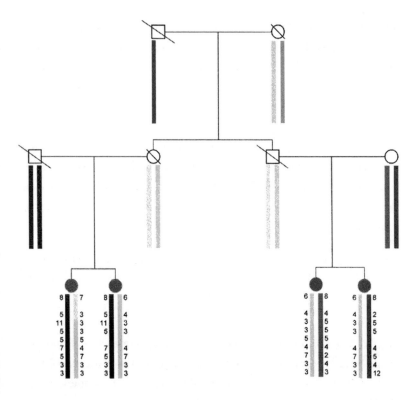

FIGURE 2.1 A pedigree with two pairs of sisters affected by osteoarthritis (source: deCODE genetics)

Occasionally the statistical results run counter to the hopes and expectations of team members who speak of statisticians "slaughtering" their lod-scores. At one point S. E. Stefánsson explained to me: "In November, the statisticians slaughtered our lod-scores. We have a new search now, on slightly different grounds. We need a score of 3.7. I am still confident. I have dense markers." There is an interesting parallel between such hunting expeditions and fishing and navigation in distant waters. Both gene hunting and navigation involve cognition in the wild. For the gene hunter, the lod-scores are what "soundings" or "echoes" from sonar are for the fishing skipper, indicating the availability of prey and the feasibility of capture.

Sometimes gene hunting proceeded randomly, with the nets cast widely. S. E. Stefánsson complained about the frustrating results of such a strategy: "the team has genotyped hundreds and hundreds of samples without any lod-scores; everything is just flat." At other times, the team focused on candidate genes considered more likely than others to yield positive results:

We mapped the chromosome region by region, rebuilt it. Then we narrowed down even further, sequencing base-by-base. There are two candidate genes left on chromosome A (a pseudonym). I think I have narrowed down to a region.

Clearly, gene hunting is a tiresome job with frustrations and disappointment. Nevertheless, the team were excited about the prospects of their study. Hitherto no one had successfully "cracked" a complex disease like OA or, in other words, identified the genetic factors involved in the phenotype. Here was an opportunity to make history.

Prior to the work of the OA team, several studies had been reported attempting to map genes that contribute to the common forms of OA. These studies revealed suggestive loci for OA which the team was bound to take into consideration. For S. E. Stefánsson, however, this invited the problem of perceptual bias:

The problem when you have a candidate gene is that you tend to shift your attention towards it. It's not unbiased. This might have been distracting me . . . I spent months for nothing. I was absolutely convinced. We are getting more and more convinced now of a perceptual bias. Everyone in the business does this. You are literally stuck.

Although knowledge of family histories and genealogical distance helped to narrow the region in which to search, there wasn't much to go by and gene hunting was still much like looking for a needle in a haystack. Hunches had an important role to play. In S. E. Stefánsson's words:

I keep on trying until something works, going by hunches. The first step is to use the lod-scores to guide us into the chromosome region. Then we add more markers to the region. If we are lucky, we can see the same markers in unrelated families with the same symptoms. Bingo!

Formal schooling was important to the OA team for the complex tasks they were engaged in – most of them, indeed, had years of academic training and university degrees behind them. Nevertheless, much critical knowledge was gradually acquired in the context of the clinic and the laboratory. Essential abilities required for gene hunting were developed largely in the course of everyday practice, in the company of colleagues and tutors. Strategies of gene hunting were adopted and revised both intuitively in the laboratory or at the computer screen and in formal or informal meetings. From time to time the research team assembled to evaluate results and to plan ahead.

In practice, this was a highly complex interactive process combining different kinds of mapping. Several kinds of maps are used in this kind of work and in molecular genetics more generally (see, for instance, Rabinow 1996a, Brown 2002, Gannett and Griesemer 2004a). It is conventional to distinguish between genetic mapping and physical mapping. Genetic mapping involves the application of genetic techniques to situate genes on chromosomes by relative distance ("genetic distance"). The first maps of this kind were constructed early last century by researchers working on the fruit fly, *Drosophila*, using genes as markers to establish the distinguishing features of the genetic landscape. Physical mapping, on the other hand, involves the use of molecular biology techniques to explore DNA molecules directly, locating the positions of sequence features, including genes, on chromosomes by absolute distance (in units of DNA nucleotides).

The social context of gene hunting was an important aspect of the work of the OA team. There was some element of competition between teams within deCODE genetics. While project leaders internal to the company sometimes leaned on each other, circumnavigating around common problems, there was competition between leaders and their teams for access to assistants and machinery where one team might slow others down. Not only was there competition between deCODE teams, there was also competition with other companies. Such competition, one of the driving forces behind the dynamics of biotechnology companies, obviously affected the way in which results were presented. As S. E. Stefánsson explained: "We could easily have published much more on various chromosomes . . . but we don't know how much lead we have. Other companies are working on this too." Thus, it was important to try to strike a balance between the need to publicly document one's findings, to publish, and the necessity to ensure competitive advantage. Publishing too early might mean losing a potential head start, disclosing information about one's hunting grounds that might provide unexpected opportunities for others who arrived late in the game or who had been searching on less productive tracks. Going to conferences, presenting posters or papers, team members had to be careful not to disclose too much, being evasive, for instance, about the chromosome or the region they were working on not to lose the lead. At the same time, they were likely to seek to extract such information from others.

While such games are not new to science, they take somewhat exaggerated forms in modern bioscience, given the huge interests and implications involved, both economic and symbolic. Traditions of publishing, of communicating findings to the public and fellow scientists, as a result, are rapidly changing. Again, there is an interesting parallel with competitive fishing. Skippers who think they have discovered useful fishing grounds on, say, edges of the seabed where fish gather and are easy to catch, are likely to avoid giving out important information on location and fishing success to prevent the whole fleet from arriving on the scene. In some cases they will even deliberately mislead by a variety of deceptive techniques in order to be able to fish in peace, diverting their colleagues' attention to other locations.

How do gene hunters become competent at what they do, navigating the genome and mapping diseases? Polanyi observes that as we become skilful practitioners we assimilate technology as *a part* of our own body. In the process of learning, he suggests, "we shift outwards the points at which we make contact with the things that we observe as objects outside ourselves"; as tools become "part of ourselves, the operating persons," we "pour ourselves into them and assimilate them as parts of our own existence. We accept them existentially by dwelling in them" (1958: 59). Skilled genome analysts pour themselves into their machinery, not so much focusing on them as dwelling in them, and, as a result, the key equipment involved in the situated practice of gene hunting – including polymerase chain reaction (PCR) machines, robots, and computers – have a tendency to disappear. Indeed, as Knorr-Cetina suggests for molecular biology (1999: 97), the acting body itself is a kind of robot: "Sensory performance and action go together, especially when, as in molecular biology, almost all experimental work is *manual work.* The acting body is perhaps the first and most original of all automats." Professional clinicians, as Shaw points out, "speak of the 'gestalt' or diagnostic intuition of particular practitioners, a form of tacit knowledge that denotes an intuitive response to the visible features of a patient" (2003: 40). Recently, there has been a growing theoretical and anthropological interest in practical learning and tacit knowledge. At the same time, science itself has increasingly been seen as an embedded enterprise – as a local concern (see, for instance, Löwy 1996).

What is in a gene? Epigenetics

When pressed about genetic determinism, interaction among genes, and the role of environmental factors, the OA team maintained that while OA was "clearly genetic," since it ran in families it was a complex disease, with five to ten genes behind each joint. Team members suggested that while gene hunting might or might not prove successful, genetic studies were the proper, if not the sole, avenue to explore. As I extended my field site beyond deCODE and Iceland, attending biotechnology conferences in several European contexts, I got a similar impression. While speakers represented a broad range of disciplines and perspectives, discussions of the roots of common diseases were invariably dominated by gene talk, occasionally with a hint towards gene–environment interactions.

What, then, are the practical uses and theoretical implications of gene hunting? The most significant breakthroughs repeatedly promised early on by deCODE genetics and its main corporate financier, Hoffmann-LaRoche, have not been realized. The same goes for most if not all other businesses of this kind. The identification and mapping of the genes implicated in common diseases that inflict humans turns out to be a painfully slow and immensely expensive journey. In addition, so far the promise of drug developments on the basis of molecular biological research remains just a promise. Despite massive investment in the dreams of the start-up companies of modern biotechnology, genetic solutions to some of the major health hazards of the times simply do not seem to be around the corner. There is good reason, therefore, for taking new claims about revolutionary biomedical developments and "miracles" with a grain of salt. The comparison with the "hard" social science of neo-classical economics may be illuminating. Just as some economists tend to emphasize what may be called the "alchemy of capturing rent," not only fetishizing an abstract economic construct but also making the world conform to their virtual vision, some geneticists have tended to reify the gene and elevate it to a supreme status. In his portrayal of economics and its preoccupation with the objective, the harsh, and the mathematical, McCloskey describes neo-classicists as a motorcycle gang (1993: 76). Perhaps the promoters of biotechnology are aptly described as the motorcycle gang of biology.

Keeping in mind the disappointments associated with gene hunting and the medicine it promised to deliver, it may be tempting to refer to the biotech community as a millenarian movement, a religious and political sect – much like the so-called "cargo cults" of early twentieth-century Melanesia – anticipating the return of Western goods and preparing for their landing by means of ritual exercises. After all, this is an "economy of appearances" characterized by "spectacular accumulation," to draw upon Tsing's terminology (2005: 74), based on investment in products that may or may not exist. In the world of biotechnology, a few leading personalities (including Daniel Cohen, Francis Collins, Kary Mullis, Kári Stefánsson, Craig Venter, and Hwang Woo-Suk) have become household names – the millenarian "prophets," if you like, of a spontaneous international movement announcing the imminent occurrence of amazing events. Many of them have promised wonderful cargo once the airstrips have been cleared and the planes have landed. This is a line of reasoning developed by several observers, including anthropologists. Thus, Lock emphasizes, partly on the basis of depressing results for Alzheimer's disease which she has skillfully documented, the "divinatory" aspects of the new genetics, its repeated, lofty claims in the face of "the undeniable fact that genomic 'deliverables' are as yet few and far between" (2005: 48). Surely, in some cases (in Alzheimer's research, in particular) further genomic work seems like a complete waste of time. Might it not significantly improve human well-being to reallocate much of the current global budget for medical research from genome research to other more promising avenues, incuding studies of environmental health risks?

While the reference to divination, prophets, and millenarian movements may be illuminating, drawing attention to the wide gulf between promises and results, in my view it is an overstatement. Theoretical and methodological issues should be evaluated in terms of actual results, altough it is often difficult to disentangle the real, the virtual, and the rhetoric. Important advances have, indeed, been made in studies of mutations implicated in the development of some common complex, multifactorial diseases. Thus, some of the results of the research at deCODE genetics are impressive. After the completion of my fieldwork, the OA team published an important article about its results (Stefánsson *et al.* 2003) reporting mapping hand OA to three prominent locations on chromosomes 2, 3, and 4. Moreover, it described a mutation in a gene (*MATN3*) with an association in some patients diagnosed with hand OA; deCODE also boasts of several other successes, including the mapping of a gene linked to Parkinson's disease (Gulcher, Kong, and Stefánsson 2001: 266–267), the isolation of genes associated with myocardial infarction and stroke (Helgadottir *et al.* 2004), the demonstration of a strong familial component to longevity (Gudmundsson *et al.* 2000), and the identification of a variant in a previously unknown candidate gene (designated *TCF7L2*) for type 2 diabetes, a common disease that is expected to rise in the near future due to increasing age of the population and growing obesity (Grant *et al.* 2006).

Perhaps the most impressive achievement of deCODE is a recent clinical trial involving the risk of myocardial infarction.[3] An editorial in the *Journal of the American Medical Association* suggested that while the trial, "one of the first human trials to attempt to translate genomic findings into clinical practice for cardiovascular disease," should be viewed as preliminary, it "provides an exciting attempt to translate genetic findings

---

[3] By means of a genome-wide linkage approach, the deCODE team first identified a disease gene for myocardial infarction (MI) in a particular region on chromosome 13. Having shown that the gene *ALOX5AP* may be a predictor of genetic risk for MI, the researchers undertook a randomized trial which suggested the inhibition of a particular protein (FLAP) in patients with at-risk genotypes may reduce biomarkers of cardiovascular risk. On the basis of their trial the researchers hypothesize that the inhibiting drug (DG031) "will cause reduction in the risk of MI" (Hakonarson *et al.* 2005: 2255).

to clinical applications" (O'Donnell 2005: 2278). Results such as these may have important practical implications, paving the way to diagnostic tests to identify people carrying the variant genes, preventive measures in terms of lifestyle, gene therapy (a particularly controversial procedure), and, possibly, the development of drugs that affect expressions of the proteins involved. Establishing genetic risks can itself be a major advance. While there is no such thing as a "breast cancer gene" and the "shorthand of the phrase *breast cancer gene* is . . . highly misleading" (Condit 1999: 231), whenever any of a series of mutations in the BRCA1 gene occurs or is inherited the likelihood of breast cancer developing increases. Many people take deliberate preventive measures to avoid health hazards on the basis of such knowledge (Finkler 2000). As we shall see, these developments raise interesting questions about genealogies, relations, and identities.

The twentieth century may well be characterized as the "century of the gene" (Keller 2000). Despite the advances of gene hunting, it has become increasingly clear that the narrow focus on the gene itself provides limited explanatory power in biomedical studies. There is a growing awareness, in fact, among both practicing biologists and theorists of development and evolution, of a tension between empirical results and interpretations based on the orthodox view of the causality of genes (Neumann-Held and Rehmann-Sutter 2006). A growing body of evidence indicates serious difficulties in predicting phenotypes from DNA due to the complex web of interactions between genes, their products, and the environment. As Jablonka and Lamb point out, "something else" is going on: "on the one hand you can have identical genes leading to very different phenotypes, and on the other you can have dissimilar genes producing exactly the same phenotype" (2005: 62). While Boas's reading of human biological development and differences which informed a whole generation of anthropologists battling eugenics and other biological reductionisms may sound old-fashioned, framed as it was within early twentieth-century debates, he nevertheless seems to have anticipated some of the doubts about the phenotype/genotype distinction expressed by many modern scholars. To underline "environmental" contributions to physical appearance he suggested, half-seriously, perhaps, since he didn't make much use of it, the alternative notion of "ecotype" (1940: 77). Given such a vocabulary, faithful to the broad notion of the Greek *Oikos* (the "house" of life), the architecture of human ecotypes is much too fleeting and complex to allow for any kind of either tight compartmentalization or simplistic determinism.

Why the paradigm of gene centrism persists in spite of a fairly common awareness of the difficulties it confronts is an intriguing question. One reason is that challenges to the paradigm are often easily dismissed with the mantra of gene–environment interaction which to many people evokes futile chicken-and-egg speculations of the kind pursued for decades if not centuries in debates in several contexts on the relative impact of nature and nurture. Another possible reason has to do with the peculiar logic of financial markets and start-up companies exploiting biomedical resources. Hoping for immense profits in the tapping of biovalue in the case of success – in particular, the development of medical products – businesses are able to tolerate high risks and long and even embarrassing delays – the absence of cargo. Oyama (2000), Griffiths (2006), and some others have suggested an important further explanation emphasizing the semantic notion of the gene. As long as genes are seen as privileged messengers containing essential information about development, they argue, they will keep on being regarded as determining causes despite mounting contrary evidence. Given such an interpretation, only the proof that "developmental information is not localized in the genes . . . will lay the vampire of genetic determinism to rest" (Griffiths 2006: 176).

It is difficult to tell where the future will take us, but a broader perspective beyond genes and cell-centered accounts seems inevitable. Rheinberger anticipates (2000: 232) that while we have "come a long way with molecular biology from genes to genomes," there is "still a way to go from genomes to organisms that will need the efforts of a new generation of molecular developmental biologists"; "the path from there to populations and communities, and vice versa," he predicts, "will not be shorter and left for still another generation." Significantly, an "epigenetic" discourse that draws partly upon the notion of "epigenetic landscape" developed by C. H. Waddington in the 1940s has recently emerged as an appealing alternative to the paradigm of gene centrism, underlining the unity of genes, organisms, and environment. Not only does this discourse conflate the inside and the outside, it also emphasizes that organism and environment literally define each other. Thus, Lewontin insists that "just as the information needed to specify an organism is not contained entirely in its genes, but also in its environment, so the environmental problems of the organism are a consequence of its genes" (1995: 132).

Mappings

Impressed with their ability to zoom in on the minute details and contours of hereditary material and their power of visualization, geneticists and molecular biologists have firmly reinforced their language of cartographies, a language that echoes the modernist notion of expansion and mastery. Textbooks represent a useful source of information on the language and imagery involved. At the turn of the new millennium a standard textbook described molecular genetics in the grand terms of discovery and voyaging:

After many centuries, we have built up an approximate understanding of our external universe, but the universe within us has only very recently been the subject of serious study. The application of microscopy to the study of cells and subcellular structures provided one major route into this world, to be followed by pioneering advances in biochemistry and then molecular biology. Now, as we enter the next millennium, we are on the threshold of a truly momentous achievement that will have enormous implications for the future. For the first time, we will know our genetic endowment – the sequence of our DNA. Then our voyage into the *universe within* really will have begun. (Strachan and Read 1999: 295; emphasis in original)

The apparently innocent language of voyaging, of course, is somewhat misleading. Keller points out that while star-gazing has always been an important metaphor for biology it "certainly . . . has no place in the biology of today" (1996: 108). Gazing, she suggests, is increasingly enmeshed in actual touching, if not aggressive bombarding, of the object in question. Thus, to obtain her famous X-ray photograph in Figure 1.1, Franklin needed to manipulate the cellular material she was working with, eventually destroying its vital functions. Perhaps, though, the development of cosmic maps beyond the Milky Way represents an appropriate parallel to genomic maps. Both projects have significantly altered the scale and meaning of the cartographic enterprise. Never has "anything," to paraphrase Wilford, encompassed so much and so little space; in the case of cosmic maps, the subject of mapmaking is infinitely larger than the maps themselves, while for genomic maps the reverse is the case (2000: 463). One project puts parts into context, another zooms in on the parts: "Telescope or microscope, aggregate or particle: whatever is within one's field of vision makes other things either part or context, either intrinsic elements within or ecosystem without" (Strathern 1992: 133).

Maps, like photographs and other forms of visualization, are obviously powerful tools for scientists and other explorers of the unknown. Clearly, the mapping of genetic material was greatly enhanced by Franklin's photographs, the model of the double helix, and the map of the human genome. At the same time, mapping deserves attention in its own right as the product of situated, historical activity. Maps have, indeed, become objects of critical attention in the social sciences and the humanities. Cosgrove (1999) attributes the extensive rethinking of maps, the "spatial turn" as he calls it, to several factors, including the dissolution of a "Eurocentric" geopolitics, changing techniques of seeing, and poststructuralist theorizing. For him, the growing critical interest in maps and mapping corresponds to fundamental doubts about grand narratives "and to the concomitant recognition that position and context are

centrally and inescapably implicated in all constructions of knowledge"
(Cosgrove 1999: 7).

In some ways, recent advances in the mapping of the genome remind
one of the nineteenth-century scramble for colonies. While maps, however, are often about appropriation and alienation, they need not be.
Corner, for example, suggests some techniques (including that of the
rhizome) that allow for creative and emancipating mapping:

As we are freed from the old limits of frame and boundary – preconditions
for the survey and "colonization" of wilderness areas – the role of mapping
will become less one of tracing and re-tracing already known worlds, and
more one of inaugurating new worlds out of old. Instead of mapping as a
means of appropriation, we might begin to see it as a means of emancipation
and enablement, liberating phenomena and potential from the encasements
of convention and habit. (1999: 252)

A series of images, "Birthmarks," by the Icelandic artist Katrín
Sigurðardóttir underlines the creative and liberating aspects of mapping. At the same time, it nicely captures the cartographic aspects of the
new genetics. The seven images involved (one of which is reproduced in
Figure 2.2) represent tiny birthmarks on the artist's body as geographical
maps of islands, with the relevant spatial scales and contours. To make
these works, the artist had three-dimensional images of the birthmarks
fed into a computer program, transforming them so that they would
resemble infrared aerial photographs. In the artist's reading of her own
work, the "Birthmarks" series underlines both her "feminist motto" on
autonomy and strength – "starting with one's own body to establish one's
sphere of power and the perspective from where one can watch, talk, and
create" – and her wish to "play with, and thereby challenge, traditions
that reflect a shallow worldview where everything is classified in terms of
binary oppositions: man/woman, nature/culture, observer/observed . . ."
(Sigurðardóttir 1998: 374–375).

More recently, considering the effects of her work on viewers,
Sigurðardóttir seems to have revised her own understanding of the series

Anthropology and the New Genetics

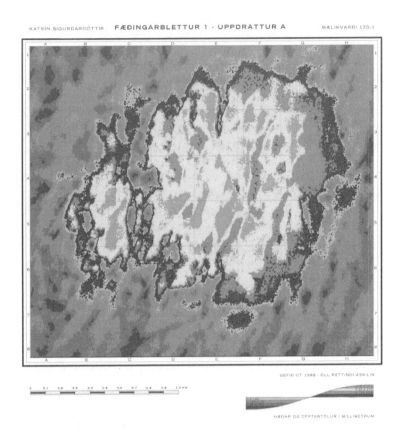

FIGURE 2.2 "Birthmark 1, Map A" by Katrín Sigurðardóttir

to include an implicit threat of the grotesque, hinting at the danger of malignant growth. In her perceptive interpretation of the series, Heisler suggests that it might be read as a critique of the biotechnological gaze that renders the body as a site, in particular the female body:

In this work, the body's small "monstrosities" are charted and magnified; the body is visible as "a field of inscription." Another reading is that the artist's play with the visual languages of medicine and cartography is an attempt to picture the relationship of body to place. (2004: 8)

52

Indeed, the representation of birthmarks as islands invites questions on roots and belonging. Perhaps the "Birthmark" series emphasizes the seriousness of ongoing debates in many contexts of the representation and commodification of "national" bodies and the nexus between person, body, and market. In the process of commodification, the fleeting body is fragmented and inscribed with fixed coordinates. As birthmarks become landmarks, the "islands" of the body are removed from their natural history, circumscribed by stable coastlines. Paul Carter has argued (see Cosgrove 1999) that maps and photographs render the "coastline" – the necessarily unstable space between high and low – as a fixed line, not as a fleeting zone. Likewise, bodily mappings, including the Birthmark series, freeze the continuous, changing body as an assemblage of stable and closed forms. At the same time, to paraphrase Cosgrove, "mapping has become an installation art" (Cosgrove 1999: 6).

While for the artist the "map" and the making of it may be an end in itself, for most mapmakers cartographies, much like other representations, are not what "it" is all about. As Ingold argues from a phenomenological perspective, one becomes a competent and skilled practitioner not through the acquisition of representations but at the point where one is able to dispense with them:

representations . . . are like a map of an unfamiliar territory, which can be discarded once you have learned to attend to features of the landscape, and can place yourself in relation to them. The map can be a help in the beginning to know the country, but the aim is to learn the country, not the map. (2000: 415)

This applies to genetic maps just as other maps. The ultimate aim is not to construct and collect maps but to take some kind of "trip," to understand organisms and to be able to influence their life course, partly for the purpose of mining them, and turning them into a resource.

The pioneers of biometrics – the description and identification of individuals using biological traits – would have welcomed the mappings of the new genetics. In his book *Finger Prints*, published a little before the rediscovery of the laws of Mendel, Sir Francis Galton wrote of his biometric dream in the following terms: "I have an inquiry in view, which has not yet been fairly begun, owing to the want of sufficient data, namely to determine the minutest biological unit that may be hereditarily transmissible" (1892: 187). An important advantage of fingerprints, in his view, related to their potential use in "indicating Race and Temperament"; this was "a branch of the subject" of which he had "great expectations" (1892: 17). While some of the pioneers of eugenics hoped that fingerprints would turn out to yield useful information about ancestry, results did not meet their expectations. On the other hand, fingerprints were seen to be useful for individual identification, especially in detective work. Early forms of fingerprint identification were used for centuries in China and India prior to its European "discovery" in the late nineteenth century by Galton and some others (Cole 1999: 147). A Scottish physician, Henry Faults, who served at a hospital in Tokyo in the late 1870s, brought fingerprint patterns to the attention of Charles Darwin in a letter that Darwin forwarded to his cousin Galton. Galton suggested that fingerprints were "in some respects the most important of all anthropological data. We shall see that they form patterns, of a curious variety of shape, whose boundaries can be firmly outlined, and which are little worlds in themselves" (Galton 1892: 1–2). A small gadget originally made for the purpose of counting the number of threads in a sample of linen, a folding lens sold at opticians' shops under the name of "linen tester," had made it possible to explore these "little worlds in themselves," to map them and to speculate about their nature, variety, and, possibly, inheritance. Galton's work thus foreshadowed in some ways the new genetics and the mapping of the human genome.

Linkage analysis of sequences that show common patterns of inheritance with the phenotypical condition involved has proved to be useful in research on Mendelian or monogenic diseases in relatively isolated and homogeneous populations. In both deCODE's early investment and

marketing statements which were quite successful, and its database proposal, Iceland was presented as a particularly valuable site. Iceland, it
was argued, provided the ideal context for the production of biovalue
because of the small size of the population, its isolation and history, but
also because of the detailed genealogies available and the accuracy and
completeness of disease diagnoses. It need not be surprising that numerous geneticists throughout the world have been focusing on research on
relatively homogeneous populations, studying a whole range of mutations and diseases. These researchers form an extensive, informal network
associated with international conferences on the "Genetics of Complex
Diseases and Isolated Populations" (Genetic Isolates 2005). A somewhat
similar insular notion, as we will see, is underlined in the populations-of-
historical-interest approach developed by the Human Genome Diversity
Project.

Small, however, is not necessarily beautiful. Generalizations for other
populations may not hold well and, moreover, homogeneity may not
allow for the genetic variety needed to research the genetics of a complex
disease. For many common diseases that may involve several or many
genes, larger populations and datasets and more heterogeneous genomes
may be more useful. Brookes suggests that deciphering the genetics of
complex diseases is like "the challenge of reassembling a jigsaw puzzle to
create a view or understanding that did not previously exist" (2001: 512)
and, as a result, a thorough rethinking of "genetic strategies" is needed.
The ultimate test, however, of the usefulness of a genome – of the relative
worth of a small and homogeneous population such as the Icelandic
one, a heterogeneous population such as that of Manhattan, or, indeed, a
gigantic and complex population like that of China – is success in terms
of actual results.

The notion of maps is used here in a fairly broad sense, for any kind
of visual surrogates of spatial relations. It is tempting to refer to genomic
cartographies as "mere" metaphors and, indeed, an important avenue
to explore in relation to the new genetics is: what do people mean when

they speak of charting the "geography" or the "regions" of human genetic material? Recently, *Scientific American* presented an account of a biologist who has been exploring the Y sex chromosome under the heading: "Geographer of the male genome" (Stix 2004). When launching their high-resolution recombination map of the human genome, deCODE scientists referred to "peaks," "valleys," "deserts," and "jungles," partly drawing upon earlier work:

Most interesting is the large number of local recombinations of peaks and valleys through each chromosome . . . Yu *et al.* identified 19 recombination "deserts", defined as regions with crossover rates less than 0.3 cM Mb^{-1}, and 12 recombination "jungles", defined as regions with crossover rates greater than 3cM Mb^{-1}. (Kong *et al.* 2002: 243)

While this topographical language is clearly metaphoric in that it refers to the abstract visual representation of "crossover rates" (the layout of graphs and charts), it also seeks to realistically describe particular regions in the genome. In fact, a radical distinction between the "metaphorical" mapping of genomes and the "realistic" mapping of landscapes may not make much sense. The mapping of chromosomes – estimating their size, charting their layout, and positioning genes – is just as real a procedure as topographic mapping and, conversely, cartographic mapping may be just as metaphorical as genome mapping (Gugerli 2004: 214). Maps may look deceptively simple and straightforward. However, a critical engagement with them is essential in the sciences and the humanities. Genetic maps, much like geographic maps, are performative constructs, "bringing genes into existence . . . making them manipulable, mobile, and assemblable" (Turnbull 2004: 215). Inevitably, maps, whether geographic or genetic, are informed by the interests and perspectives of the people and the regimes involved in their making.

The biotech industry seems focused on the roles of big men of science, much like the ethnography of Melanesia. Strong leaders who are dependent upon their skills in managing and negotiating extensive social networks and establishing trust seem to characterize accounts of both contexts. Recent theoretical discussions of the personification of the power of big men (and their relatives, "great men" and "chiefs"), a longstanding and contested issue in the ethnography of Melanesia, have emphasized the relational nature of leadership. Similarly, I think, popular accounts of big men in science need decentering. Skill, authorship, and creativity are properties of social persons firmly rooted in communities of practice, not autonomous individuals. Work on the double helix and the copying mechanism of genetic material is a case in point. The final breakthrough in 1953 was the culmination of a series of efforts, technical, experimental, and theoretical, involving the cooperation of a whole group of people only some of whom were credited with the discovery. Another telling case is the "making" of the PCR machine at Cetus Corporation in California, a critical innovation in the development of biotechnology (Rabinow 1996b). Still another case is the making of Dolly, the world's first cloned sheep, at the Roslin Institute in Edinburgh. In 2006, a decade after Dolly's birth, Professor Ian Wilmut, who has usually been credited for the research involved, admitted that his role had been grossly exaggerated. Notions of agency, creativity, and innovation are not, of course, simply interesting topics for social theorists, they are central issues in many property regimes.

The theory of skilful practice developed by Polanyi and several others helps to decenter the notion of creativity. Collectively, these theorists suggest the proper unit of analysis is the whole person in action, acting within the contexts of that activity, not the individual separated from the social world by the surface of the body, a natural being who passively internalizes the mental scripts of the cultural environment. Such an approach – informed by the notions of situated action, mutual enskilment, and communities of practice – emphasizes the continuity of the social world. Recent studies in anthropology emphasize that "personal" capacities *arise from* the collaboration of person and context. Much research on scientific practice tends to shift the agency behind the system in question not only from the inventive researcher mixing his or her labor with the productive material to teams and communities, but also to the material itself (Hanson 2004). The material, literary, and social technologies that constitute the world of experimental science – so-called experimental systems – are inherently unstable and path-dependent, driven "from behind" by their own history and dynamics rather than a teleological quest for a given future (see Rheinberger 1997: 28). Echoing the position of Latour (1988), Kohler (1994) and Creager (2002) emphasize that the "standardized" laboratory fly, virus, and mouse are organic machines endowed with an agency of their own, colonizing the landscapes of laboratories and taking the centre stage of experimental genetics. Knorr-Cetina treats cells and organisms used in the production systems of laboratories as biological machines – and, in fact, they do a lot of work (1999: 149). So do family histories, as we will see in the following chapter.

THREE

Genealogies, relationships, and histories

The notion of "mapping" emphasized in Chapter 2 may be applied to the social space captured by family histories, a central component of the new genetics. To think of the tracing of family histories in terms of mapping is not, in fact, as farfetched as it may sound. Ingold points out, quoting Edmund Leach, that "the generation of persons within spheres of nurture, and of places in the land, are not separate processes but one and the same" and, therefore, "'kinship is geography'" (Ingold 2000: 149). As we shall see, some representations of kinship have drawn upon spatial imagery. Inevitably, family histories play an important role in the mapping practices of the new genetics. Genealogies established by or for researchers tracing the presumed genetic roots of common diseases have proved to be a powerful navigational aid in the cartography of the human genome, much like GPS technology and remote sensing are essential for modern travelers and explorers. In a digital form, they become efficient tools for exploring the nature and distribution of disease, generating useful information on feasible hunting grounds, the causes of diseases, and their eventual treatment and management. As a result, there has been a rapidly growing interest in biomedical research that combines genealogies, on the one hand, and genetic information and medical records, on the other.

Emphasizing the changing implications of genealogies as they become enmeshed in biomedical projects, this chapter discusses the tracing of family histories in the genome era, the figurative modes involved, and competing assumptions about identities and relatedness. I shall argue that genealogical records and family trees are never innocent phenomena. I first give a brief account of the imagery associated with family trees in European history and the tension between alternative modes of visual expression. I then compare two kinds of genealogies – in the public domain and in the context of biomedicine. This is followed by a discussion of the negotiations between the makers and the users of genealogical databases as well as some of the larger implications of the digitalization of family histories for notions of belonging. While the fascination with genealogical trees and family histories is a common theme, in some contexts the attraction to family histories is somewhat extreme due to the depth of available records, urban nostalgia for the rural past, and the emergence of new imagined genetic communities. As we shall see, the digital family history of the "Book of Icelanders" has an aura of science fiction, combining elements of the cumbersome hypertext of late-medieval ancestral albums and the rhizomatic kinship of Artificial Life (see Helmreich 2001) – and yet it is ethnographically salient, a part of the everyday world of Icelanders.

The construction of pedigrees is a widespread commodity industry, a critical component in the mapping of genes and bodies. In the modern era of molecular biology, genetics, and bioinformatics, kinship diagrams are routine figures. As genealogies have become gold mines, the pages of many scientific books and journals are teeming with "family trees." The significance, however, of genealogies is not restricted to biomedical laboratories and scientific circles. In her ethnographic description of medical encounters in the analysis and treatment of cancer, Gibbon contrasts the highly visible, and the hidden, "technologies" involved in the production and use of family trees, emphasizing that "clinical family trees gain much of their 'force' from being both a form of family genealogy and simultaneously a type of scientific pedigree" (2002: 433). In some cases, the visible version of computerized genealogies produced for the general public justifies the largely hidden version, in Gibbon's terms, exploited in the context of private industry.

Anthropologists have sometimes taken the role of kinship relations as given and primary, eager to force such "structural" relations upon their ethnography to see order in, and make sense of, the seamless flow and chaotic nature of everyday life. Thus, the formal traditions of anthropology, focusing on the ways in which social life is embedded in relations of kinship and affinity, have informed one generation of anthropologists after another, turning the ethnographic gaze away from other realities, including the concept and practices of friendship. With the works of Schneider (1980), Strathern (1992), Carsten (2004) and some others, however, the "classic" issue of kinship has been denaturalized and destabilized. Kinship, it has been argued, does not necessarily represent "the same thing" in different contexts. Moreover, kinship, or rather relatedness, is best regarded as a complex processual thing, not a fixed, abstract geometry of social relationships. Relatedness, in sum, is continually under construction.

To some extent, recent developments in biotechnology have provoked such a conclusion. With artificial reproductive models, gene therapy, and genetic engineering, relatedness has become not simply a matter of genealogical history but also a matter of consumer choice in a quite literal sense (Bestard 2004). While, however, new reproductive technologies may have challenged the structure and phenomenology of kinship, their deconstructive impact should not be overrated. As Laqueur points out (2001: 79) in his survey and evaluation of the "strangeness" of connectedness in the age of sperm banks, ovum brokerages, surrogate motherhood, and similar reproductive techniques and practices:

This strangeness . . . is not born of technology. It is at the root of kinship: heterodox ways of making families – high, low, or no technology – only expose it for what it is, as if our own, Western, structures were exposed to the scrutiny anthropologists more usually reserve for other people.

Laqueur concludes that "so far blood and flesh, mother and father, and sire and dam are as clear or as muddled as they have ever been" (2001: 94). Moreover, DNA analyses and molecular biology have given genetic relatedness a renewed, supreme status where there seems little room for culture and social construction. The implication here is that relatedness is simply connection by birth through a genealogical tree. And kinship diagrams are back on the scene, "deeper" and more elegant than before.

The life of family trees and the genealogy of genealogies

The temporalization of experience, the notion of time as a framework within which life unfolds, is not a universal one. One of the early means of tracking time in medieval Europe was the imagery of the tree. Initially, the "genealogical tree" was adopted by agrarian elites for documenting social honor, the symbolic and social capital on which political alliances were based. Honor was frequently claimed with reference to properties of the human body, the essence of families and lineages. "My lineage, my branch, my name, my coat of arms," as Connerton emphasizes (1989: 86), "all these terms . . . allude to something that is distinctly and directly corporeal: blood." The genealogical tree, however, is necessarily an historical artifact and, indeed, it has taken many forms. For one thing, its visual representation exhibits more diversity than the popular reference to the key metaphor of "trees" may suggest (Klapisch-Zuber 1991, 2000). In addition, family trees are embedded in different kinds of projects, cultures, and property regimes, much like the living organisms we call trees (Rival 1998, Jones and Cloke 2002).

Pedigrees and genealogies are necessarily historical artifacts. Thus, drawing upon the ideals of his society and literature, Charles Darwin attempted to locate man in the genealogy of life: "He sought the restoration of familial ties, the discovery of a lost inheritance, the restitution of pious memory, a genealogical enterprise" (Beer 1986: 221). Just as genealogical diagrams were essential for tracking the paths of human nobility, Darwin reasoned, they were indispensable for naturalists inter-ested in describing the diversity of living things and relations among them:

> As it is difficult to show the blood relationship between the numerous kindred of any ancient and noble family, even by the aid of a genealogical tree, and almost impossible to do this without this aid, we can understand the extraor-dinary difficulty which naturalists have experienced in describing, without the aid of a diagram, the various affinities which they perceive between the many living and extinct members of the same great natural class. (Darwin; cited in Beer 1986: 221–222)

It may be tempting to think of genetic and genealogical models as being "pure" descriptions of relations and histories, untainted by the contexts that produce them. This, however, is not the case. The kinship diagram, as Bouquet argues (2000: 187), has "its own historicity, making it an anything but neutral instrument." This historicity is manifested in a family resem-blance of "pedigree thinking" in a variety of academic contexts, including the formal diagrams of kinship studies, evolutionary biology, philology, the "Ethnologia" or *Völkerkunde* of museum collections, literary the-ory, and the history of language (for a recent phylogenetic approach to language, see Dunn *et al.* 2005). The genealogical view of the world out-lines the common roots and relatedness of different groups and nations, providing the classificatory rationale for various kinds of collections, museum cabinets, ethnographic records, and zoological collections. Lin-guistics and biology present a purified vision of languages and organisms as timeless artifacts with parallel roots and histories. For some literary historians, genres of fiction exhibit a "branching process" similar to that of life forms and languages; "if language evolves by divergence," Moretti asks, "why not literature too?" (2005: 70). In anthropology, the genealogi-cal method had important implications for both theory and the empirical approach: it "fixed birth as the defining moment of kinship, and fixed the instruments for its recording accordingly" (Bouquet 2000: 187).

Klapisch-Zuber (1991, 2000) has nicely documented and analyzed the history of the family tree in medieval Europe. As she points out, the Middle Ages inherited a series of concepts, representations, and formal traditions from classic Antiquity, all of which combined to construct an elaborate language of genealogy. That language was figuratively expressed in a series of highly symbolic medieval paintings, including "The lineage of Saint Anne" (see Figure 3.1). While we tend to take this language for granted as it is firmly rooted in Western imageries of kinship, in fact it was the result of complex experimenting with visual tools and organizing metaphors (Klapisch-Zuber 2000: 339). After 1550, the imagery of the family tree was spectacularly successful. Europeans were obsessed with genealogical details and their visual tree-like representation. Some family diagrams drawn on rolls of parchment nicely demonstrate this; avoiding the interruption of a new page some of them were no less than 10 meters in length.

Over time, European lineage imagery was subject to conflicting ideologies. On the one hand, some genealogies suggested reading from top to bottom, with the ancestors, the trunk, at the top and the descendants below. A lower position in such a scheme not only indicated a chronologically later moment, it also suggested deterioration or demotion, a departure from the honored distant past. Such imagery both documented the continuity of the lineage, the direct line between the present and the past, and the humble status of contemporary humans underlined in eschatological, Christian schemes. The alternative, the up-ending of the lineage in terms of the flowering tree, however, had an even greater appeal, underlining the joyful proliferation of the lineage drawing its vital energy from the earth and stretching into the divine light of the heavens. Such a horticultural metaphor appeared in various forms from at least the eleventh century onward, but it was only in the fifteenth century that it acquired its canonical imagery, with a founding ancestor in the trunk of a tree and his descendants scattered above among its branches.

FIGURE 3.1 The lineage of Saint Anne (Gerard David (1455–1523), Musée des Beaux-Arts de Lyon)

Despite its joyfulness and its success in representing and reinforcing kinship, the metaphor of the flowering tree was also seen to be theologically problematic. Given the need to project the past in magnificent terms, the image of the ascending, growing tree, with the ancestors (and the gods) in the mundane soil and degenerated contemporaries in the glorious heaven, was bound to be met with resistance if not disgust. Not only was there tension between the competing images of ascending and descending, the ups and downs of kinship, there was also tension between the language of roots and branches. The tree metaphor, in fact, was riddled with tension, a tension that "obliges us to ask questions about the connections between language or text and the logic of graphic means of expression which are used to give a visual account of it" (Klapisch-Zuber 1991: 112). The highly nuanced graphic metaphor of the tree which keeps reappearing in a variety of radically different contexts at the intersection of science and art invites a profound but simple epistemological question, namely "*What do we know when we see?*" (Jones and Galison 1998: 7, italics in original).

The medieval imagery of the tree was not exclusively focused on "blood" connections. Interestingly, sixteenth-century genealogical trees showing the kings of Navarre in Portugal included their wives on discrete branches, mixing blood relationships and marital alliances in the same imagery. Nor was the tree imagery the only one employed. In fact, as Klapisch-Zuber points out (1991: 110), it is "quite possible to adopt other graphic systems, simpler but equally effective, for visually presenting the obsessive repetition of genealogical descriptions." Rival metaphors, including those of the human body and the house, appeared from time to time in artistic representations of relatedness. The flowing river of descent captured the Christian imagination; some medieval mnemonic devices merely linked names of descendants with a series of curving lines. Much later, one may note, Lewis Henry Morgan developed a language that allowed him to discuss genealogical and geo-hydrological issues – the "channels" of blood as well as water – in identical or similar terms (Feeley-Harnik 2001).

In due course, the family tree was transformed into an abstract diagram where the trunk has more or less disappeared and only the end points, the leaves, are clearly visible. According to Klapisch-Zuber (2000: 332), this transformation of the genealogical tree had been more or less completed in Italy, one of the key sites of her analysis, around 1600. Yet the family tree continues its evolutionary course. In the age of molecular biology, bioinformatics, and digital design, the abstract diagram is the focus of intensive visual experimenting for the purpose of economizing and packing information in an appealing and readable form (see, for instance, Brown 2002: ch. 16). Given the history of the graphic expression of family trees one may ask: What are the constraints on the representation of family trees in the age of biotechnology? To what extent are genomic projects mapped onto implicit practices of genealogical imaging and tacit assumptions about citizenship and the "nature" of kinship?

Increasingly, family histories are explored and celebrated on the web by the curious and enthusiastic public. Thus, in the United Kingdom, several websites – including Ancestry.co.uk, Genes Reunited, 1837online.com, and Achievements.co.uk – offer a range of genealogical services, either free of charge or for a certain fee. Some allow for the making and storing of family albums with details of family events, photos, and videos, others help users to create family trees, and still others provide access to records of births, baptism, deaths, and marriages. TV programs such as Channel 4's "Extraordinary Ancestors" and BBC2's "Blood Ties" testify to an extensive interest among the general public. In the United States too there are several powerful genealogical websites, among them MyFamily.com, and FamilySearch.org. The latter is run by The Church of Jesus Christ of Latter-Day Saints, in Utah, drawing upon the extraordinary genealogical sources assembled by the Mormons over the years.

Some of the genealogical projects on the web are a by-product of the new genetics, combining in one fashion or another genetic and genealogical research (Tutton 2004a). The Huntsman Cancer Institute of the University of Utah has assembled life and health histories for 1.6 million Utahans, living or dead, into the Utah Population Database. "Mormon Genes Are Hot," as a front-page article in *The New York Times* had it (Johnson 2004), mainly because of the wealth of family histories but also because of the practice of polygamy in the past that has amplified the genetic imprint of a relatively small number of males. Another Utah-based project is that of the Sorenson Molecular Genealogy Foundation. Appealing to volunteers from all over the world to participate in its project, it combines Y chromosome, mtDNA, and autosomal genetic markers with established genealogies. About 40,000 people from different countries have participated in the project so far, providing genealogical information and donating a DNA sample taken through mouthwash. The sole purpose of this enterprise is to identify possible genealogical links on the basis of "molecular genealogy."

The "Book of Icelanders"

The Icelandic context is a useful avenue for exploring some of the issues discussed above. Genealogical interest in Iceland has a long history although the enthusiasm and the motives have varied from time to time. During the settlement of Iceland, genealogies were carefully established and recorded in order to justify claims to land. This is underlined in a medieval manuscript called The Book of Settlement (Landnámabók, written around 1125), which lists settlers, farms, and family histories. General interest in such details seems to have faded in the following centuries as cultivable areas were fully settled and property claims were well established. Later on, however, genealogies gained a renewed significance in the turmoil of a sudden population decline in the wake of epidemics and volcanic eruptions during the eighteenth century (Helgason 2001).

Property had to be reallocated on a large scale among surviving family members, even to distant relatives. Several kinds of historical records on families and genealogies, besides The Book of Settlement, have survived into the modern age – the Family Sagas (Íslendingasögur), church registers, administrative records, censuses, and published registers and national databases. Some of the censuses are only partial lists of farmers and taxpayers while others are relatively complete. Contemporary genealogists draw extensively upon earlier efforts, including the records of a certain Jón Espólín (b. 1769), a knowledgeable and enthusiastic collector of manuscripts.

Not only did these early documents chart a person's position within a web of natural and social relations, they also outlined his or her history, character, and appearance (Grétarsdóttir Bender 2002, Pálsson 2002). Sometimes, the records combined genealogical and "medical" information: "Half of his body had contracted in the autumn, and so had his tongue. As a result, his speech was barely recognizable (a man born in 1740)." Many of the comments indicate concerns with inbreeding, incest, and adultery: "She had four children with her brother and killed them all, except the youngest one (a woman born in 1799)." Sometimes a folk theory underscores the continuity of familial characteristics, the passing of individual characteristics from one generation to another: "Among his descendants, certain family characteristics have persisted, including tremendous energy, endurance and dexterity (a man born in 1755)." The idea that a person's character, capabilities, and dispositions are partly determined by what one would now translate as "inheritance" appears early on in some of the sagas. Thus one of the better known Family Sagas, Njál's saga, comments (Íslendinga sögur og ættir, 1987, ch. 42) that "nurture accounts for one quarter" of a person's dispositions (fjórðungi bregður til fósturs).

A Genealogical Society was founded in Iceland in 1945 to foster genealogical studies, to sustain important historical and demographic documents, and to publish censuses and family histories. The Society now has 800 members, it organizes several lectures a year, and publishes a newsletter. A few Icelandic companies specialize in the tracing of family trees and the computerization of genealogies. Also, a number of genealogy enthusiasts specialize in particular families, both for personal reasons and for anyone interested in their expertise. All of this testifies to the Icelanders' current interest in genealogies. Some years ago, Frisk Software in Reykjavík developed a computer program for handling genealogical information (named "Espólín," in honor of the early collector) that sold well on the market, in more than 1,000 copies. The maker of the program, Friðrik Skúlason, director of Frisk Software, pointed out in an interview that many of these were bought for birthday presents, emphasizing that genealogical interest comes with age, "like the consequences of a slowly-impending genetic defect."

In the 1990s, Frisk Software began the construction of a genealogical database on Icelanders, starting with three censuses (1703, 1801, and 1910) that covered the whole country at sufficiently different points in time, to minimize overlap, as well as the up-to-date national records (þjóðskrá). Skúlason happened to be a genealogical enthusiast eager to use his programming skills for his hobby. Later on, deCODE genetics signed an agreement with Frisk Software to speed up the construction of the database by adding information from a variety of available sources, focusing on twelve censuses taken from 1703 to 1930. "Pretty much everybody," as Skúlason put it, "is included." The emerging database, the "Book of Icelanders," records approximately 700,000 people, the majority of people born in Iceland since the Norse settlement in the ninth century. A team of about fifteen researchers and computer programmers compiled the information contained in the Book of Icelanders and designed the necessary programs for displaying and analyzing it. The whole point, of course, is not simply to record individuals but rather to be able to connect them to each other. The "connectivity rate," the rate of documented connections between an individual and his or her parents, is close to 95 percent.

There are a number of empty spaces in the genealogical database. Part of the problem stems from missing information about paternity. The scale of the problem – the missing pages in the "Book of Icelanders," so to speak – varies from one century to another and from one region to another. Generally, the further one goes back the more erratic the records. For some districts, however, most of the records of the past have been lost due to fire or negligence. Not only are there empty spaces in available records, there are errors, too. Sometimes, families have "purified" their records, possibly to prevent disclosing information about teenage mothers or to avoid an image of inbreeding. However, recent estimates indicate that the problem is a minor one, for example with an error rate of 0.7 percent in maternal connections (Sigurðardóttir *et al.* 2000). Often, the genealogical team of deCODE genetics and Frisk Software have had to "socially construct" the information they have, in the light of their understanding of Icelandic history and culture and the nature of the sources at their disposal, making inferences, for instance, about births, marriages, deaths, and family connections. Skúlason has likened his task to "working out a puzzle the size of a football stadium, with half of the pieces missing and the rest damaged and randomly scattered" – a gigantic enterprise indeed.

The chief aim of deCODE genetics by the construction of the database was to advance genetic and biomedical research. One version of the Book of Icelanders is only available to deCODE researchers. In this case, no names are included, only numbers or IDs that allow for the combination of different datasets on a limited basis for particular research purposes. A complex process of encryption, surveillance, and monitoring has been designed to prevent any illegitimate use of the data. Such a database, it is argued, combined with genetic and medical data, provides an invaluable historical dimension to the exploration of potential causes of common diseases.

Some of the diagrams produced by the Book of Icelanders take the form of a circle, others are more like a horseshoe, and still others are

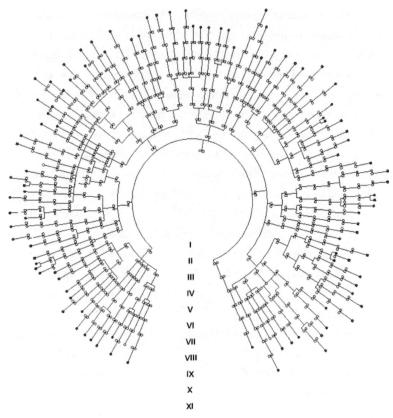

I
II
III
IV
V
VI
VII
VIII
IX
X
XI

FIGURE 3.2 An asthma pedigree with eleven generations (source: deCODE genetics)

more like trees proper, unfolding from left to right, from bottom up, or top down. Some are narrow and egocentric while others are fairly inclusive, and so on. Figure 3.2 shows a pedigree with eleven generations. The current-day Icelanders diagnosed with asthma (black squares and circles in the figure) are limited to the last generation or two, but their relationships are known through eleven generations and all of them are descendants of a single founder born in the seventeenth century. This powerful image, reproduced on deCODE genetics' tee-shirts and web pages, has functioned as the informal logo of the company. What are the figurative modes developed by deCODE genetics and the Book of Icelanders and what could they possibly signify?

Perhaps, given the variety of representation of genealogies in the deCODE genetics/Frisk Software project, one should not read too much into the differences between figurative modes such as these in terms of the graphics and layout of pedigrees. To some extent, the designers are "simply" motivated by straightforward visual concerns and the practical constraints of their tools, their programs, and computer screens, much like medieval genealogists were constrained by the properties of vellum, paper, and rolls of parchment. On the other hand, the different kinds of images are likely to represent particular aspects of the deCODE genetics/Frisk Software genealogical project: one underlines the rhetoric of the common roots and interests of the enclosed Icelandic "circle" (Figure 3.2), and another, as we saw in Chapter 2 (Figure 2.1), represents the search for genes with mutations passed "down" through the generations.

Apart from its visual appeal, the circular image of Figure 3.2 underlined in the public-relations material of deCODE genetics may serve, consciously or not, to foster a sense of unity and belonging. The reference to the "circle" of the community, the "Book" of Icelanders, and the continuity with the Viking past may, therefore, indirectly suggest a rather narrow genetic notion of citizenship. While most of those living in Iceland at present are included in the Book of Icelanders, in public perception some Icelanders are less equal than others, namely, "recent immigrants" or "latecomers" (*nýbúar*, in current jargon), whose genetic and genealogical "roots" lie elsewhere. Metaphorically speaking, in reference to the notion of the Book of Life in Christian eschatology, "recent immigrants" may be thrown into a lake of fire; while they live and work in Iceland, they do not belong, from the point of view of the majority, to what Finkler terms the circle of the "significant same" (2000: 15). A somewhat similar idea is captured in the notion of "French DNA" discussed by Rabinow (1999). Iceland, however, in particular Reykjavík the capital city, is rapidly becoming a multicultural community with a growing number of immigrants from different parts of the world. The genetic notion of citizenship suggested by the database project competes with other notions of citizenship which have increasingly been gaining force, emphasizing human rights and the empowerment of ethnic groups marginalized in the past.

The web of kin: kinship goes online

While one version of the Book of Icelanders, the encrypted edition, was produced for deCODE genetics, another version has been available since January 2003, free of charge, on the Worldwide Web (www. islendingabok.is). Those who are interested in exploring the database have to request a password, and as long as they have an Icelandic social security number they are provided with access by mail a few days later. This version, of course, includes personal names; there is no encryption. It enables Icelanders to trace their family histories and to explore their genealogical connection to almost any Icelander living or dead.

The response to the genealogies on the web was overwhelming. Overnight, the Book of Icelanders became a popular pastime. In a few weeks, 100,000 Icelanders, about one-third of the total population, requested a password, exploring their relations with neighbors, colleagues, and friends. Soon the database became a party game. Newspaper reports and discussions on the web indicate that families actively search for genealogical connections at informal social occasions, including dinner parties. Sometimes young people playfully explore connections with each other at drinking parties, joking and speculating about potential spouses and good matches. Also, there are reports about people checking on connections at work, to establish rapport at meetings, and to facilitate some kind of collaboration.

Much of the coverage of the Book of Icelanders in local media plays with both humor and vanity. Apparently, many people have explored their connections with public figures such as the prime minister and the musician Björk, celebrating the fact that they are "closely" related to important people. On April Fool's Day 2003, one of the local newspapers made up a story indicating the database had shown that a certain Lord Dillon turned out to have had Icelandic blood in his veins. That day, about 300 users logged into the database to see if they were related to Lord Dillon. Sometimes when browsing their web of kin users sadly discover that they have a closer connection than they would like to admit, with well-known crooks and criminals. In some cases, users' discoveries turn out to be shattering. One woman was shocked to discover that she had a half-brother in town (*Morgunblaðið* 2003). She knew that at some point her mother had given birth to a boy, but she had been told that he was stillborn. The facts of the boy's existence had been published in a family history which the makers of the Book of Icelanders had access to, but the woman only found out decades later when she was browsing the web that she had a brother alive.

The password provided for the Book of Icelanders only allows for limited access in the sense that the user cannot freely explore other families or the database in general. Access, in other words, is egocentric; a person can trace *his or her* relationships to any other Icelander, not the relationships between *any* two Icelanders. Thus, the designers of the Book of Icelanders have deliberately, it seems, avoided legal hurdles involving competition with published works. At the same time, such a restriction prevents others from downloading extensive information from the database, securing the property rights of the companies involved.

Following the launch of the Book of Icelanders on the web, the public responded enthusiastically by sending corrections, complaints, and additions to the company responsible for updating and maintaining the database. In a few months, the company received thousands of e-mail messages from users. These messages provide a fascinating window into Icelandic kinship, offering insights into genealogical concepts and practices. Here I can only explore a few aspects, the tip of the iceberg.

Below are some extracts from these messages to give the gist of users' responses. Many comments expressed the enthusiasm of thankful users of the database:

Gosh, this is really exciting!!! Now we finally have a point of departure. I got thinking of this when I was having my hair done. On both sides were women saying "Listen, my son-in-law turns out to be your husband's cousin" etc. Suddenly all cocktail parties have been turned into family reunions. I have no doubt that this has increased solidarity among us. This is wonderfully Icelandic. Again, congratulations!

Some of the comments were written in a humorous style, sometimes with a sarcastic undertone, correcting sensitive information about paternity, marriage, and cohabitation:

I don't know this woman. And, in any case, I am not married to her. But if this, indeed, were the case, by all means don't tell anyone about it.

I just wanted to say that this is a fantastic web site. The problem is, however, that my dad is not registered as my father. I have raised this with my parents and they guarantee that I am their daughter. Would you please correct this. Thanks. I know I am related to my dad as I inherited a disease from him; that is my proof.

The other day I was browsing through information on myself. My spouse was listed as my partner and when I clicked on him the name of his former GIRLFRIEND since high-school days appeared. Today we are married and the only thing that my husband and his former girlfriend have in common is a dog that was executed in 1998. So, I don't see any point in listing this woman there, at least not as part of my information . . . I am not going to explain to my children who this woman is; she has never been part of our life. THANK YOU.

Other comments seem to have been written in an angry and desperate mood: "I am the brother of this boy . . . And we are full brothers. Do you have to label our mother as a tart? I suggest you fix this before my father and my mother go on the web and have a fit."

A few comments underline serious concerns with belonging and exclusion from the community of Icelanders. Some people who, because of some error or lack of information, have not been "connected" to their parents in the database, have expressed their existential anxiety, as if the lack of digital connection forced them into exile or even non-existence:

I registered for the Book of Icelanders and according to the records I have no parents! Am I a clone? . . . It would be fun to know what went wrong . . . I have enjoyed telling my friends that I am a clone composed of all the best material that the human race has to offer . . . But it would be good if you could fix the error so that I can convince myself that I actually do exist.

Judging from such comments, being included and connected in the database is equivalent to a declaration of citizenship.

Many of the comments and corrections are fed simultaneously into the database on the web to comply with public understandings of kinship and belonging. Often, however, this is problematic due to conflicting positions and demands. The most sensitive comments involve illegitimacy and the children of single parents, as Skúlason explains in a newspaper interview (*Morgunblaðið* 2003). One contested issue involved a man who had a child outside marriage. The child's mother requested that the father be linked to the child in the Book of Icelanders. The wife of the biological father, however, insisted that this information was not published as the children she had with her husband remained unaware of his infidelity. Skúlason draws attention to an inherent gender difference in the treatment of information about the children of single parents:

A child of a single parent is by default linked to the parent that has the custody. If the parent is male, this is straight-forward. In that case, we call the man and ask him about the mother. This is never a secret. If on the other hand the child is linked to its mother – and, indeed, single mothers are far more numerous than single fathers – we have a problem. We cannot ask the mother as this would be against the working rules of the Book of Icelanders and, indeed, violate rules of ethics. Neither can we ask the child itself, at least not until it has become legally autonomous.

The Book of Icelanders would not have been brought into being had it not been for the genealogical enthusiasm of Icelandic scribes and collectors through the centuries and the gene talk of the modern age, but once in existence it had important repercussions, operating like a machine.

Genealogical machines

The standard dictionary definition of "machine" (from the Latin noun *machina* corresponding to the verb *machinari*, "to plot") is any contrivance for the conversion of motion, an apparatus for doing some kind of work. In Mumford's analysis a machine is a "minor organism" in that it "involves the notion of an external source of power, a more or less complicated inter-relation of parts, and a limited kind of activity" (Mumford 1962: 11). Given such a definition, machines can take many forms. The political economy of human–machine relations also varies from case to case. Some relations may be seen as mutual subjugation, others are more properly characterized as slavery, and still others represent symbiotic cyborgs. Machines are constructed by humans for specific purposes, but sometimes they seem to acquire autonomous, self-generating powers, constituting society, "plotting" its course. Much like viruses and other subjects of experimental biology "have taken researchers to unanticipated destinations" (Creager 2002: 325), machines sometimes open up new vistas and avenues. The perspective of "co-production" is useful for addressing some of the ways in which technology and the social order mutually constitute each other, "highlighting the often invisible role of knowledges, expertise, technical practices and material objects in shaping, sustaining, subverting or transforming relations of authority" (Jasanoff 2004: 4). The Book of Icelanders is a case in point.

The original fascination with the Book of Icelanders has slackened, but nevertheless figures supplied by deCODE genetics show that public use of the database has been maintained at a somewhat surprisingly high level (see Figure 3.3). The frequency of visits to the web reached its peak of almost 18,000 log-ins per day around two weeks after the launch of the Book of Icelanders. During the following three months it slowed down until it reached the stable level of about 1,000 log-ins per day during weekends and 1,500 on working days.

The launching of the Book on the web encouraged Icelanders to think that they are all fairly closely related, suggesting an imagined community based on kinship ties. In a sense, Icelandic society has been celebrating itself by digital means and on the web. Most Icelanders, in fact, are related through an ancestor seven or eight generations back. But if the imagined community of Icelanders turns out to be a huge extended family, kinship and belonging seem bound to change. The implications are complex and only the future will tell which way things will go. For Icelanders, the strength of the kinship bond has usually been more a matter of degree than an either/or, relational space and distance being opportunistically defined according to context. Perhaps this will be even more the case in the future than in the past, keeping in mind Icelanders' playful use of the genealogical machine. Given that most people are related through a common ancestor only several generations back, there are virtually no non-relatives, apart from the relatively few immigrants whose parents represent other cultures, nations, or populations. If practically everyone turns out to be fairly closely related to everyone else the notion of "relatives" becomes a bit too broad to have much significance.

Obviously, whatever the implications for Icelandic notions of kinship, which for the time being must remain only good guesses if not pure speculation, the "complete" genealogical database is revolutionizing genealogical practice in Iceland. Genealogical enthusiasts and family historians need not struggle with a variety of obscure documents, past

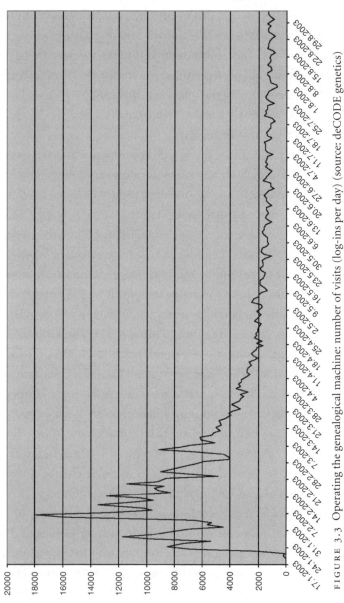

FIGURE 3.3 Operating the genealogical machine: number of visits (log-ins per day) (source: deCODE genetics)

and present, as most available material has now been digitalized and compiled in a single database. Interestingly, the typical user of family histories is no longer an elderly, scholarly male. The Book of Icelanders seems to be used by both men and women from most walks of life. Among the most enthusiastic early users of the Book were groups of young girls who apparently wanted to explore kinship connections with their friends.

The web version is bound to give priority to legal notions of social kinship, not genetics. Some of the corrections by the users of the database on the web, corrections involving genetic kinship, are obviously relevant for the encrypted version used in deCODE's biomedical project. Gradually, these corrections are incorporated in new "editions" in the continuous remaking of the Book of Icelanders. Occasionally, the staff of deCODE discover a mismatch in their anonymous database, a contradiction between genetics and social paternity. In that case, the records are simply dropped from the database as they are useless for genetic and biomedical purposes. Since, however, these corrections relate to the encrypted version and no one knows the names or identities of the persons involved, they obviously cannot be introduced on the web even if one wanted to.

A recent study of photocopier repair technicians emphasizes the triangular relationship and negotiation among technicians, customers, and machines (Orr 1996: 3):

The problems encountered by technicians are most fundamentally breakdowns of the interaction between customers and their machines, which may or may not include a malfunction or failure of some machine component. Diagnosis requires negotiation with both customers and machines, first to assess the breakdown and determine the problem and then to produce an acceptable solution.

Running the digital machine represented by the Book of Icelanders requires similar negotiation. Frisk Software rightly observes that through the enthusiastic cooperation of the Icelandic public the company has effectively "hired" a substantial part of the population for free to correct and "finalize" the genealogical database. The public, then, has been both busily fine-tuning the machine, ensuring that it runs smoothly and accurately – and, at the same time, reflecting upon relatedness and redefining community.

The machine metaphor, no doubt, is one of the seductive metaphors of our times. Rothenberg argues that the machine "suggests feedback, and new machines extend feedback into new situations" (1993: 131). "Can we," he adds, however, "see nothing more than machines anymore in the world around us?" Digital genealogies, I have suggested, can be usefully regarded as machines, generating – for social, commercial, managerial, as well as epistemological purposes – connections, questions, and answers. In Iceland, a rich local tradition of collecting and storing family histories, a tradition established and developed during the Middle Ages, has been adopted and enhanced by the tools of computers and modern informatics. Clearly, digital genealogies represent a powerful machine. The deCODE edition of the Book of Icelanders may significantly advance the monitoring of public health and the management of the body politic, speeding up the search for genes and the improvement of health. Equally, the search-engine available on the web has established connections that would otherwise remain hidden, "plotting" at the same time histories and identities, personal, familial, and national. Much like ice-core isotopic records from glaciers extracted through the application of heavy machinery give some hints regarding the past climate of the Arctic, building up a detailed account of environmental change that extends hundreds of years into the past, drilling into the past by means of the online genealogical machine helps to establish social connections and reinvent family histories.

Often, biomedical projects represent a curious pooling of rather different sources of information that have not previously been combined – genealogical, genetic, and medical. While each source has its own trajectory and use rights, their collective, synergic assembly for the purpose of exploring the potential genetic bases of common diseases necessarily redefines each of them. Given the importance of genealogical records for many biomedical projects, the issue of access and owner-ship may become a central one in genealogical research and record-ing (Pálsson 2006). In January 2000, the Icelandic genealogist Þorsteinn Jónsson and his publishing company Genealogia Islandorum challenged deCODE genetics and Frisk Software in the courts for using previously published genealogies whose rights, it claimed, belonged to the company. The spokespersons for Genealogia Islandorum suggested that scholars working for them had searched original documents in local archives throughout the country (genealogies, farm histories, and folklore), com-piling massive amounts of information and arranging it in readable fash-ion, in a series of costly commercial publications. Now, they claimed, their property rights were being violated as others, deCODE genetics, punched in the records, copying and marketing the products of earlier efforts for profit, partly through biomedical research. In compensation for the "vio-lation" of its property rights, Genealogia Islandorum demanded millions of dollars.

The staff of deCODE rejected the claimants' arguments, pointing out that, on its own, genealogical data did not constitute private prop-erty. Also, they suggested that along with Frisk Software the company had added extensively to earlier compilations by independent research and, moreover, designed its own electronic format of storing and usage; deCODE further claimed that genealogical information about Icelanders constituted a common heritage and by taking the makers of the Book of Icelanders to the courts Genealogia Islandorum was effectively trying to appropriate genealogical information that had been the collective posses-sion of the Icelandic nation for centuries. Finally, deCODE announced that it would be offering its genealogical program and database for free, in the public domain, so as to ensure public access to this important resource. In 1999, one may note, one of the architects of the database, Skúlason, estimated that on a CD-ROM it would become a bestseller.

The case was taken to the Icelandic Supreme Court. During its proceed-ings the claimants requested that two evaluators be appointed to examine the way in which the digital database was being constructed. In particular, they suggested, the evaluators should "establish whether the spokespersons for the Book of Icelanders had chiefly constructed the database ... on the basis of published genealogies or chiefly through their independent scrutiny of original documents. . . ." (Supreme Court of Iceland 2000, no. 292). The court accepted the claimants' request and appointed two independent evaluators. Their report concluded that the description of the construction of the Book of Icelanders offered by deCODE and Frisk Software was essentially correct.[1] Eventually, the company Genealogia Islandorum was declared bankrupt and its spokespersons withdrew the case against the Book of Icelanders. Many of its databases and publications were bought by deCODE and Frisk Software, adding to the companies' already vast storehouse of biomedical information on the national body. The Book of Icelanders is bound to affect the market for books on genealogies, a market that in the past has been a fairly lively one. However, these are radically different kinds of publications. The Book of Icelanders only includes basic facts on dates of birth and death, residence, and occupation, while available printed books tend to provide much "thicker" descriptions of family histories, sometimes adding photographs of individuals, families, and farms, descriptions that the consumers tend to be interested in.

From trees to rhizomes

The imagery of the tree has had a strong hold on the human imagination, as a metaphoric aid for talking about diversity and relationships, whether human or non-human. There are countless examples in the ethnographic literature of the metaphoric association of trees and kinship relationships, from Europe, Africa, South America, and elsewhere. Atran suggests that

[1] In the court's reasoning: "As a genealogical database, the Book of Icelanders is based on original sources, but in the process of its construction many printed or published sources have also been consulted ... All published genealogies naturally add to previously available information . . . making it easier at the same time to connect persons and accelerate the process" (see *Morgunblaðið* 2002).

as a life form trees may be evolutionarily significant for human cognition; trees, he argues, may be "phenomenally compelling" (1990: 35) to humans generally due to their ecological and historical role.

Such a claim may, however, need to be qualified in the light of both history and ethnography. As we have seen, some medieval European genealogical concepts associated descendants with a series of curving lines without any botanical reference. For some people, for instance Inuit groups in the barren Arctic, the idea of trees is probably radically different from, say, the trees experienced by inhabitants of South American rain forests (Fernandez 1998: 81). Klapisch-Zuber (2000) leads one to believe that the Western preoccupation with the tree metaphor has much to do with agrarian domination and succession, and Deleuze and Guattari (1988) would seem to agree, emphasizing a contrast between the patriarchal West, on the one hand, and the democratic South or East, on the other hand. While the imagery of the tree is neither cognitively necessary nor an ethnographic universal, trees seem to "make perfect natural models for genealogical connections" (Rival 1998: 11). As Rival suggests, trees may "be potent symbols of vitality precisely because their status as living organisms is so uncertain" (1998: 23); trees die slowly, unlike animals they do not seem to have a "natural" life-span, and, finally, trees may be intensely alive and half-dead at the same time, composed of a mixture of dead and live tissue. Much like, perhaps, family trees.

The metaphor of the tree may be central to several academic disciplines, but it also has its critics. Fernandez (1998) suggests that the trope of the banyan tree, a trope drawn upon in Linton's book (1955) *The Tree of Culture*, offers a "more accurate and compelling metaphor" for anthropologists "than the common tree metaphor with the unidirectionality, hierarchy and finality of its spreading and diversifying fruitions":

The banyan tree suggests a circularity, if not a tensile netlike interconnectedness of parts, in human affairs, both as regards cultural evolution and the evolution of understanding, that the normal tree metaphor either conceals or cannot manage to convey. The circular intertwined metaphor of the banyan tree, indeed, offers a different imaginative vision of the human condition, a different order of "necessary connections" between human variety, than the tree metaphor pure and simple. (Fernandez 1998: 99)

Instead of the metaphor of the tree, Deleuze and Guattari similarly suggest the notion of the rhizome, a decentered cluster of interlaced threads where everything is potentially interconnected with everything else; whereas the tree "always comes back 'to the same'," the rhizome has "multiple entryways" (1988: 12), connecting any point to any other point. Kinship research has usually relied on tree-like diagrams, a mode of representation heavily informed by literacy, print cultures, and textual metaphors. In order to make our accounts more authentic, perhaps we need to pay greater attention to the multiple ways in which kinship is manifested and represented during ethnographic encounters. Enfield explores the ways in which people use their body as a "cognitive artifact" for the expression of kinship, emphasizing that "speakers' gestures during interviews on kinship and kin terminology are ethnogenealogical diagrams which have been in front of our eyes all along" (2005: 51). Speakers of Lao, and, in fact, most of us, Enfield suggests, draw more upon hand movements and other bodily signals to flesh out and mediate relatedness than pencil, paper, and diagrams, "sketching with bare hands in mid-air" (2005: 73).

Traditional notions of human relatedness, indeed, seem to have taken a general "lateral" shift, undermining the "vertical" determinism of many contemporary discourses on genetics and relatedness. Echoing Deleuze and Guattari, Ingold suggests there is "a world of difference between the real, living tree in the forest and the abstract tree of the genealogical model":

For the former is caught up in a dense network of entanglements with the vegetation that clings to it, the animals that forage and nest in it, and the humans that live under it. In short, the tree is but one part of that vast rhizome that is the forest as a whole. Only when it is abstracted from these rhizomatic entanglements does it appear in its "pure", dentric form. (Ingold 2000: 145)

If the paradigmatic family tree is being radically refigured along these lines, the evolutionary tree seems bound to change as well. After all, throughout the history of the tree imagery, the evolutionary tree and the family tree have co-evolved, nature and society (evolution and history) mutually informing each other (Bouquet 2000, Feeley-Harnik 2001). In fact, the phylogenetic tree of evolutionary biology has been shaken by recent research. Darwin posited a universal phylogenetic tree that united the great kingdoms of nature, but now it looks as though the kingdoms have been swapping genes back and forth for a very long time (see, for instance, Doolittle 1999), introducing fundamental messiness into biological classification. Thus, some early organisms (eukaryotes) picked parts of their genome from their food. Such "horizontal" transfer of genes – prehistoric equivalents of modern gene hunting and genetic engineering, perhaps – may be the major evolutionary source of true innovation. According to researchers at the Human Genome Project, some human genes seem to have been horizontally acquired, from bacteria. While that claim is currently being contested, it underlines the possibility that part of the human genome is second-hand – or, to paraphrase Bakhtin (1986) on words in language, half somebody else's. Under certain conditions, genes, then, pass across organisms, adopted much like children – or ethnographers in the field. Quite possibly, as a result, the notion of the universal evolutionary "tree" needs to be revised.

Some scholars have suggested fungus – with its open-ended, subterranean network of mycelial fibers – as a paradigmatic life form (Ingold 2000). Perhaps, the discovery of gene swapping invites a gestalt shift in biological and evolutionary perspectives, from trees to fungi. Recently, the phylogenetic tree has been revised on the basis of computational analyses of existing genetic databases; through the mining of genetic data researchers have rearranged millions of species on what they call a "supertree" (see Crandall and Buhay 2004). Some suggest that with the sequencing of complete genomes, phylogenetic analysis, the reconstruction of the tree of life, is entering a new phase of "phylogenomics" (Delsuc, Brinkmann, and Philippe 2005).

Latour has argued that "*whenever we learn something about the management of humans, we shift that knowledge to nonhumans and endow them with more and more organizational properties*. . . : industry shifts to nonhumans the management of people learned in the imperial machine" (1999: 207–208; emphasis in the original). Digital genealogies, a by-product of experimental biomedical projects, are a case in point. Such genealogies, I have argued, can be usefully regarded as machines, as vehicles for generating connections and histories and for changing existing notions of kinship and belonging – in short, for "revealing" or "bringing-forth," in Heidegger's sense. "[W]hat is decisive in techne," Heidegger argued, "does not lie in making and manipulating, nor in the using of means, but rather in . . . revealing . . . It is as revealing, and not as manufacturing, that technē is a bringing-forth" (1977: 319). Perhaps the negotiations on relatedness described above, involving consumers and makers of digital genealogies and their collective fine-tuning of genealogical machines, will in the long run highlight and reinforce a rhizomic notion of relatedness. Fusing the horizontal and the vertical, the order of law and the order of nature in Schneider's (1980) and Strathern's (1992) terms, "authoritative" digital genealogies become a complex tight-knit web, more like subterranean fibers than trees. The web of kin, indeed, is increasingly digitally explored on the Worldwide Web. Like the rhizome, to borrow from Deleuze and Guattari, the web has "multiple entryways" (1988: 12); everything is potentially interconnected with everything else.

Ethnographically, siblings are sometimes represented as "one stomach." Perhaps trafficking in the Book of Icelanders and similar web-based genealogies reinforces old notions of intercorporeality, of bodies of kin, mother tongues, and national wombs. Han (in press) presents an interesting analysis of what she calls the "belly talk" of American middle-class women and men when preparing for parenthood – talking, singing, and reading aloud to the expected child *in utero*. Some of Han's informants, both men and women, regularly told bedtime stories to the child and one woman "checked in" with her baby during her morning drive to work. "Belly talk," Han suggests, does important cultural work, constituting kin and kinship, socializing parents, gendering them as mothers and fathers, and enabling men to become active partners in childbearing, "making room for daddy." When browsing web-based genealogies such as the Book of Icelanders, people engage in a kind of "belly talk," constituting kin through logging-in, by talking to the national circle of kin.

One somewhat surprising result of the application of the Book of Icelanders in genomic studies is the demonstration of regional subdivisions in the Icelandic gene pool. Such divisions are likely to be even more marked in contexts characterized by more complex geographies and population structures. Taking them into account rather than assuming regional homogeneity is likely to reduce the risk of being misled by spurious associations of alleles with disease phenotypes and of overlooking true associations, thereby advancing the genetic research on common diseases (Helgason *et al.* 2005).[2]

Few people would seriously claim that genetic and/or genealogical connections encompass all forms of relatedness. It is one thing, of course, to argue that population histories can be written on the basis of genetic substance and quite another to suggest that the phenomenological experience of relatedness is dictated by DNA material. Ethnography, in fact, suggests a variety of models. In some societies, the transmission of substance is regarded as an ongoing process that includes breast-feeding,

---

[2] Another surprising by-product of the Book of Icelanders is the discovery by deCODE researchers of positive selection of an inverted segment on a particular chromosome (in technical terms, an inversion polymorphism on chromosome 17q21.31). This discovery suggests that carrier females have more children than non-carriers, a conclusion that is likely to hold for European populations where the inversion is found at a frequency of 20 percent (Stefansson *et al.* 2005). Such results are not only important for the understanding of biological evolution and regional differences (the arrival of the inversion around 3 million years ago resulted in two distinct lineages that apparently occur in different proportions in different populations), but also they may have implications for the understanding of disease.

a process that may take several years after the moment of birth. More importantly, in some contexts kinship connections have little to do with shared substance. Bamford argues that while at first glance the notion of "one blood" among the Kamea of Papua New Guinea seems to resonate with substantial notions of kinship, local notions, in fact, have little in common with Western understandings. Unlike the Western notion of descent, the "one-blood" idiom only connects people within the same generation. "In order to understand what connects and disconnects people in this world," Bamford concludes, "it is necessary to move from a substantive to a relational point of view" (2004: 302).

The powerful discourse on the "book of life" established during the last century (Kay 2000) and the recent achievements of genetics and biotechnology have fostered a renewed interest in family histories and kinship diagrams. As Chapter 4 shows, genealogies are a critical component of a number of large-scale genetic databases that seek to advance biomedical knowledge by studying regional or national populations. Family trees, however, have a social life of their own, a biography informed by the contours of the cultural landscapes to which they belong. Not only is the inclusion of genealogies in biomedical projects a contested issue, their graphic representation also invites controversial notions of identity and citizenship. Moreover, the linear notion of kinship as the business of transmission of substance has been challenged on several fronts. The genealogical notion underlined in early anthropological notions of kinship has become fuzzy and rhizomic; family trees, it turns out, to paraphrase Turner (1967), are a forest of symbols.

FOUR

Biobanking: medical records and genetic databases

Moving from the laboratory to larger contexts, this chapter explores the structures and histories of large-scale biomedical projects somehow combining, or allowing for the combination of, genetic, medical, and genealogical information. I argue that while such projects differ in many ways, they represent the extension and intensification of governance and the biomedical gaze. For Foucault, the eighteenth century gave birth to biopolitics, the rationalization of "the problems presented to governmental practice by the phenomena characteristic of a group of living human beings constituted as a population: health, sanitation, birthrate, longevity, race." "We are aware of," he added, "the expanding place these problems have occupied since the eighteenth century, and of the political and economic issues they have constituted up to the present day" (1994: 73). Foucault's approach was rather Eurocentric, ignoring the emergence of "modern" government both in empires such as that of China and in European colonies (Inda 2005: 12). Nevertheless, his concepts have relevance today, at a time when power over life is expanding into new domains: "These concepts are particularly useful in understanding the politics of life at the collective level of the population, a domain of politics that has been little explored" (Greenhalgh and Winckler 2005: 27).

Human bodily components differ in the extent to which they can be extracted, stored, and exchanged. Their "candidacy" for exchange and commodification, in Appadurai's sense (1986), is highly variable; blood transfusion and heart transplants, for instance, represent radically different contexts. Much depends, of course, on people's conceptions of the body, the social context, and the technology available for the extraction, storing, and circulation of body parts. Harvey's discovery in 1616 of the circulation of blood signaled the revisioning of the body of Early Modern Europe (Paster 1997), paving the way for the banking and transfusion of human blood. The history of blood, in fact, provides a special case, as Titmuss shows in his work *The Gift Relationship: From Human Blood to Social Policy* (1997). While blood is frequently donated in an altruistic fashion, other modes of exchange also apply. Such differences are indicative of social relations and ethical codes: "To give or not to give, to lend, repay or even to buy and sell blood leads us . . . into the fundamentals of social and economic life" (Titmuss 1997: 124). In some cases, in the United States, for example, people increasingly "donate" blood to themselves, placing it on reserve in a personalized blood bank for potential later use (Godbout 1998: 54). The practice of blood banking has undergone significant change as a result of a number of different developments, including the discovery of the AIDS virus, the development of new technologies for monitoring blood quality, and the manufacture of blood substitutes. As Casteret points out, in France and some other countries faith in the state system of blood banking has been seriously undermined (1992); "blood scandals" whereby contaminated blood products were passed on with the knowledge of those responsible to hundreds of hemophiliacs have cast doubt on the role of the state and the spirit of the gift in the context of blood donations. As a result, blood is not flowing as freely as before through the veins and arteries of the medical system. These are reminders of the contested and unstable cultural biographies of blood, other human biological material, and biomedical information.

Ongoing developments in biotechnology and bioinformatics have opened up a new world, shifting the focus to bodily information, genes, and DNA sequences; the critical issue is the use and control of the information that can be derived from body components rather than the components themselves. Throughout the world there are numerous specialized biomedical collections such as cancer registries and general health records. Recently, a new kind of biomedical collection has taken center stage in public discussions of biomedicine, namely DNA banks. One of the world's largest DNA banks, it seems, has been operated by the United States military since 1992. All military inductees and all active duty and reserve personnel have been requested to provide blood and saliva samples for a DNA Specimen Repository. A potential biomedical collection can be said to exist wherever tissue samples are stored, whatever the stated purpose of the storage. Thus, the archives of newborn screening cards in the United States – so-called "Guthrie cards" – that many public health laboratories have retained (after testing the blood spots on the cards for inborn errors of metabolism) collectively constitute a gigantic DNA bank. McEwen suggests that "because DNA may be found wherever biological materials are present, even such places as post offices (where DNA may be found on millions of licked stamps), barbershop floors (where DNA may be found in hair roots), and manicure salons (where DNA may be found in clipped fingernails) can be viewed as at least potential DNA 'banks'" (1997: 247). A daunting scene perhaps.

Is the notion of "banking" in the context of biological material and information, one may ask, simply a catchy metaphor or are biomedical collections no less bank-like than the financial institutions we call banks? Apparently, the word for a *bank*, which is common for most European languages, is of Teutonic origin, meaning bench, table, and counter. Likewise, the ancient Greek word for a banker, *trapezites*, comes from *trapeza*, a money-changer's table. The first bankers were living in Babylon over 3,000 years ago, exchanging goods from the bench or across the counter in temples and royal palaces that provided security against the threat of confiscation or destruction. At first, grain was the main form of deposit; later, other crops were added as well as cattle and, eventually, precious metal and coins. Originally, the deposits were transferred to the order of the depositor but later on also to a third party. Handwriting probably developed in association with keeping accounts. Before double-entry bookkeeping arrived transactions were recorded by varying the case ending of the names of those involved, "credit entries being naturally enough in the genitive or possessive case and debit entries in the dative case" (Davies 1994: 53). Seed corn, the basis of both the economy and banking, was administered by an official, *Oeconomus*, who ensured that it was used properly. How, then, can the reference to the concept and history of the ancient institution of banking – a product, as we have seen, of the Neolithic revolution, state formations, and agriculture – help to illuminate discussions of the new genetics of the contemporary world?

Structures and histories: seven cases

Banking "proper" invites a series of important questions that may facilitate comparison of the governing, structures, operations, and histories of biomedical collections. What is being assembled in each case – blood, organs, tissue, genetic material, bodily information, genealogies? What is the purpose of its collection and what are the rules of bookkeeping? Do transactions take the form of a gift, barter, or commodity? Are deposits transferred to the order of a third party and, if so, in return for what? Who is the *Oeconomus* governing what is assembled and the ways in which it is used, and on what grounds is governance based? I shall address some of these questions with reference to several national biomedical projects.

Many people nowadays use the term "biobank" as a generic. Thus, Cambon-Thomsen refers to "biobanks" as "organized collections of biological samples and data associated with them" (2004: 866), one subset of which is "population biobanks." Since the term is rather broad and fuzzy, several others have been suggested for the kind of large-scale biomedical assemblies employed by the new genetics, including "genetic databases," "biomedical collections," "population biomedical collections," "genebanks," and "biothèques" or "biolibraries." Here I shall speak of "genetic databases," following Tutton and Corrigan: "we see these databases as involving the collection, storage, and use of physical tissue (usually blood, but by no means exclusively), genotype and other biological information derived from that tissue, and a variety of personal data from populations of various sizes" (2004: 3). In such a definition, a genetic database typically combines (temporarily at least) two kinds of banking, one corporeal (DNA samples) and another informational (including medical records). A brief comparison of seven genetic database projects and proposals (in Iceland, Tonga, Sweden, United Kingdom, Estonia, Quebec, and Taiwan) suggests similar concerns with health, monitoring, research, and commercialization, revealing at the same time different contexts, scales, and designs.

Iceland: the Health Sector Database

In 1998, the Iceland Ministry of Health dramatically and abruptly announced its plans for the construction of a Health Sector Database on the entire Icelandic population of 300,000 people. These plans, initiated by deCODE genetics and emphasizing a research strategy outlined by Gulcher and Stefánsson (1998), specified how and under what conditions national medical records could be assembled and exploited. The first bill for the Health Sector Database was presented in Parliament as an item demanding urgent action. Immediately, there was strong public reaction. Critics argued that the measures introduced for the encryption of personal data were insufficient and, moreover, that clauses on patient consent and the monitoring of the database as well as the rules of access were poorly developed, at best.

Given the pioneering nature of the enterprise, a legal and ethical model or framework for such a comprehensive, national project was non-existent. The bill was withdrawn and a second and extensively revised version was soon introduced. Finally, the Icelandic Parliament passed the second bill authorizing the construction of the database (Icelandic

Parliament 1998, Act no. 139). The license to construct it was open to competition; the licensee would finance it, and the resulting database would belong to the National Health Service, with the licensee retaining privileged rights to commercialize it for twelve years. Eventually, deCODE genetics was granted the license to construct the database. The text for the license specified that the company should pay the Icelandic state a certain fee for the assembly and use of the records of the medical service; deCODE genetics was requested to cover the cost of the agreement on the database, its construction, and marketing. Also, it had to forfeit 70 million Icelandic kronur annually (about $US 1 million) for the license that would be used to further medical research and development. Furthermore, the Icelandic state would receive 6 percent of the annual profit that deCODE genetics would make from using the database. A rival biotechnological company, Iceland Genome Corporation (UVS), was established in the heat of the legal debate, partly to challenge deCODE genetics.[1]

The public debate in Iceland frequently referred simply to "the database issue" (*gagnagrunnsmálið*), subsuming medical records (the Health Sector Database), genetic information, and genealogies as well as their combination. International discussion also emphasized the combination of these three datasets and their collective commodification. This is not surprising as original plans suggested combining medical records and the other two databases for scientific and commercial purposes, thereby developing what is referred to here as a "genetic database." The legal framework, however, of the Health Sector Database is exclusively focused on the assembly of medical records, on the principle of presumed consent. Genetic samples (*blóðsýni*, blood samples, or *erfðasýni*, genetic samples)

---

[1]   In January 2006, deCODE genetics acquired the Iceland Genome Corporation for $5.5 million in common stock. By then, the latter company had built up a strong program for cancer research with a large number of patients and control groups. The two companies had used similar methods and the same genealogies. Prior to the deal, the relevant ethical authorities gave permission for combining the medical data obtained by the two companies.

would be collected for specific research purposes, on the basis of informed consent, and only combined with medical records on condition of scientific and ethical screening and approval. Family histories, as we have seen, are already in the public domain.

For the spokespersons of the Health Sector Database, the power of genetic and epidemiological analyses would be greatly enhanced by the database. The medical records available since 1915, it was argued, would allow for the exploration of a set of new questions on the interaction among a number of variables apart from genetic makeup and genealogical connections, including variables pertaining to lifestyle, physical and social environments, the use of particular medicine, and degree and kind of hospitalization. While the Icelandic project seems to have been cancelled or put on hold at the time of writing, as we have seen, it has nevertheless indirectly generated interesting results and products. Moreover, it has inspired biomedical planning in several contexts. The project has appeared to be plausible and scientifically promising not only because the Icelandic population has been small, relatively homogeneous, and comparatively isolated but also because Icelanders have a passion for keeping genealogical records. A relatively homogenous population with good genealogical as well as medical records (for precise phenotypic identification of symptoms), it is argued, is the ideal experimental site for biomedical analysis. According to deCODE genetics and their investors, Icelanders meet such conditions better than most other populations. Similar arguments were advanced in some other contexts.

There were several kinds of motives for the establishment of the Health Sector Database. From the point of view of members of Parliament, ministers and representatives of the state, such a database would render the health care system more efficient, making it possible to monitor the impact of drugs, health care, and the role of lifestyle. The results might be useful, according to the Icelandic medical authorities, for pharmaceutical companies and for the medical service, producing information on potential drugs, particular genes or proteins, and possible preventive measures in terms of consumption and lifestyle. From the point of view of deCODE genetics, a database would speed up the search for genes responsible for common diseases and the development and manufacture of "personalized" drugs.

Given the historical significance of the Icelandic Health Sector Database project, a somewhat extended discussion of precedents is in order. The major biomedical collections already in place in Iceland were the Blood Bank and the databank of the Cancer Society. Established in 1953, the Blood Bank is the main collector of blood for medical purposes. It collects blood within the framework of the reciprocal gift and serves almost all of the hospitals in the country (Harðardóttir 2002). As a result, it is a major source of biomedical data, with detailed information on donors and potential recipients of blood. Launched around 1954 by the Icelandic Cancer Society, the Cancer Registry documents information about all diseases that have been diagnosed in Icelanders since the beginning of its operation. It also records personal names, gender, date of birth, day of diagnosis, how the diagnosis was made, tissue type, stage of development, as well as information about treatment, the spread of the disease, and the date of death.[2]

The idea of constructing a comprehensive genealogical database on Icelanders is not a novel one. In an essay written in 1943, the novelist Halldór Laxness suggested that an "anthropological" office or institute (*mannfræðistofnun*) be established in order to document, for the purpose of marketing and research, information on every Icelander ever recorded:

---

[2] Parallel to the Cancer Registry, the Cancer Society has kept and maintained another register focusing on the family histories of cancer patients. The aim of the two cancer registries is to provide information and knowledge about the causes of cancer, advancing epidemiological research through tracking family connections (*fjölskyldugengi*). Few databases of this kind have been constructed for an entire nation, providing information about all cases diagnosed over a period of fifty years. Many researchers elsewhere have expressed interest in collaborating with the Cancer Society.

Information on every family would be organized (*kerfaðar*) so that the employees of the institute would be able to assemble, at short notice, the family history of any Icelander . . . Thus, the study of Icelandic genealogy would reach the state whereby genealogists would be superfluous; the female [*sic*] clerk of an official institute could extract at any moment in time the family records of any Icelander, living or dead, with minor effort . . . and hand them over to a contractor in return for an inconsequential fee. (See Laxness 1962: 155–6)

As a serious social thinker and a critical commentator during World War II and in the heyday of eugenic theorizing, Laxness was well aware of the potential misuses of records of this kind. He concluded his essay on "Indexing human life" by pointing out that the German security police had constructed records on tens of millions of people in many countries throughout the world, with detailed information on social background, life histories, and political inclinations, "for the sole purpose of being able to identify them and execute them at a convenient moment": "In comparison with [Heinrich] Himmler's database, which is aimed at murder," Laxness adds, "it would be a small job to grant these few Icelanders life in a catalogue" (Laxness 1962: 157). It is only very recently, however, thanks to modern bioinformatics and computer technology, that Laxness's grand idea of granting Icelanders eternal life in a complete and easily accessible genealogical file has become a realistic one.

Laxness was expressing something that was in the air. A precursor to the Health Sector Database was a database made from the early 1960s onward under the umbrella of the University of Iceland and largely funded by the Atomic Energy Commission of the United States. At the end of World War II, critical questions about the effects of increased radiation were being asked more frequently than before. Would, for example, increased radiation from atomic bombing affect the mutation of human body cells? Scientists had already realized that in order to examine the effects of radiation they needed a well-defined control group. They reckoned that they had a better chance of finding the base frequency of mutations that could occur in the human body if they had access to small and well-defined populations. Icelandic society provided an ideal context for comparison. In 1966, a Genetic Committee was established at the University of Iceland, the role of which was to encourage and organize genetic research at the university and, more generally, in Iceland. The work of the committee focused on "the recording in one place on punch cards various genetic information on Icelanders" along with information provided by the Statistical Bureau of Iceland and the National Archives (Greinargerð um erfðafræðirannsóknir á Íslandi 1974: 2).[3]

The committee carried out extensive research on blood groups, based on information provided by the Icelandic Blood Bank. The distributions of blood groups were analyzed "in an attempt to explain the origin of Icelanders, through a comparison with the distribution of blood groups in neighboring countries." The Committee also carried out research on chromosomes, "examining most mongoloid patients with particular studies of the families of individuals with a disruption in the chromosomes." "Moreover," the report added, "there are records on mental health for many people as well as on final grades from primary school. This information has so far not been used." As to the purpose of all of this, the report elaborated (1974: 5–6):

Icelanders have for long had a special interest in genealogies and inheritance . . . Much knowledge is to be found in genealogies, biographical collections, registers of employees, as well as the records of churches and censuses . . . Until now . . . it has been difficult for several reasons to analyze all the data, but with the advent of computers a new and better context for this research has been created . . . With the completion of the collection of all of this

---

[3] In 1974, the Genetic Committee sought to ensure a broader and more permanent basis for its activities, emphasizing the importance of collecting on file available demographic and biological information on all Icelanders, from the time of settlement. Individual records would be collapsed into family records and genealogical files.

information, a database would be established with information, written on a punch card, about every Icelander, living and deceased . . . This database can be utilized for various kinds of research, anthropological, genealogical, genetic, and medical. (1974: 5–6)

While the Health Sector Database had clear scientific and managerial motives, from the point of view of the Icelandic medical authorities and spokespersons for deCODE genetics, local interest in centralized medical databases has to be seen partly within the context of "Norse" history. The nationalist discourse of Icelanders – with its emphasis on the sagas, the glories of the past, the uniqueness of the Icelandic heritage, biological and cultural, and the Scandinavian interest in Norse genetics – partly explains the fascination of modern Icelanders with genetic databases and family histories. Influenced by Euro-American discourses of racial hygiene, Finnbogason (1922), one of the leading Icelandic intellectuals during the first half of the twentieth century, invoked the "science of eugenics" to argue for the purification of the Icelandic "race" to preserve its spiritual and physical asset.

Tonga: Autogen

Plans by deCODE genetics for a national genetic database on Icelanders quickly triggered similar schemes elsewhere. Most of the projects attempted in one way or another to learn from what has often been referred to as the "Icelandic mistakes," either searching for politically acceptable ways of involving commercial enterprises or suggesting informed consent as a general rule, or both. In November 2000, a biotechnological company, Autogen, based in Melbourne, announced plans to recruit 50,000 people in the Kingdom of Tonga, about half of the total population, to donate blood samples as well as medical and genealogical information for a biomedical collection. Autogen claimed in a statement to the Australian Stock Exchange that it had signed an agreement with the Tongan authorities to use the "unique" population of the Kingdom for identifying genes responsible for common diseases, including diabetes, obesity, and cardiovascular diseases. The rationale for the project was similar to that of the Icelandic one. On the other hand, the plan was to elicit informed consent, not the presumed consent in the use of medical records in the Icelandic case.

According to one of the early newspaper reports, Autogen would build a research laboratory on Tonga's main island next to a government-owned hospital, the only one in the country (Williams 2000). Autogen's director of research and development suggested that patients at the hospital would be requested to donate blood to the company's project. One of the assets of this case, he argued, was that Tongans had "a lot of history in the family groupings; they know who is related to whom." Autogen planned to offer the Tongan authorities a profit-sharing deal, in case any drugs would be developed on the basis of its results, while the database itself would remain Tongan property. The plan was to negotiate a similar deal with other Pacific nations which would allow for genetic studies of "the entire Polynesian race."

These plans sparked concern in both Tonga and the neighboring countries, particularly amongst church leaders and human rights groups. Before long, the Tongan project was abandoned as a result of protests. Opponents suggested that the agreement with Autogen was struck in the absence of public consultation. Interestingly, there was also a kind of culture clash between Western bioethics and Tongan notions of sociality. While the narrow, individualistic emphasis on informed consent was seen as an attempt to avoid the "pitfalls" of the Icelandic project, to steer clear of public concerns, it seems to have done the opposite, violating Tongan notions of personhood and the role of the extended family in decision-making.

One of the important concerns with the database project in the Tongan case was the widespread fear, emerging from the Solomon Islands and

Papua New Guinea, of bioprospectors extracting human genetic material for the purpose of patenting cell lines. During colonial times, Western passion for Tongan artifacts was so extreme as to provoke parody in Tonga. Captain Cook was "astonished" to witness with what eagerness Western sailors "catched at everything they saw"; "it even went so far," he observed, "as to become the ridicule of the Natives by offering pieces of sticks and stones and what not for exchange, one waggish Boy took a piece of human excrement on a stick and hild it out to every one of our people he met with" (cited in Thomas 1991: 128). Now the entangled, curious object was not a human artifact such as a tool or a weapon but the Tongan genome. At the same time, parody was replaced by anger. One of the local opposition slogans ran as follows: "Three centuries ago they came after our sandalwood. Today the bastards are after our genes!"[4]

Sweden: Medicinska Biobanken of Västerbotten

In the northern region of Sweden, Västerbotten, a medical database had already been constructed at the time of the Icelandic and Tongan developments: Medicinska Biobanken, a collection of medical and genetic information on 70,000 40–60-year-old people (Hoeyer 2004). It had been known for years that certain heart and cardiovascular diseases run in families in Västerbotten. In order to examine the distribution and causes of these diseases, blood samples from most adults in the region were collected over many years and compiled in a genetic database. By the end of the 1980s, a sizeable information pool had been amassed, one of the largest of its kind in the world. Researchers and state representatives argued, however, that to systematically tap that resource a

---

[4] This is not to say that the Tongans are isolationists. While Tonga may be an extreme periphery in world-system terms, the local population has developed strong international connections at least since the 1960s, partly through a Tongan diaspora, the family networks of the national elite (Marcus 1998: 135–151).

private genomics company had to become involved. In 1999 the regional council of Västerbotten signed a contract with the University of Umeå and a newly established biotechnological firm called UmanGenomics for the use and further development of the database. According to the agreement, UmanGenomics has the exclusive right to exploit for commercial purposes genetic information obtained from blood samples collected in Västerbotten over the years and in the near future. The agreement was prepared in the absence of any debate among the public and the media.

In the early years of the Swedish database, blood donors were requested to sign a statement (a so-called "donation contract") testifying to their agreement to the use of their samples for research purposes. Samples were collected as contributions to the medical service and the Swedish welfare state, often known, significantly, by the term "*Folkhemmet,*" meaning literally "the people's home." With the arrival of UmanGenomics, the practice of informed consent entered the scene. From then on, blood donors were supposed to be informed about the specific use of their samples. In Västerbotten, there was little discussion of the database, and practically none outside of the local university. On the national Swedish scene there was no significant debate either, although the public would respond a few years later. While the media discussed the ethical implications of biomedical collections in general, early reports on Medicinska Biobanken were fairly positive, praising the people responsible for setting a new standard, the so-called "ethical model of informed consent" developed by UmanGenomics. That model was also praised on similar grounds in international journals, including *Science* (1999) and *Nature* (1999). Sweden, like Iceland, has a strong national health care system that covers all citizens. Hence, the implications of a database project are probably rather different from those in other contexts where health care is either weak, as in Tonga, or heavily market-driven, as in the United States.

Estonia: the Gene Bank Database

In Estonia, a Human Research Act was passed in December 2000 to facilitate the establishment of a Gene Bank Database that is expected to contain phenotype and genotype data as well as information about lifestyle for all voluntary participants, around 1 million people or three quarters of the Estonian population. The project was conceived by researchers at the University of Tartu and presented to politicians in early 1999 as an opportunity to strengthen the national economy and advance biological research. Again, the chief purpose was to explore the purported genetic causes of common diseases, including hypertension, diabetes, as well as cardiovascular and neurodegenerative diseases such as Alzheimer's. In this case, a non-profit public foundation, the Estonian Genome Project (*Geenivaramu*, literally "Gene Collection" or "Heritage"), founded by the government of the Estonian Republic is responsible for the making of the database that will remain public property. The financing of the project, on the other hand, would largely be the business of a private company, EGeen International Corporation, located in California. In return, EGeen would have the exclusive right to use the sources of the database for twenty-five years. The major anticipated clients of the bank are research institutions and companies in the fields of bioinformatics, biotechnology, and pharmaceutics.

Public presentation of the project emphasizes altruistic contributions to scientific research and the health service. Participants are referred to as "gene donors" (*geenidoonor*). Some people, according to local jokes, who have considered participating have raised the question: "Will I have any genes left?" Apart from the reference to altruism, prospective participants are offered the opportunity to access their personal genetic data (through their general practitioner who collects the sample), in return for their help. Unlike the other genetic database projects discussed here, the Estonian one specifically allows for feedback to the donors of genetic samples. Participants are requested to provide a blood sample, sign a consent form, and fill out a questionnaire on background and lifestyle. While personal data are encrypted, replaced with a 16-digit code, in order to protect personal privacy, the manner of encoding will allow for the possibility of "going back," in case it is deemed necessary to communicate findings about genetic characteristics and potential inherited diseases to the people involved or their physicians.

Located at a dividing line between Eastern and Western Europe, Estonia has seen large-scale intermixing of languages and populations through the centuries.[5] As a result of frequent trans-border migration, the Estonian human genome is presumably fairly heterogeneous. For the spokespersons of the national database project, the relative heterogeneity of the genome – compared to, say, the Icelandic and Tongan ones – is one of the assets of the project. Estonia regained independence in 1991 and since then the health care system has been radically revised and improved. It has national health insurance, a well-developed network of general practitioners, and strong research institutions focusing on biological and genetic research.

The Estonian economy of the communist era was a weak one, stagnant and heavily focused on agriculture. Recently biotechnology and genetic databases have been seen as potential fields of growth and expansion to sustain increasing standards of living. The success of the Finnish neighbors' Nokia has often served as an example of the dynamic innovation of "new" economies. Public discussion emphasizes the need for an "Estonian Nokia" and for many people biotechnology is one of the potential avenues to explore. Discussion of the database project has been fairly lively and usually in support of the project (Korts 2004, Tammpuu 2004). While much work has already been done, the future remains uncertain as there have been problems in sustaining necessary funding. Private funding

[5] The nature of the "border state" is perceptively explored in a recent novel by the Estonian writer Tônu Õnnepalu (2000).

has failed to materialize and despite its emphasis on "Knowledge-based Estonia" the government has refused to provide further support.

The United Kingdom: UK Biobank

In June 2003, the UK secretary of state for health presented to Parliament a White Paper, *Our Inheritance, Our Future: Realising the Potential of Genetics in the NHS* (2003), which emphasized the increasing role of the new genetics for the benefit of citizens and scientific research. The White Paper recommended massive investments in genetics within the National Health Service in England. One of the avenues in that direction is UK Biobank, a £61 million project that began prior to the White Paper. Funded by the Medical Research Council, the Department of Health, and the Wellcome Trust, UK Biobank aims to advance genetic epidemiological research by means of the largest genetic database of its kind in the world (Weldon 2004). It is expected to contain DNA samples from up to 500,000 adults aged 45 to 60 years. Samples will be linked to personal medical records and family histories.

In March 2006, UK Biobank sent out invitations to 3,000 residents of the Manchester area to take part in the start-up phase of the national database. Ongoing collection of data from research subjects is assumed, and genotyping of participants will be done in centralized facilities. Participants in the initial phase provide blood and urine samples, respond to questions about their smoking, eating, and exercise habits, and grant UK Biobank permission to track their health for many years. The aim of the project is to explore interactions between genes, environment, and lifestyle, focusing on cancer and cardiovascular conditions. Companies are expected to have access to the data on a non-exclusive basis. Important aspects of the design of the UK Biobank remain as yet undefined, including monitoring and control, and the nature and degree of commercial involvement. Tutton suggests that UK Biobank is "an example of a resource funded by and operated in the charitable and public sectors, but which will rely on in different respects commercial involvement and could have the potential to encourage future pre-competitive public–private collaborations" (2004b: 24).

The current collection of data in the United Kingdom takes place partly on a regional basis, emphasizing so-called "spokes." One of the spokes is Generation Scotland which aims to recruit between 80,000 and 100,000 people across Scotland (Marsden 2004). Generation Scotland seeks to tap the resources of the people of the region, their scientific expertise and genetic characteristics, to achieve a competitive advantage for Scotland. It will focus on understanding diseases that remain prevalent in Scotland, including heart diseases, cancer, stroke, and mental illness.

Public discussion in the United Kingdom generally of the National Health Service tends to draw upon Titmuss's notion of blood donation as "a gift." Thus blood donated to UK Biobank is said to underline a gift relationship between participants and researchers. For many Britons, the National Health Service represents an "imagined community" (Busby 2004: 309), somewhat like "the people's home" of the Swedish welfare state. While some key scientists were highly critical of the biobank project early on, they seem to have shelved their opposition, possibly due to an apparent shift in the project's focus from genetics to broader concerns with epidemiology, the development of diseases.

Quebec: Cart@gène

Early in 2002 the outlines of a Canadian genetic database project, Cart@gène, focusing on Quebec were announced. The plan was to approach 90,000 people aged between 25 and 74 years, randomly selected from medical records (*La Régie de l'assurance maladie du Québec*). It was hoped that two thirds of those approached would respond positively and serve as the foundation of the database through their biological samples. The participants would then respond to questionnaires about family history and health profile and donate blood for DNA analysis. The

Cart@gène project is a joint venture of the Balsac project of the University of Quebec, research institutes at McGill University, and the Faculty of Law at the University of Montréal. The aim is similar to that of the deCODE project – to throw light on the "predispositions" of particular groups for developing certain diseases (for example, hypertension, diabetes, asthma, and cancer), to explore the relationship between genetic characteristics and environmental variables, and to establish the local economy as an important site in the globally emerging genomic research (Bibeau 2004).

During the planning process, important changes were made to the original outlines, partly as a result of debates on the relative roles of the state and private companies as well as demands from the Commission on Information. For one thing, information entered into the bank would remain anonymous. Originally the spokespersons for the Cart@gène project hoped that the design of the database would allow for the possibility, as in the Estonian scheme, of getting back to people with particular profiles, within five years or so, but this was later seen as unacceptable. Eventually, the project was redefined as a "population" health survey, a non-profit enterprise with no specific commercial involvement. Bibeau suggests that despite differences with respect to commercial involvement, the contexts of Quebec and Iceland have much in common, in terms of public confidence in researchers, the progress of medicine, attitudes to the pharmaceutical industry, and support for the public health care services (2004: 100). Last but not least, Quebec and Iceland share the scientific advantages provided by great interest among the public in family histories.

About 10,000 French immigrants settled in "New France" in Quebec between 1608 and 1760 and, apparently, many people in Quebec can trace their roots back ten or even fifteen generations. The success of modern genealogy companies can be partly explained by the desire of the descendants of the pioneers to trace their roots to a particular region in France and, obviously, the Cart@gène project benefits from this interest in roots. According to the spokespersons of Cart@gène, a founder effect should be exerted on two fronts: in the Quebec genome from the first two centuries of Quebec's history and, secondly, certain regional genomes, in particular the regions "colonized" in the first half of the nineteenth century. Bibeau suggests, however, that the Quebec genome has never been "homogeneous" and that the true reason for interest among academics and industry in genome research, irrespective of the rhetoric of a strong founder effect, has to do with the fact that Quebec has demographic files and genealogical information "without a doubt more complete than those in Iceland and just as rich in information as the genealogical sources of the Mormons in Utah" (2004: 120).

Taiwan: the Super Control Genomic Database

A Taiwanese genetic database, the Super Control Genomic Database or the Chinese Genetic Database, has been in the making in Taiwan since 2003 under the auspices of the Institute of Biomedical Sciences of the Academia Sinica in Taipei. The aim is to conduct genetic research on "ethnic Chinese-related" diseases such as high blood pressure, manic-depressive psychosis, and arthritis (see Cheng and Li 2004: 45).

Established in 1998, the National Health Record Databank of Taiwan now has records for more than 20 million Taiwanese. Genealogical information for Taiwanese is both abundant and detailed due to the National Census Register System and the traditional Chinese respect for family pedigrees. Information from these databases will be combined with genetic information from blood samples, as well as a series of rather idiosyncratic facts on lifestyle, including habits of drinking, smoking, and betel nut chewing. Participants in the Taiwanese project are requested to sign informed consent forms. On the other hand, no specific legal framework has been developed for genetic databases nor have principles of research licensing and benefit-sharing been made explicit to the participants. Public discussion on the making of the database and its social and ethical aspects has been minimal.

The Taiwanese project applies statistical sampling methods, collecting roughly 3,000 DNA samples from 34 towns. In doing so, it draws upon the two main ethnic groups of Taiwan, the Hoklo and Hakka, jointly representing about 98 percent of Taiwan's population. Assuming a close genetic relationship between the Chinese and the Taiwanese (Cheng and Li 2004), this database could, theoretically, become the largest genetic database in the world, representing more than 1 billion Chinese people. Researching the populations of the People's Republic of China and the Republic of China is, however, exceedingly complex and invites a series of conceptual, political, and methodological problems. It is by no means obvious what constitutes a "population," on what basis a definition should be grounded, and how the historical and genetic relationships between different subpopulations should be interpreted (Jiayou *et al.* 1998). Some of these problems, as we shall see later on, are shared by the Human Genome Diversity Project.

Many other national or regional genetic database projects have also been suggested or planned, in Germany, Israel, Japan, Latvia, Newfoundland, Norway, Sardinia, Singapore, and Wisconsin – and many other contexts. All of these projects, it seems, have some fundamental properties in common that distinguish them from other kinds of biomedical projects and assemblies, although they sometimes take hybrid forms that elude any clear-cut categorization. To return to the questions posed at the beginning – concerning the purpose, rules of governance, and modes of exchange and bookkeeping – databases differ on several scores. Table 4.1 outlines some of the dimensions of comparison.

Some database projects obviously involve tiny and rather homogeneous island populations, others are set up for "ethnic" regions, and still others cover huge and complex populations, potentially a substantial fraction of humanity, much like the plan for the Human Genome Diversity Project. Apart from differences in the scale of the populations involved, database projects differ with respect to the processes and criteria of sampling, property arrangements and management regimes,

TABLE 4.1 A Comparison of seven genetic database projects

	Sample or population	Ownership, management, and returns	Consent and confidentiality
Iceland	300,000 total pop.	National ownership Company license (12 years) deCODE genetics Fees	Presumed (med. records) Informed (DNA) Encrypted
Tonga	50,000 Half of the total pop.	Company license Returns to the community Autogen	Informed Encrypted
Sweden	70,000 Aged 40–60, A region	Public ownership? Company license UmanGenomics university involvement	Informed Encrypted
Estonia	1,000,000, 3/4 of the total population	Public foundation Private company EGeen	Informed Traceable Possibility of feedback
UK	500,000 Aged 45–60	Public foundation University involvement?	Informed Encrypted
Quebec	90,000 Aged 25–74 Regional sample	Public ownership	Informed Encrypted
Taiwan	3,336 Random sample Total pop. 20,000,000	State ownership	Informed Traceable Possibility of feedback

the nature and degree of commercial involvement, forms of consent as well as measures for the protection of personal information. Furthermore, there are differences in terms of what some observers refer to as "language." Inevitably, genetic databases reflect the cultures and contexts to which they belong, in particular notions of sociality and the level of trust between participants on the one hand and, on the other, general practitioners, scientists, and the state. Database projects, as Tutton and Corrigan emphasize, are necessarily shaped by the assumptions and vocabulary applied to them:

Through these languages people are conceived as certain kinds of research subjects within fields of governmentality in relation to institutions. These languages are informed by assumptions about the nature of people's involvement with research, their motives for doing what they do, which draw on concepts from domains such as bioethics, philosophy, anthropology or law. (2004: 6)

Several kinds of languages are being used and developed in biobanking, including the language of exchange ("gift," "donations") and involvement ("participation," "agreement," "opting out," and "refusal").

There are important similarities as well. While the Icelandic context is somewhat unique, with its nationalistic rhetoric and its emphasis on roots, as a welfare state Iceland shares many of the characteristics of other contexts, including "the people's home" of Sweden and the rest of Scandinavia. All contexts represent a concern with the governing of bodies, populations, and welfare, monitoring the health of the national or ethnic body. One of the implications of this monitoring is the geneticization of notions of citizenship and belonging. Israeli databases are an illustrative example, given their close alliance with notions of governance, citizenship, and nationhood. Prainsack suggests (2006) these databases operate as "important stabilizers" for national identities within Israel. Since independence, Israel has committed itself to being both a democracy and a Jewish state. Therefore, in order to be widely acceptable, genetic databases and other medical innovations should resonate with religious teachings and rabbinical rulings. This does not necessarily mean that genetic databases are slowed down or hampered by Israeli law; on the contrary. The Ashkenazi Jewish population, Shohat comments, "is a resource that must be harvested quickly – before the 'melting pot' effects of intergroup marriages in Israel result in the mixing of different ethnic subpopulation" (2000: 441). According to Jewish teachings, it is even mandatory to build and change the world for the benefit of human beings, which seems to include developing and operating genetic databases.

Genetic databases draw upon a series of developments in the history of states and bureaucracies, including practices of writing, accounting, and monitoring represented by "statistics of sickness." Thus, in nineteenth-century England the medieval bioinformatics that traditionally had focused on documenting births, deaths, and marriages was extended to statistics and probabilistic methods to describe the health risks and tendencies of the population and its subdivisions: "Disease, madness, and the state of the threatening underworld, *les misérables*, created a morbid and fearful fascination for numbers upon which the bureaucracies fed" (Hacking 1982: 287). Developed in one nation state after another, such statistics represented biopolitical concerns with monitoring and governing the health of the national population. While this new "avalanche in numbers," Hacking suggests, was rarely efficient in managing the population of study, it had subversive effects, namely "to create new categories into which people had to fall, and so to create and to render rigid new conceptualizations of the human being" (1982: 281). Keeping in mind that the term "nation" is etymologically derived from *nascere* (to be born), health statistics, in a sense, establish the birthmarks of the national body.

While genetic databases differ in several respects, and the *Oeconomus* governing what is assembled and the ways in which it is used vary from case to case, they all represent the extension of the biomedical gaze. As Lyotard points out, data banks are "the Encyclopedia of tomorrow. They transcend the capacity of each of their users. They are 'nature' for postmodern man" (1984: 51). For Foucault, the medical clinic represented a complex cognitive and political history, a "mutation in discourse" – "A new alliance was forged between words and things, enabling one to *see* and *to say*" (1973: xii). The clinic, however, as Foucault emphasized, has continued to evolve as an important element of governmental politics. In the 1970s, the term "medicalization" was coined to address the extension of political authority as social problems such as alcoholism and drug abuse became redefined as "sickness" (Zola 1972). With the new genetics, the medical gaze has been extended even further – again transforming, expanding, and intensifying the clinic.

Biomedicalization

"Biomedicalization" is a term that has been suggested to denote these developments, "the increasingly complex, multisided, multidirectional process of medicalization that today is being both extended and reconstituted through the emergent social forms and practices of a highly and increasingly technoscientific biomedicine" (Clarke *et al.* 2003: 161–162). For Clarke and colleagues biomedicalization began around 1985 as biomedicine began to be transformed "inside out":

the shift to biomedicalization is a shift from enhanced control over external nature (i.e., the world around us) to the harnessing and transformation of internal nature (i.e., biological processes of human and nonhuman life forms), often transforming "life itself." Thus, it can be argued that medicalization was co-constitutive of modernity, while biomedicalization is also co-constitutive of postmodernity. (2003: 164)

Despite the national or regional rhetoric of many database projects, there is much formal and informal collaboration among them. Recently, Cavalli-Sforza, one of the pioneers of the Human Genome Diversity Project, has suggested that national genetic databases might contribute to the Project's collection by donating blood samples, "representing a minute fraction of their collection, ideally forming a geographically (and if necessary, linguistically and ethnically) stratified sample of the country" (Cavalli-Sforza 2005: 340).

One of the new "El Dorados" of biomedicine is the move away from "national" genomes to comparative datasets such as that of the International Haplotype Map Project, drawing upon the power of genome-wide scans and related technological and methodological advances. Already, several companies are betting on the value of the Haplotype Map Project, scrambling for a place in the global competition of pharmacogenomics. Such a shift in emphasis in the biomedical hunting for genes may, somewhat unexpectedly, make anthropology, with its knowledge and understanding of human variation and the history of the species, central to the new genetics. Quite possibly, in the future, large-scale genetic databases will be operative at numerous sites, either permanently or from time to time. This is indicated by the initiative of the Public Population Project in Genomics (P^3G Consortium), a consortium of several population database enterprises in Europe and North America begun in 2003. As Brookes observes (2001: 516), real success will require "teamwork that involves all countries . . . Meta-analyses and project consortia will need to be larger than ever before, whilst isolated projects and overly cautious data-protection philosophies will only serve to stifle real progress." For gaining larger numbers and samples, which may be important for analyzing many common diseases, different database projects may find it feasible to temporarily share data, hunting and gathering in the human genome on an unprecedented scale under some kind of permanent institutional umbrella. Collectively they become "global assemblages," in Collier's and Ong's sense (2005: 4), consisting of abstractable, mobile, and dynamic phenomena that move across and reconstitute social boundaries, redefining material, collective and discursive relationships as various kinds of bodily material and information is being reassembled and reterritorialized in specific situations.

Genetic databases of the kind discussed here suddenly appeared on the biomedical agenda in 1998. Soon they became the subject of intensive discussion. One of the reasons for the fascination with such databases is that they may make it possible to design and manufacture personalized drugs that are potentially safer and more effective than mass-produced "blockbuster" drugs. In fact, a Japanese genetic database project goes under the name of "Personalized Medicine Project." The problem with mass produced drugs is that they are often aimed at some unrealistic ideal patient; genetic differences may cause some people to react positively to a drug while others fail to respond. As a result, there is lots of waste, disappointment, and even harmful side effects. So-called Cox-2 inhibiting drugs, for instance, that have become staples for the treatment of osteoarthritis have proved to invite an increased risk of heart attack. Therefore, the pharmaceutical industry is investing heavily in research that may lead to the development of personalized drugs, tailored, in a sense, to the genetic signatures of the person involved.

Critics suggest, on the other hand, that personalized drugs are unlikely to be technically feasible in the near future. It is too early to tell if such drugs represent a sensible avenue and even if they appear in the marketplace – and they do seem to be on the horizon – they may prove to be too costly for many health services already burdened by the extreme costs of medicine. Some approaches to pharmacogenomics try to have it both ways, suggesting that the production of drugs be custom-made for particular groups, presumably sharing some critical genetic characteristics that distinguish them from others. Given such an approach to production, drugs should be, up to a point, both personalized and mass produced. Obviously, this raises fundamental questions about the "mapping" of race, some of which will be addressed in Chapter 7.

Much of the fascination with "national" or "ethnic" genomes evident in database projects stems from the fact that they represent relatively demarcated populations, apparently appropriate for genome mapping and research due to presumed genetic homogeneity. In some cases, homogeneity has been overstated, minimizing so-called "melting pot effects." This includes deCODE's early statements about the value of biomedical research in the Icelandic context. Genetic analysis, however, underlines that the Icelandic population is, indeed, among the most homogeneous populations of Europe: "The overwhelming conclusion . . . is that the Icelandic gene pool is less heterogeneous than that of most other

European populations" (Helgason *et al.* 2003: 283).[6] The problem, on the other hand, of describing and ranking a population in terms of genetic homogeneity is likely to remain under debate, keeping in mind its relevance for biopolitics of all kinds, including contending claims about competitive advantage. Through the ages, theorists of human–environmental interactions have often concluded that the ideal conditions for human activity are right at home. Numerous observers on the impact of climate, from Hippocrates to Ellsworth Huntington, have argued that the ideal conditions for the development of civilization are the ones they are used to themselves; the ideal site – in terms of precipitation, temperature, seasonal differences, etc. – shifts from one location to another depending on the habitat of the author one happens to read. No doubt, a similar rhetoric and ethnocentric element is involved in the debate on genomes and populations ideal for genetic research on common diseases. Drawing upon genetic samples from Ashkenazi Jews, who are presented as one of the most genetically homogeneous populations in the world, one of the Israeli database projects is reported to engage in a kind of "homogeneity war" with the Icelandic project (see Prainsack 2006).

To what extent, one may ask, are genetic database projects and the biomedicalization they represent rooted in eugenic thought? The development of eugenics had much to do with colonial contexts which were predicated on concepts of citizenship, the problem of deciding who was "white" and who was "native" – "métissage emerged as a powerful trope for internal contamination and for challenges to rule that were morally, politically, and sexually conceived" (Stoler 2002: 80). In the heyday of the colonial regime in the 1920s, metropolitan bourgeois discourse emphasized notions of national "purity" and biological "degeneracy." In Britain,

---

[6] Some geneticists have challenged the assessment of the relative genetic homogeneity of Icelanders (see, for example, Árnason 2003). A review of the literature of human genetic diversity in Europe, however, supports the conclusion of Helgason *et al.* that "Icelanders do show evidence of greater drift effects than most other European populations" (Barbujani and Goldstein 2004: 138).

Germany, North America, the Nordic countries and several other contexts, a strong eugenic lobby was developed, calling for the sterilization of what were considered the mentally, morally, or physically unfit members of society. All kinds of social "progressives" participated in attempts to appropriate eugenic discourse and ideas for birth-control programs. As we have seen, such ideas informed some of the first Icelandic database proposals in the 1960s.

The extreme case of eugenic policy, however, was that of the German National Socialist regime. A few weeks after Hitler's rise to power in 1933, the Nazi regime ratified a law for the prevention of the continuance of hereditary disease, stipulating that "those afflicted with a hereditary disease may be sterilized by a surgical operation if there is medical evidence to suggest that their descendants will most likely be afflicted by serious hereditary disorders of the body or the mind" (see Agamben 1995: 149). Within months, this legislation was extended to marriage, by the law for the "protection of the hereditary health of the German people" which stated that "No marriage may be performed . . . when one of the betrothed suffers from a contagious disease that might seriously threaten the spouse or any descendants . . . [and] when one of the betrothed suffers from one of the hereditary diseases provided for by the law . . . " Agamben emphasizes that the first concentration camps were the work not of the Nazi regime but of the German Social-Democratic government, which interned thousands of political activists in 1923 on the basis of *Shutzhaft* (literally, protective custody). For him, the camp should not be seen as "an anomaly belonging to the past . . . but in some ways as the hidden matrix and *nomos* of the political space in which we are still living" (Agamben 1995: 166), a space characterized by the politicization of "bare life," the new biopolitical body of humanity.

Are genetic databases, then, bound up in the eugenics of the early twentieth century, as some observers argue (Rose 2003), or are these radically separate projects? All genetic disease studies have at least a eugenic touch in the sense that their aim is to neutralize or eradicate particular genetic disorders or characteristics (Wikler 1999). It may be difficult, as a result, to draw a firm line between strong and weak eugenics. It needs to be emphasized, however, that there are radically different concepts of eugenics, with different assumptions about coercion, positive or negative aims or impact, and reproductive decision-making. While for some critics the term *genetics* can never escape the social implications of coercive eugenics, failure to distinguish between eugenic biological citizenship and the one that follows the new genetics obstructs understanding of ongoing developments (Rose and Novas 2005). It seems, indeed, quite a stretch of the imagination to apply the label of eugenics to the database projects discussed here, as none of them seems coercive and truly eugenic motives are difficult to find. Perhaps a test case would be one of the genetic projects in Israel, Dor Yeshorim ("The Generation of the Righteous"). This project offers genetic testing to young people for the purpose of checking the "genetic compatibility" of future spouses, and for preventing dating and marriage between two carriers of a recessive genetic disease, in particular Tay Sachs, which affects about one in every 2,500 Ashkenazi Jewish newborn. Since the launch of the project in 1983, the genetic tests of Dor Yeshorim have identified 500 "at-risk" couples whose children would be likely to be afflicted with a serious genetic disease. Apparently, most of the courtships and proposed marriages involved were cancelled as a result (Prainsack and Siegal 2006). And who can blame them? There is an element of social pressure involved, but there is no coercion. While the parallels between the Nazi marriage law and the "suitability" tests of the Dor Yeshorim project may be both bizarre and ironic, to juxtapose the eugenics of the Third Reich and the Israeli struggle with Tay Sachs and other hereditary diseases is not particularly illuminating.

In my view, the new modes of reasoning or "genetic imaginations" (Simpson 2000) made possible by the mapping of the human genome do not by definition suggest a eugenics movement; indeed, it is difficult to see why they should follow a predetermined, linear path. Given, nevertheless, the social context – a context characterized by, say, unemployment and a prior history of ethnic conflict and racist thought – genetic projects can easily serve as the rationale for local eugenic regimes. The task remains to explore ongoing developments in biomedicine and the ways in which they inform, reflect, or interact with the social context. This includes spelling out what may be termed the "epidemiology" of eugenics, outlining both the kinds of historical conditions that help to explain why eugenic ideas may become "contagious" (to continue the metaphor) and the social "antibodies" that may prevent their spread.

A focus on bounded, homogeneous populations necessarily conveys an image of islands, an image that seems to have a peculiar and powerful hold on the Western mind. As Gillis remarks, they are the locus of both desires and fears:

We feel extraordinarily free there, but also trapped . . . Isles remind us of our individuality while sustaining our sense of family and community; and though they are unparalleled as places of solitude, they are also among the few places we feel cosmically connected . . . It is on islands that one feels closest to the secrets of both origins and the world that lies beyond life itself. (Gillis 2004: 3–4)

Despite its appeal, the island imagery invites certain risks, including those of essentialist representation and commodification. The image of insular and homogenous genomes seems to engender two responses at once, a fascination among geneticists, bioprospectors, and investors with "local" genes and a passionate fear of objectification and exploitation. Perhaps the notion of the gene "pool," engendering a cozy image of bounded-ness and unity in contrast to the complex and fleeting *ocean* of genes, calls attention to a similar notion in the case of genome mapping and banking.

With the growth and expansion of genetic databases, a lively public and academic discussion on their implications has emerged. Such innovations, much like other biomedical developments, need to be considered as embodying social contexts, not as independent variables. Franklin and Lock rightly caution that biomedical innovations do not develop on their own and that it is inadequate to refer to changes in terms of their following "after" technological developments:

the phrase "social implications" is often annexed to "the new genetics" to bookmark a space for dealing with the consequences of technology – an equation that places society and sociality after the fact of technological innovation. This flies in the face of everything practitioners of sociology, anthropology, science studies, and feminism have argued about how the social precedes and is embedded within any kind of technoscientific project, initiative, or discovery. (2003: 4)

One of the contributions of anthropology to the study of genetic databases is to provide a reasonably "thick" description of ongoing developments and a comparative perspective of existing plans and projects.

Clearly, the banking of medical records, family histories, and genetic material and information has been a major development in genomics and biomedicine in recent years. Recently, Francis Collins, the director of the US National Human Genome Research Institute, suggested, drawing attention to biobank projects proposed or under way in the United Kingdom, Iceland, Estonia, and Japan, that the United States could ill afford not to invest in its own population-based cohort study (GenomeWeb News 2005). Such projects in progress around the globe, he argued, had left the United States behind in biobanking endeavors: "[if] we wait until we get data to start setting [the project up] then we have waited too long." Collins emphasized that while current "case-control" studies are valuable, in order to understand the effects that environmental factors play on genetic diseases in the United States researchers would need a "cohort that's selected to cover all ages, all races," and all states of wellness. In his estimate, the project would aim for a large sample size, perhaps from 2 million to 3 million individuals. As we will see, the optimism and promises of many genetic database projects have seen serious setbacks, partly due to concerns with ethics, privacy, and bioprospecting.

FIVE

ᕠᕤ

For whom the cell tolls: bioethics

Inevitably, the growing intersection of biomedicine and the market gives rise to disputes on the collection, storing, exchange, and control of human cellular material and information. Returning to the "great dry fog" of biomedicine mentioned at the beginning, this chapter discusses public debates associated with genetic databases, emphasizing the notion of moral landscapes (Appadurai 1986, Hirsch and O'Hanlon 1995, Helgason and Pálsson 1997). Such a notion I suggest both offers a powerful tool for the comparative study of biopolitical debates and facilitates understanding of the dynamics of local concerns. A comprehensive understanding of debates about genetic databases and the commodification of the body they may entail needs to be based on an empirical approach that confronts the ethnographic complexities involved, a point emphasized by Sharp (2000). The metaphor of landscape offers a useful approach with regard to people's responses to developments in biotechnology and helps to determine the options available for informing public decisions on contested issues such as those surrounding modern biomedicine and biotechnology.

There are, indeed, noticeable differences across the globe – among, for instance, Europe, Japan, the United States, and the Islamic countries – in attitudes towards body components, the consumption of biotechnological products, and its moral values. One point of difference in the discourse on the human body is the extent to which it is morally "right" or "permissible" to reproduce and market as commodities components of the body (including cell lines, clones, and blood) or information based on them. Although in every case a fairly clear distinction is made between the permissible and the unethical, the line separating the two seems to vary from one context to another. These differences can be observed at different levels, ethnically and locally as well as nationally and internationally. The consequences, then, of the realignment of the market and the bodily domain vary widely with the social, religious, and political context. I shall take a closer look at the genetic database project of Iceland and, for comparison, Britain, Estonia, Quebec, and Sweden, the ways in which these projects have been discussed domestically and internationally, and the kinds of "bioethical" issues that have emerged in the process. One of the contributions of anthropology to recent developments in biomedicine is to explore how and why people moralize about them and how the responses may differ from one context to another.

Sudden and firm demands for tight moral regulation necessarily reflect the anxieties and concerns of their times. This is illustrated, as we will see, by responses to the Icelandic genetic database project. While it may be tempting to refer to such responses as "moral panic," this would be misleading: "The term 'panic' implies that the response to some social problem is an over-reaction or exaggerated . . . To assume that such movements involve over-reaction and irrationality is but a short step from a conspiracy theory in which some agent . . . actively sets out to fan the smoke of anxiety into flames of panic" (Hunt 1999: 19). A growing literature explores how certain phenomena become formulated as problems, "investigating the sites where these problems are given form and the various authorities accountable for vocalizing them" (Inda 2005: 8).

Moral landscapes

Biotechnologies, their methods, projects, and implications, are currently embroiled in a global controversy. This controversy is focused on many aspects of the new genetics, including cloning, stem-cell research, human genetic engineering, genetically modified foods (sometimes called "Frankenfoods"), and the assembly and operation of a variety of biobanks and genetic databases. One of the by-products of the Human Genome Project was a large-scale effort to address such controversies, to study the ethical, legal, and social implications of human genetic research. This was the so-called ELSI Research Program established in 1990 as an integral part of the Genome Project. The ELSI Program identified several research areas as "grand challenges" for the future of genomic research which were listed and described in detail in "A Vision for the Future of Genomics Research" (*Nature* 2003). Among the issues involved were intellectual property concerns surrounding access to and use of genetic information; ethical, legal, and social factors that influence the translation of genetic information to improved human health; the impact of genomics on concepts of race, kinship, and social identity; the implications for both individuals and society of uncovering genomic contributions to human traits and behaviors; and how different individuals, cultures, and religious traditions view the ethical boundaries for the uses of genomics.

While formal bioethics began soon after World War II, with the Nuremberg Code of 1947 and its focus on voluntary consent in biological research on human subjects, the ELSI Research Program and a variety of smaller programs in national and multi-national contexts opened up a vast space for ethical as well as legal and social scientific research on genome projects. This space was quickly occupied by a large number of scholars and research institutions. In the process, the discipline of "bioethics" was professionalized as a significant component of the governing regimes and "audit" cultures of states, universities, and medical institutions. The rapid expansion of bioethics during the second half of the last century need not be surprising. "One of the powers of bioethics," as Strathern points out (2004: 13), "is the way it can simultaneously stand for the whole person and the whole society." By definition, the emergence of the new genetics invited concerns with both individual liberties and the collective rights and responsibilities of nations, populations, and ethnic groups.

No doubt, the highlighting of the ethical helped to flesh out some of the pressing issues of the genome era, advancing the development of appropriate legal and ethical standards for the future. But whereas ethical perspectives and practices have been indispensable, it is important to take a critical look at them. To some extent the development of ELSI programs departmentalized "ethical" issues pertaining to the new genetics, relieving the practitioners of biotechnology of much of the responsibility of reflecting on what they were doing and the likely wider implications of their works and ideas. Molecular biologists, geneticists, and their industrial collaborators could thus continue their work with relative ease, despite public anxieties and concerns, with the mentality summed up decades earlier in Tom Lehrer's song about the makers of nuclear missiles: "'Once the rockets are up, who cares where they come down? That's not my department,' says Wernher von Braun." If true virtue is an embodied disposition evident at the moment of action as a result of a long process of cultivation (Varela 1999), the removal of such cultivation from the laboratory with the relegation of ethics to ethical experts who make the rules is likely to result in the erosion of ethics. The departmentalization of the "ethical subject" and the "truth-seeking subject," to borrow Foucault's terminology, was unthinkable before the arrival of modernity; "to know the truth one had to be virtuous, that is, capable of knowing" (Rabinow 1996a: 137).

Some philosophers and social scientists who address the implications of biotechnology focus on ethical issues, challenging the rhetoric of the protagonists of bioscience. There is good reason to respect academics who speak out on public issues, taking responsibility as both scholars and citizens to critically examine new developments in science and technology. A sustained, critical engagement with our field sites is essential, for both intellectual and ethical reasons. While humanist scholars and social scientists, including anthropologists, are "always on the verge of activism" (Marcus 1998: 122) and modern multi-sited fieldwork is necessarily highly complex, professional activism can simply become an excuse or an alibi, leading to conditioned reflexes and theoretical stagnation – and, as a result, loss of credibility. Some social scientists, ethicists, and philosophers who have explored the implications of the new genetics within the space carved out for them by ELSI programs have been committed to this kind of activism, restricting their commentaries to voicing the rules of normative ethics. To the extent that they subscribe to a tree-like model of human differences emphasizing the branching of cultures and populations, they seem to think of themselves as particularly sentient primates, skillfully moving from one branch to another in an attempt to mediate or translate notions of genetic rights and wrongs.

In the case of anthropology, this is a particularly worrying development. Traditionally, anthropologists have prided themselves on suspending ethical judgment until late in (or after) fieldwork; ideally, anthropologists have attempted to "get it right" before passing judgment on others' practices. Such neutrality, informed by a profound ethical premise of the worth of all cultures, has been held to be necessary to carry out fieldwork at all (Pálsson and Rabinow 1999). And surely we need to be open to the unknown; if we think we know all the answers in advance, what would be the point in doing fieldwork? Humanity may have reached an "ethical plateau" (Fischer 2003: 37) in the sense that the issues that have arrived with our exploration of our own genome, and the escalation of efforts to manipulate genetic material – including the "ethical" issues surrounding genetic databases, personalized medicine, genetic engineering, human cloning, and the possibility of a new eugenics – at least *seem* to be fundamentally new or on an unprecedented scale. Canguilhem characterizes some of the "dreams" associated with the new genetics as "another world," in rather strong language (1989: 280–281):

in dreaming these dreams, we enter another world, bordering on the bravest of Aldous Huxley's from which sick individuals, their particular diseases and their doctors have been eliminated . . . At the beginning of this dream we have the generous ambition to spare the innocent and impotent living beings the atrocious burden of producing errors of life. At the end there are the gene police, clad in the geneticists' science.

The challenge of anthropology is to provide rich ethnographies and comparative frameworks that facilitate understanding of what is going on, taking a critical stance with respect to the hype of biotechnology and the new genetics as well as the politics of mainstream Western bioethics.

This is not to say that anthropology itself is exempt from the critical scrutiny of its ethics. Recently, several anthropologists have called for a renewed focus on ethics, including the standards of the discipline. In fact, the discipline does not have a particularly good record with regard to its own ethical practices, given its longstanding application of Orientalist perspectives, in Edward Said's (1978) understanding of the term, and its historical association with colonial regimes. Biological anthropology, in particular, which routinely works with human genetic samples with all the complications this invites, has been embarrassingly slow, in comparison to medicine, in engaging with ethical issues (Marks 2005, Turner 2005). Recently, during the so-called El Dorado "scandal," anthropology had to face serious public accusations of unethical practices in biological research among Amazonian communities, following claims in 2000 about a noted geneticist deliberately starting a measles epidemic among the Yanomami. While these accusations were grossly overblown, the anthropological community was forced to take direct measures to avoid similar troubles in the future (Pelts 2005).

As Rabinow and I have suggested (Pálsson and Rabinow 2005), following Dezalay and Garth (1996, 1998), it is important to examine the transnational developments and practices of bioethics, to identify the principles it operates under and the forces and interests behind it as symbolic, academic "capital" is moved from one market sphere to another.

Thus, it is imperative to try to understand why the ethical gaze is focused on some themes and issues and blind to others. Dezalay and Garth suggest that there are parallel principles and forces at work in the market of humanitarianism and the capital markets. The world of bioethics with its rapid professionalization and its accumulation of symbolic capital in the wake of the Human Genome Project is one example.

The neo-classical theorizing of economics has played a growing role in most places in policy discussions of medical services. Such an approach, however, assumes the "flat" landscape of supply and demand; moral issues, in other words, are simply ignored. Proponents of property-rights ideology even revel in the fact that their suggestions to apply the neo-classical approach to body commodities are frequently met with repugnance, seeing themselves as the vanguards of reason against "shibboleth and shamanism" (see Joralemon 1995: 345). By ignoring social context and the hostility to the process of commodification, standard neo-classical theory is effectively ruled out from having much to contribute to a study of differing responses to biotechnological and market innovations. Yet another approach is that of the bioethics developed by moral philosophers and legal experts. In this case the ethical dimension is, indeed, included as a central one. Bioethics, however, is usually normative, much like the universal monetary standard of neo-classical economics, based as it is on some of the yardsticks of classical Western philosophy. Most philosophically trained bioethicists, as Kleinman (1995: 46) observes, draw upon "the orthodox sources of the self in Western philosophical tradition," emphasizing the autonomy of the person, partly in an attempt at balancing the interests of the individual and society. Neither the approach of bioethics nor, obviously, that of neoclassical economics, then, is "thick" enough anthropologically speaking to illuminate the topography, dynamics, and comparative context of moral debates.

The perspective of landscapes, spheres, and boundaries proposed here demands an important qualification. The driving force behind the moral economy is ultimately derived from the intentionality of individuals, not from normative scripts or blueprints. Debates about biomedicine and the commodification of body components take place in a changing social environment. It is the protagonists and consumers of these debates, with their diverse range of perspectives, values, strategies, and interests, that weave the moral strands that result in legislation and the formation of policy and tradition. Such a generative approach to ethics resonates with the pragmatism of Meskell and Pelts (2005) who call for a novel attitude in anthropology that gives priority to practical ethical engagement. They criticize the anthropological conception of ethics that "turns the ethical code into a kind of 'constitution' for the profession and the professional into an adjudicator who, on the basis of this ethical constitution and his mastery of expert information, assumes a position of unquestioned (and often implicit) superiority" (2005: 3). For them, it is essential to "embed" ethics, to locate ethics not in a lawlike universal or a ready-made scheme but in practices of interaction. Similarly, Brodwin suggests an ethnographic emphasis on "bioethics in action"; "the discourses and apparatus of today's conventional bioethics," he argues, "require the same analysis as the facts and machines of technoscience. Employed as a black box in daily professional work, they demand a critical and relativist analysis that shows how they were produced and stabilized in the first place" (2005: 146).

A critical step for tackling "ethical problems" associated with modern biomedicine is to adopt an approach that focuses on the social and cultural contexts into which new forms of biomedicine are introduced and the actual practices, reactions, and concerns of the actors – of scientists, interest groups, policy-makers, and the general public. Inevitably, the social biographies of biomedical research and bodily commodities are defined and charted through biopolitics, through the activities and concerns of the actors involved. While the use of spatial metaphors is by no means essential to the study of the exchange of bodily commodities, it presents a useful way of conceptualizing contrasts, similarities, and differences. Comparative ethnographic research on people's responses to the development of biomedicine and the moral landscapes which they constitute provides a better understanding of the market and the economic system in question as well as the options available for informing decisions and regulating production and consumption. In this endeavor, anthropology – medical, economic, cognitive, and otherwise – can play a crucial role, given its routine attention to context and detail.

Actors and interests: an Icelandic debate

As we have seen, many national genetic database projects have been introduced in recent years. The first project, the Icelandic Health Sector Database, was at the center of controversy from the start. There were several hundreds of articles about it in the Icelandic press, numerous television programs, a series of town meetings, and endless discussion and debate in Parliament, in shopping centers and cafes, and around dinner tables. One sign of the important role of the genetic database issue in Icelandic discourse early on was the popular thriller *Jar City* (also published as *Tainted Blood*) by Arnaldur Indriðason (2004) that centered on some of the biomedical issues involved, bodily signatures, hereditary diseases, and biobanking. Understandably, Icelanders were quite attentive to the issues invited by the database project. There was extensive coverage as well in the world press of deCODE genetics, its director, its scientific project, and the database under construction.

Here I explore the domestic discourse on the database project, focusing on a single Icelandic newspaper, *Morgunblaðið.* Along with Kristín E. Harðardóttir I collected and analyzed all the material mentioning the project published in *Morgunblaðið* for twenty-eight months after the introduction of the first bill on the database in the Icelandic Parliament (see Pálsson and Harðardóttir 2002). Our sample comprised 569 items – news reports and submitted articles. Such coverage of issues is exceptional in the Icelandic context; certainly no other "medical" issue has been debated to such an extent. The only equivalent, perhaps, in Iceland's recent history is the massive debate on privatization of fishing rights, following a decision by the Icelandic Parliament in 1983 to regulate access to the major Icelandic fisheries by a system of individual transferable quotas (ITQs).[1]

There were three main reasons for focusing on *Morgunblaðið*. First, it was seen at the time by almost every household in Iceland. According to surveys, about 64 percent of Icelanders and 71 percent of the inhabitants of the capital city Reykjavík read it every day. Secondly, *Morgunblaðið* printed almost every article sent to it, independent of its own policy on the issue in question and therefore provided a fairly good idea of public discourse in the country. Finally, it was, and remains, the only paper that can legitimately claim to be the newspaper of record, with a long and continuous history and an extensive on-line archive. *Morgunblaðið*, of course, not only reflected Icelandic discourse, but actively *shaped* it as well through its near-monopoly of the newspaper market on the local scene, its historical links with the governing Independence Party, and its strong stance on many public issues. This, however, did not minimize its usefulness for the analysis of public discourse. While the newspaper generally supported the database project in its editorials and its news coverage, most of the submitted articles it published on the issue were highly critical.

There were important shifts in both the volume of the discourse and the proportion of items for and against the database, depending on

---

[1] Our method of analyzing the newspaper material was as follows: in the first round, we scanned all the newspapers, extracting items specifically focusing on the database. Then we searched the newspaper's web site (www.mbl.is) and downloaded all material mentioning the database. All the items collected in this manner were then carefully read and classified into news and submitted articles. Next we divided the material in each category into "for," "against," and "neutral" in terms of its take on the issue. Finally, we explored in more detail the content of the newspaper material, focusing on ethnographic content. This is important to indicate the flavor of the Icelandic debates and to situate the actors, issues, and arguments.

the formulation of concerns and issues during the course of the public debate.[2] The news items were typically neutral, in contrast to submitted articles, which by definition usually had a rather strong and clear agenda. The articles are perhaps more interesting in the sense that they represent the voice of at least some segments of the public. A breakdown of the articles, the relative proportions of those that were for, against, and neutral, shows that there were few neutral pieces, and in most months there were more negative items than positive ones. Out of 190 articles published during the period in question, 121 (64 percent) were against the medical database, 65 (34 percent) supported it, and 4 (2 percent) were neutral. This conclusion is in striking contrast to the findings of opinion polls suggesting that an overwhelming majority of the public supported the Health Sector Database. In June 1998 a Gallup survey concluded that 58 percent of Icelanders supported the database, while 19 percent were opposed, and 22 percent neither for nor against. In April 2000 a Gallup survey concluded that 81 percent of Icelanders supported the database, while 9 percent were opposed, and 10 percent were neither for nor against.

Physicians wrote no fewer than 28 percent of the items – understandably, perhaps, since they compile many of the medical records that are the subject of debate. Their contributions turned out to be overwhelmingly against the project. It should be noted, however, that only a few doctors were responsible for most of the negative items. One doctor was the author of 27.8 percent of the items, 15 of the 54 items in this category. What were the concerns, then, of critics and supporters of the database project? A strong ethical and political body – the Association of Icelanders for Ethics in Science and Medicine (*Mannvernd*) – was formed in direct response to the project. Its main spokespersons were

---

[2] During the period discussed, four major events occurred: in April 1998 a bill on the Health Sector Database was first introduced in Parliament; in July 1998 a revised bill was introduced; in December 1998 Parliament ratified the second bill; and in January 2000 the Ministry of Health granted deCODE genetics the license to construct the database.

physicians, biologists, geneticists, and philosophers. For one thing, the database project has raised important concerns about the protection of personal information. One member of the Association of Icelanders for Ethics in Science and Medicine, a university employee, wrote an article entitled "I Don't Want to Be a Code Bar" (April 14, 1999): "I choose to trust neither the expected licensee nor the state, and to practice instead my own personal protection by requesting that no information about me will be transferred into the Health Sector Database."

Another important concern for much of the opposition was that of informed consent. The Health Sector Database was to operate on the basis of the principle of *presumed* rather than informed consent; people could refuse to be included in the collective medical records, but if they did not, information on them would be automatically entered. One of the leading Icelandic geneticists and a board member of the Association of Icelanders for Ethics in Science and Medicine remarked in an article entitled "The Bill for the Database is Sinking in the Harbor" (November 24, 1998):

To legalize presumed consent is to violate the positive attitude currently shown with respect to scientific research. The concept of presumed consent is an absolution for those who do not want to respect the individual right of self-determination.

Much of the discussion of the genetic database focused on issues of property, ownership, and control. Thus, a fundamental debate took place concerning the ownership of and access to genetic information and medical records. One physician commented as follows (October 17, 1998):

I think it is a gross insult to my practice as a physician to appropriate documents that I record as memos and then to turn them into scientific data. This would be an assault if done by force. Therefore I protest, and so will others.

The property issue has often been discussed with reference, or in comparison, to ongoing debates about another thorny common-property issue, namely, the allocation of individual transferable quotas to rights in fish. Medical (and possibly, genetic information), it has been argued, are common-pool resources with some of the characteristics of the fishing stocks in Icelandic waters. Privileged access, permanent or temporary, should therefore be granted only in return for a fee to ensure equity and fairness. An editorial in *Morgunblaðið* made the following comparison (January 23, 2000):

Don't we all agree that the industries should be treated equally? Why should boat operators not be requested to pay anything for their use of a resource belonging to the nation when deCODE genetics Inc. has to pay 6 percent of its profits from using the right to exploit medical data? Everyone must see that this doesn't make sense. Exactly the same arguments that are used to ensure returns for the use of the right to use medical data . . . apply to the main national resource, the fishing grounds.

For many of the critics, however, the commodification of biomedical data was problematic. Thus a physician commented (October 16, 1999): "The resources are no longer metal or spices but medical data and blood for entire nations. The returns will supposedly come later on in the form of free medicine. The rebirth of bartering!" Another physician emphasized the differences between fish and patients (December 4, 1998):

The authorities can maneuver various things that they do not own in the legal understanding of the term, for instance the fish in the sea . . . Because of their lack of understanding of scientific ethics . . . the authorities have failed to realize that patients have rights that fisheries' products . . . have not.

Perhaps the dominant focus in the debate was the fact that a private multinational company proposed to explore the genetic bases of common diseases in the entire Icelandic population and to commercialize its results. A philosopher commented: "The nation has probably never before in Icelandic history come so close to being sold" (November 21, 1998). Some of the comments in this genre echoed claims about "biopiracy" popular in debates on genetic research on indigenous groups and the Human Genome Diversity Project.

Opposition to the database project, then, seems to have been motivated by several concerns, including potential infringements of personal autonomy and privacy, the ethics of consent and commodification, and the threat of biopiracy. The debate about the database and deCODE genetics focused above all, however, on the use and control of several kinds of information – derived from medical records, blood, and genealogies – which had not necessarily been controversial in the past. Much of the heat of the opposition was driven by an apparent sense among physicians of rather suddenly lacking authority in the biomedical domain, of losing dominion over information largely constructed and controlled by them in the past.

The Icelandic public, on the other hand, supported deCODE genetics and the database project. One sign was the strong positive initial response of the Icelandic stock market, although the reaction of the market later on has been mixed and shifting. Significantly, in both 2000 and 2001 the local business magazine *Frjáls verslun* ("Free Trade") declared deCODE genetics the most popular company in the country. Understandably, proponents of the project represented a more complex professional and social spectrum than the opponents, given the fact that they by far outnumbered the critics. Those who contributed articles in support of the project emphasized concerns rather different from those of the opponents; deCODE genetics and the database project, they argued, would advance biomedical research in Iceland, creating many new positions for scientists and laboratory assistants both within the company and at the University of Iceland. It was often pointed out that deCODE genetics had attracted much investment from abroad and created numerous jobs for Icelandic scientists, many of whom in the absence of deCODE genetics would have been forced to seek employment abroad. The author of one article commented (April 28, 1998):

When we at last envision a grand new plant in the economic flora, a project that draws upon science and human capital rather than pollutants . . . many of us respond with fierce opposition. On its own, such a change in economic policy should improve public health.

Proponents of the project, some of whom represent particular patient groups, also tended to emphasize medical advances. Thus, an article suggested (April 25, 1999):

Personally, I don't mind if someone makes a profit from using information about me, particularly if the person in question produces in the process new knowledge about inheritance and an untreatable disease that has colored my entire life and that of my family.

Moreover, the supporters pointed out, there was a significant gap between current bioscientific and medical practices in Iceland (the practices of many of deCODE genetics' main opponents) and the types of protection of privacy and provisions for informed consent appropriately demanded for deCODE genetics (February 3, 2000):

People do not seem to realize that information from these medical records that apparently have to be guarded so carefully is, in fact, provided with far better protection in an encrypted database than in the archives of the cellars of medical centers throughout the country.

Some of the support for the database project reflected an underlying discontent with a loosely defined medical establishment, in particular the control and expertise of physicians. A former teacher argued (April 7, 1999):

The outspoken encouragement for people to participate in group action in order to prevent the advance of knowledge is a shameful one, echoing perhaps the prejudices of the church in the early days of modern science. Such a campaign is not fitting in the case of people who belong to respected academic communities.

Interestingly, the different components of the database project did not raise identical ethical questions of privacy and consent. Unlike the medical and genetic data, the Book of Icelanders did not raise major ethical concerns, despite the fact that it was partly in the public domain. Icelanders were not bothered by such an exposure of identities and relationships. The public has generally welcomed the opportunity to explore genealogies electronically and on a grand scale. A novel by Einar Már Guðmundsson referred to a "national sport" in this context, making some ironic comments about the detailed personal information readily available to everyone interested and its potential use in fiction:

Novelists state in their defense that the characters in their stories have nothing to do with reality, being their own brainchildren. In this case, however, all the characters are so real that the story can be read with the telephone directory at one's side.

If some characters have passed away or have no telephone – perhaps because they lived before the days of telephones or even because they were against telephones – censuses, church records, or genealogies should be consulted.

I say this here to comply with our national sport to know the characters in stories. (Guðmundsson 2002: 20)

While restrictions along the lines of those applied to medical and genetic information, would probably cause a public outcry among genealogy enthusiasts, family histories *were* mentioned in public debates on the database project. One commentator offered the following remark, in an article entitled "Will the Interest among Icelanders in Family Histories Disappear with the Arrival of deCODE genetics?" (October 8, 1998):

Now a company in Iceland is recording in one place every piece of information documented in previously published works, including genealogies . . . and censuses. Unfortunately, the company is doing this without asking anybody for permission.

With the introduction of the Health Sector Database, the role and representation of genealogies underwent some shift. The legal treatment of genealogical information was increasingly along the lines of that for other personal information.

The different actors in the domestic debate all sought to influence decision-makers (in particular, Parliament, political parties, and the Ministry of Health) at various stages, through the media, public meetings, and informal lobbying. The outcome of the database issue – the laws themselves, the details on the recording of data, the monitoring of the construction and use of the database, and the encryption of data as well as the contract between the authorities and the licensee and the operating regulations on the license – was the result of a long and complex battle. While the two governing parties (the Conservatives and the Progressives) were committed to the project throughout the political process, sometimes pushing their agenda through the political machinery with the force of their strong majority, the opposition significantly shaped the course of events and the outcome. Both sides, then, lost and won.

Discussion of the database project clearly thrived on nationalism. Many Icelanders seemed proud of their "Nordic" roots and their genetic make-up, eager to "offer" their "unique" blood samples and medical records, as the rhetoric went, to science and the advancement of human well-being. Such a phenomenology of genetic citizenship is rather different from the discourse on "faulty" genes (Finkler 2000). As we have seen, for biomedical and pharmaceutical companies the Icelandic gene pool is valuable capital precisely because of its reported homogeneity and the direct genealogical link of "real" Icelanders, through a few lineages, with the medieval past. For some of the critics of the database, it signified a return to early eugenics.

The premature birth of a biobank

A comparison of the discussion of some of the early database projects helps to pose the issue of how and where biomedical issues become bioethical problems. While, as we have seen, the projects of Iceland,

Britain, Estonia, Quebec, and Sweden were somewhat different, in important respects they were fairly similar and launched about the same time. Kaye and Martin point out (2000: 1146) in their legal comparison of UK Biobank and the Icelandic Health Sector Database that "the parallels are striking and the social and ethical issues raised are almost identical." Given the family resemblance of the British, Estonian, Icelandic, Quebec, and Swedish projects, in particular, one might expect similar debates in the respective countries. This was not the case, however. While the Icelandic database project was the center of controversy and widespread local discussion, in the other contexts there was virtually no public debate on a comparable scale (see, for instance, Busby 2004, Korts 2004, Bibeau 2004). Later on, a somewhat critical discourse emerged in some of these contexts, in particular Sweden (Hoeyer 2004) and Britain. As regards the latter context, a public statement by GeneWatch UK suggested (May 9, 2001) that because of lack of appropriate legislation to safeguard genetic privacy and human rights, "plans to develop a national gene-bank – or 'bio-collection' – should be shelved." However, when sampling eventually began in 2006 opposition appeared to have disappeared.

The Icelandic debate was not a closed national case. The international press, the trans-national scientific community, and the emerging informal international network of bioethicists were heavily focused on the Health Sector Database. Icelanders were pictured as the guinea pigs of the new genetics, equivalent to model organisms such as the fruit fly. In February 1998, *Scientific American* published an article on "inbred Icelanders" with the title "Natural-Born Guinea Pigs" and later the same year (October 3) the Swiss newspaper *Der Tagesanzeiger* ran a piece under the title "The Icelanders, Our Lab Mice." The other cases, however, only received scant attention, and, if anything, praise rather than critique. Thus an article appeared in *Nature* in 1999 under the title: "Sweden Sets Ethical Standards for Use of Genetic 'Biobanks'." "Expert" witnesses from the trans-national world of science and bioethics often addressed the key issues internationally at conferences, in the media, and on the web (see, for instance, Chadwick 1999, Lewontin 1999, Fortun 2000, Greely 2000, and Rose 2003). The Icelandic plans were fiercely opposed, usually from a bioethical vantage point emphasizing patients' rights, informed consent, and the protection of privacy (see, for example, Árnason and Árnason 2004). Part of the reason why the Icelandic case was frequently reported, usually in a negative fashion, had something to do with the somewhat risky but skilful handling by deCODE genetics of public relations, including its frequent reference to genetic "roots" and the "Viking" past (see, for instance, Árnason and Simpson 2003, Thorgeirsdóttir 2004).

There must be more to the story, however. It seems that the differences in responses in the international press and the trans-national bioethical community had as much to do with partisan accounts, pre-formed narratives, and international competition as any differences between the projects in terms of design and implementation (Pálsson and Rabinow 2004). While it is tempting to conclude that the architects of UK Biobank, the Estonian Gene Bank Database, the Cart@gène project of Quebec, and the Swedish Medical Biobank have somehow avoided the "pitfalls" of the Icelandic case, available evidence does not seem to lend support to such a conclusion. Both the Swedish project, for instance, and the Icelandic one emphasized the role of private, commercial initiative in human genome research, in collaboration with the public health service, assuming public access to the database proposed for research purposes as long as the commercial interests of the licensee were not being violated. And both involved the use of public medical records collected for decades.

Much preparatory work was carried out in the Icelandic context. Pilot projects involving specific health care institutes explored the problems of assembling data, precursory computer programs were tested, and ethical and legal frameworks were discussed and revised. However, at the time of writing work on the database seems to have ceased. Most of the key people involved seem to assume that it is no longer on the agenda although the death certificate has not so far been issued. Several kinds of problems emerged and caused delay. Interviews with the people involved in the construction of the database revealed some of the reasons. Some of those interviewed experienced a growing disillusion with the database inside the company. One scientist, a former employee of deCODE genetics, commented: "I lost faith in what I was doing, thinking 'this will never be realized'. I was asked to move to another company project. Later on I applied for a job elsewhere."

The fate of the project and some of the other national projects proposed illustrates the contrast between the real world of biomedicine and the hype and expectations associated with genome projects early on (Taussig 2005). When it was launched, the Icelandic Health Sector Database was presented as a fundamentally new avenue to biomedicine, drawing upon the successes of the new genetics and the dynamics of the market. A few years later it seemed to have collapsed. Given the fuzz represented by the "great dry fog" surrounding the plan for the database, the first of its kind, one is entitled to ask if it was prematurely born and, if so, was it abortion or miscarriage?

One of the reasons for the delay or collapse of the project has to do with what might be called the "biopolitics of the dispossessed" (Pálsson 2007), the strategies of resistance developed by the Medical Association and the Association of Icelanders for Ethics in Science and Medicine. The Health Sector Database can only become useful if records from local clinics are passed on to the licensee for assembly. The Icelandic Medical Association claimed from the beginning that the database would violate the relation of trust between physician and patient, since it operated on the basis of the principle of presumed consent. As the database was under construction, some directors of local clinics, who are also physicians, refused to hand over "their" records, emphasizing their responsibility to their patients and pointing out that the latter had not consented to any such transfer of information about them. Dealing with the physicians' resistance demanded costly and heavy negotiations with fifty health clinics throughout Iceland. Often the negotiators of deCODE were confronted with the demands of rural politicians for "returns" to the community in terms of jobs and financial support. The main organized opposition to the project, the Association of Icelanders for Ethics in Science and Medicine, supported the doctors' refusal to hand over local records. Critics of the physicians, however, charged them with "patronizing" their patients and "medicalizing" the database issue. Some patient groups complained that the doctors were not consulting patients and that they had no right to make decisions about medical records on their behalf. In effect, they argued, the doctors were claiming ownership and control of information that properly belonged to the community – the Icelandic state that financed their recording and assembly. The association for patients with multiple sclerosis, which cooperated with deCODE genetics from the beginning, issued particularly strong statements in favor of the construction of the database.

Some of the problems encountered by the deCODE team were technical ones. Digitalizing and assembling massive amounts of data from different periods and different health care institutions demanded extensive work on developing new, powerful software. Another problem involved the security targets set by the Office for Personal Data Protection. deCODE staff suggest the targets set for protecting the anonymity of samples and data were too high and too cumbersome to work with. A tight "wall" or "curtain" was established between the researcher and the data for protection against potential "malicious users," making meaningful work on the data nearly impossible. This was partly the result of miscommunication between two groups with radically different training and perspective: deCODE scientists and state lawyers.

One more stumbling block in the making of the database project was the fact that a growing number of people opted out of it, refusing to pass on their personal information. By June 2003, roughly 20,000 people had opted out, a significant figure. A further setback to the project was a decision by the Supreme Court in November 2003. The case, *Ms. Ragnhildur Guðmundsdóttir* vs. *the Icelandic State*, centered on the legality of presumed consent with respect to medical information regarding children, incompetent adults, and the deceased (Supreme Court of Iceland 2003, no. 151). Ms. Guðmundsdóttir protested against the transfer of data pertaining to her deceased father to the database. Would it be meaningful to apply the principle of presumed consent to people who were not in a position to opt out of the database? The Court acknowledged the rights of relatives of deceased persons to make decisions about the data involved, thereby adding one more complication to the database project.

Faced with increasingly winding and time consuming negotiations and legal battles, rising costs, and growing economic difficulties in the biotech industry, deCODE genetics may have decided to back off and resort to an alternative strategy, expanding its own internal patient-group database and escalating its work on drug development. Currently, the company has acquired genetic samples from about one third of the population through its work on specific common diseases. The health authorities and the state may also have decided to define their own alternatives to the Health Sector Database although officially they are still committed to it, developing scattered databases and collections which might later on be somehow combined. The digitalization of national medical records is proceeding under the Ministry of Health and a centralized database on medical prescriptions and drug use is already in existence. In a sense, the Health Sector Database has been broken up, much like a fragmented human body, recombining with other projects serving different times and agendas.

Domestic responses to national database projects have been highly variable. Britons, Estonians, Quebecians, and Swedes have paid minimal attention to developments in their own contexts, whereas in Iceland there was extensive public debate for over two years. No doubt, there are complex historical, cultural, and political reasons for these contextual differences, including differences in the organization of biomedicine, research, bioethics, and law. One reason that the Icelandic debate was so hot has to do with earlier and ongoing debates on the reorganization of fisheries represented by the privatization of fishing rights. The tension surrounding the commodification and biomedical use of the encrypted version of the Book of Icelanders issued for the deCODE project helped to ensure that the other "short edition" appeared in the public domain, easily accessible on the web to Icelanders with access to computers.

Analysis of the material from the newspaper *Morgunblaðið* revealed the main concerns of both the opposition and the proponents of the Icelandic project (Pálsson and Harðardóttir 2002). The opposition to the database project emphasized ethical concerns, particularly those of consent and protection of privacy, as well as concerns with ownership and control. Above all it revealed concerns about potentially dramatic changes in the practices and structures of Icelandic bioscience and medicine, changes that are also taking place elsewhere. Some academics alleged that the restrictions of access to information and resources implied in the privileged contract of deCODE genetics with the Icelandic state would inevitably result in the stagnation of bioscience. They claimed deCODE genetics would restrict access to medical data, although theoretically access would be free to independent researchers as long as they worked only with data that would not violate the commercial interests of deCODE genetics. Many of the spokespersons for the Association of Icelanders for Ethics in Science and Medicine seemed to see their scientific dominion as being threatened or devalued by deCODE genetics and the database project. Thus, the sub-text of some of the debates centered on where cutting-edge research on human genetics occurred and where it should be located in the future. The arguments of the proponents of the database project, in contrast, tended to emphasize the opportunities it provided in terms of medical advances, work, entrepreneurship, and private initiative, in the age of stagnant or declining fishing stocks and the challenging "new economy."

Both supporters and opponents seemed, however, to be informed by "deeper" cultural and political considerations. While the general support of the database was partly rooted in the concept of the Nordic body developed during the nationalist era, the opposition was partly driven by both potential structural changes in Icelandic biomedicine and concerns with "capital." With the construction of the database, physicians and academe were being removed from the discursive center of local biomedicine, making way for state officials, biobankers, and shareholders in deCODE genetics. Channeled through a globalizing discourse on ethics and human rights, the dissent was directed, with some success, at resisting radical changes in the moral landscape of body components, in the process, however, introducing other changes to the scene. Some of the contours of the moral landscape were being altered in this process, but others remained intact. The legal framework of the past specifically exempted genealogical records from the restrictions generally applied to the recording and use of personal information. This underlined the ruggedness of the moral landscape of the commodities I have been discussing.

At the same time, the case of the genealogies demonstrates how the debate about the database project leveled out some of the contours in the moral landscape. Increasingly, genealogical records, which have traditionally been in the public domain without restrictions on recording and publishing, were being treated in the same legal fashion as other "sensitive" personal information (Icelandic Parliament 2000, Act no. 77). It remains somewhat unclear, however, how the new laws on personal information will be interpreted and applied with respect to genealogical records and their publication. Genealogical information still represents a diverse and gray area in a legal sense. Church records enjoy certain legal protection for a given number of years while the National Records of the Statistical Bureau are open to the public. Nevertheless, with the globalizing momentum of bioethics and its language and concepts of privacy and personal autonomy the local ethical and legal framing of family histories seems to have been transformed.

The cell is one of the most important icons of the modern world, drawing attention to a number of issues relating to the universe within, including the governance and exchange of human bodily components. With the advance of microscopical investigations, the cell "came to be thought of as the atomic unit of vitality, displacing the organism from its prior position as the most basic unit of life" (Keller 1996: 114). The commodification of cellular material and information and the discussions and debates associated with it can be addressed, I have argued, by means of the language of moral landscapes underlining the cultural process during which barriers to exchange are being created, blocked, or removed. It is the ideas, projects, and interests that motivate changes in the topography of the moral economy that become the focus of attention. At the same time, the Icelandic database project provides an excellent case study to observe, in the fashion of Dezalay and Garth (1998), the trans-national market of civic virtue. Here, a strong ethical and political body – the Association of Icelanders for Ethics in Science and Medicine – provided an important platform for bioethical criticism in Iceland. The Association was well connected to the international scene of bioethics, providing the base from which many observers positioned themselves. The failure of bioethicists to take a comparative perspective, or to acknowledge the need to achieve some distance from their own opinions or to clarify the bases for their own pronouncements are symptomatic of the emerging global market for civic virtue at a time when the terms of trade are being radically redefined, following structural changes in biomedicine and biotechnology.

Growing evidence indicates that bioethical practice may not have the same meaning to bioethicists and the "lay" people they claim to speak for. Thus, a recent survey focusing on the case of the Swedish Medical Biobank concludes that donors' awareness of what they "consented" to is not necessarily along the lines anticipated by those who requested consent; informed consent "seems to be an inadequate measure of public acceptance of biobank-based research" (Hoeyer et al. 2005: 97). Similarly, Almarsdóttir et al. suggest (2004), on the basis of focus group discussions in the Icelandic context, that the issues of confidentiality, privacy, and data protection tend to be framed in a communitarian fashion which is rather different from the perspective of personal autonomy prescribed by orthodox bioethics. Prainsack's discussion (2006) of the case of genetic databases in Israel gives a similar impression of a sense of collective responsibility and trust in health authorities. In some parts of the world, in contrast – including Russia, with its memories of Soviet authoritarianism and regime surveillance – the standard forms and practices associated with informed consent are likely to be met with distrust, and suspicion of corruption and espionage.

Public discussion of genetic databases necessarily draws upon the genetic discourse of the last century. This has not, however, been a uniform or static thing. Condit emphasizes (1999) that genetic discourse has been established through "rhetoric formations" where people have established different ways of seeing the world. For her, public discourse should be understood as "appropriating science for its own ends, ends which are perfectly valid and necessary – ultimately more necessary than science itself. From this perspective, 'public rhetoric' is not what is left over after the science, logic, action, or other substance is left out, as is implied by the frequent misuse of the phrase *mere rhetoric*" (Condit 1999: 12). The notions of genetics and inheritance currently popular in most countries are complex and contradictory, much like the theoretical discourses of biology, genetics, and anthropology. One strand of public discussion reduces many aspects of human behavior (aspects as diverse as alcoholism, gay culture, violence, and the ability to play chess) to the action of specific genes, while another emphasizes the role of context, the interaction of genes and environments, or epigenetic processes.

Database projects of the kind discussed here are not just innovative technical, scientific, and economic enterprises; they are radical experiments in biopolitics with potentially diverse social implications for individuals, families, communities, and the public at large. The broad responses by the international community to such experiments, however, vary from one case to another, depending on the moral landscapes of body components and biomedical information and the articulation of local and trans-national concerns with civic virtue. While the construction of the databases of Britain, Estonia, Quebec, and Sweden went largely unnoticed at the international level, the Icelandic project was the center of controversy.

No doubt, there are several reasons why the Icelandic case was particularly contested. One important reason probably relates to the fact that the population of an entire nation was involved, not just a sample. Many critics found such an inclusive approach shocking, evoking an image of a totalitarian, if not eugenic, regime. Another reason has to do with neoliberal politics, the privileged access to medical records granted to a single multinational company. Finally, given the relative scale of the Icelandic database project, its completion would have meant a radical shift in the balance of power in the domestic medical sector, suddenly pushing key players to the sidelines. Local critics, in particular physicians, who imagined they had important stakes in halting the scheme skillfully lined up with international bioethical networks in launching an outspoken and effective campaign.

SIX

Biovalue: appropriating genomes

One of the contested issues in the debate about genetic databases and many other biomedical innovations is that of ownership and access. Medical records and genealogies have suddenly become contested "resources" in the competition for biovalue. This contest is only one example of a much more pervasive debate about the objectification, fragmentation, and commodification of body material and information and the application of property rights. With the new genetics, a vast terrain has been opened up for the legal definition of rights, patents, and prospecting. This chapter discusses the chasing of some of the most minuscule elements of human cells, a matter of control over what Strathern calls "aspects of life and body":

The way in which people organize their relations to one another as a matter of control not just over things . . . but over aspects of life and body (that define "people") will loom large on the world agenda over the next decade. We can expect an explosion of concern with ownership. (Strathern 1998: 216)

The issue of ownership still looms large and is likely to do so for the time being. How is property in the components and products of experimental systems established? Following a discussion of the so-called "genome war" in the mapping of the human genome, I turn to the issue of inequality and exploitation, and, finally, the extent to which rights in bodies are likely to differ from those associated with other "resources." Drawing upon Humphrey and Verdery (2004) and some others, I suggest a fruitful avenue for anthropological analysis is to understand the pragmatics of property, the "work" property concepts do, rather than seek to establish what property actually "is."

The issues of possession and property have often been framed with reference to the capture of wild animals in a state of nature. In *Moby Dick* (ch. 88), Herman Melville discusses the problem of deciding when whales, "loose fish," become somebody's property or "fast fish." After a "weary" chase and capture, the body of the whale might get loose from the ship and "drifting far away to leeward, be retaken by a second whaler, who in a calm, snugly tows it alongside, without risk of life or line" (1962: 422). Did a whale become fast fish as soon as a whaler invested his labor in the chase or, later on, at the moment of capture? In drawing the contrast between the "weary" chase of the first whaler and the "snug" capture of the second, Melville seems to opt for a labor theory of property, much like the one of John Locke which suggests that one becomes an owner of a thing by "mixing" one's labor with it. For Locke, in "mixing" his or her labor with a particular resource base, in the course of production, the appropriator claims possession over the resource. Many legal traditions emphasize one form or another of such a notion of rights over the "fruits of labor" (Grubb 1998).

One of the early scholarly commentators on Melville's principle of rights over the fruits of one's labor, Veblen, objected that it was difficult to see "how an institution of ownership could have arisen in the early days of predatory life through the seizure of goods," adding that "the case is different with the seizure of persons" (1898: 363). For Veblen, captives, chiefly women, originally served as personal ownership, acting like trophies or insignia of masculine prowess; "it becomes a relatively easy matter," he said, "to extend this newly achieved concept of ownership to the products of the labor performed by the persons so held in ownership" (1898: 365). The "seizure of persons," to extend from Veblen, in the sense of the commodification of the body and biomedical information, in particular cell lines and DNA sequences, is one of the important new forms of potential property in the current age of biomedicine.

The genome war

In his study of the "fly people" researching the fruit fly, Kohler (1994) developed the concept of "moral economies" of science. For him, moral economies "regulate authority relations and access to the means of production and rewards for achievements" (1994: 6). Several historians of science have followed Kohler's lead, including Creager (2002). The moral economy of the fly people was characterized by reciprocity, gift relations, and the absence of personal property; ideas "that were engendered in the group's informal shoptalk were treated as a communal resource and not as personal property" (Kohler 1994: 103). Modern experimental science, however, is not a unified category in this respect; while the science of physics is typically communitarian, molecular biology is highly individualistic (Knorr-Cetina 1999). In much recent biomedical research, the gift economy has increasingly given way to the commercial circulation of patented biological material and technological innovations. Biomedical knowledge and biovalue is more and more produced within multinational companies and corporations that claim ownership of the material they use and the knowledge and technologies they produce. The history of the Human Genome Project (HGP) is a case in point, illuminating some of the strains in the moral economy of the new genetics.

Officially, the HGP was launched on October 1, 1990. Funded by the US National Institute of Health and the Department of Energy, the project planned to decode the chemical units of DNA that make up the genetic pattern of humans and to openly share the results. To do this, the HGP would break down the vast expanse of the human genome into chunks and then puzzle out the letters in each of them using available DNA-coding technology. The ultimate aim would be to publish the results, the full genetic map, on the Internet by 2003. The estimated cost of the task of sequencing the genome was around $1.5 billion, about 50 cents for each of the DNA letters in the 3-billion-letter sequence. In the late 1990s the HPG was internationalized in terms of participation, including sequencing laboratories in Great Britain, France, Germany, Japan, and China. Developed by the US National Human Genome Research Institute, GenBank became the main repository for publicly available genome data, regularly adding information in the process of sequencing (US GenBank 2005). The "global" extension of the project underlined its communitarian nature, its eventual contribution to human self-understanding and well-being. The head of the genome project, Francis Collins, director of the National Human Genome Research Institute, described it as a spectacular undertaking that would truly make history, "bigger than splitting the atom" (quoted in Shreeve 2004: 20).

The plan of the non-profit government project was challenged by a private enterprise organized by Craig Venter. In May 1998, Venter declared that he was going to establish a company to unravel the human genetic code. His company, Celera Corporation, announced that not only would it complete mapping the human genome three years earlier than the government project, but also it would do this at a tenth of the cost of the other project. The company suggested it would apply a "whole-genome shotgun" in order to blast the genome into tens of millions of tiny pieces and, when the DNA letters in each piece had been spelled out, reassemble them in correct order by using enormously powerful computers. It helped to add credibility to these stunning claims that three years earlier Venter had been able to announce the first revelation of the entire genetic code of a living organism, the bacterium *Haemophilus influenza* ("H flu," as it is often called). Venter's motive, apart from establishing his name even more firmly in the history of science, was to sell information developed by the mapping enterprise to pharmaceutical companies, research institutes, and others who might be interested through a pay-for-view database as well as to acquire patents that might prove profitable later on.

As was to be expected, here was an intense tug-of-war between the communitarian and private perspectives represented by the two human genome projects, each side actively engaging in a tense and complex public relations battle. Celera's job obviously benefited from the publicly available data produced by the international project, pushing the international project to try to finish its job sooner than planned. These developments raised interesting questions about ownership and property which were actively contested among the academic community, the biotech industry, and the legal and political realms. Did the human genome belong to humanity or was it up for enclosure by private interests and industry much like the high seas many years ago? Attempts were being made to reconcile the plans and interests of the two projects, but negotiations repeatedly collapsed. In March 2000, US President Bill Clinton and British Prime Minister Tony Blair issued a joint statement in an attempt to bring things under control, urging nations, scientists, and corporations to freely share their information on the human genome, emphasizing that the "book of life" belonged to every member of the human race.

The effect of this statement was immense. Billions of dollars were drained from the biotech sector, more than $2 billion from Celera alone (Shreeve 2004: 324). Stock prices on the Nasdaq exchange collapsed, with serious consequences for biotech companies throughout the globe. Some genetic database projects in Europe, including the Icelandic Health Sector Database, were slowed down or scrapped, testifying to the global nature and implications of developments in biotechnology and biomedicine. Finally, under heavy political and economic pressure, the two genome projects reluctantly collaborated, each of them making some concessions in return for sharing a place in the hall of fame. In June 2000, a joint statement about the completion of the sequencing of the human genome was issued at the White House with much fanfare. In February the following year the two projects again celebrated their joint achievements, this time heralding the simultaneous publication of their landmark genome papers in *Nature* and *Science*.

Drawing upon the theoretical vocabulary of Bourdieu, Rabinow suggests (1996a: 135) that while "until recently producers of truth in the biosciences were rewarded mainly in symbolic capital . . . [d]uring the 1980s means were developed to turn symbolic capital into monetary capital and back again. Conversion of one form to the other has been facilitated and accelerated within this sector of the field of power and culture." The HGP was instrumental in this respect, turning bioscience into an increasingly competitive business with potentially enormous financial stakes. While it was small compared to the Manhattan Project of particle physics, in the long run its institutional impact was like that of big science; not only did it necessitate a series of technological breakthroughs in DNA sequencing and bioinformatics, it also required the joint problem-solving skills of different kinds of expertise, including biochemists, physicists, engineers, mathematicians, and computer scientists (Rosenberg 1998: 578). In the process, rights in genes and genetic information became a central concern. Critics suggest, however, that in terms of direct production of biovalue the contribution of the HGP has been less than impressive. Sarkar goes as far as to argue that judged by the promises of the proponents of the project it "has been an unmitigated failure, the most colossal misuse ever of scarce resources for biological research" (2006: 86).

Haraway's analysis of an advertisement, "Mapping the Human Genome," by New England BioLabs (see Figure 6.1) provides an interesting critical reading of the politics of enclosure in the HGP and its representation. For Haraway, the conflation in the image of the female body and an antiquarian map of Africa – the animated Mercator projection of the dancing, native map-woman – emphasizes exploration and domination. Part of the fetishism is the idea that the gene is the "chief actor and point of origin in the drama of life itself" (Haraway 2000: 112). While genome maps may seem to be purely representational and bias-free, in reality cartographies and the biology that produces them are firmly rooted in the power game of technoscience: "the gene and gene maps are ways of enclosing the commons of the body – of corporealizing – in

FIGURE 6.1 "Mapping the Human Genome" (New England BioLabs)

specific ways, which, among other things, often write commodity fetishism into the program of biology" (2000: 120). Apparently, the analogy of map and human body excited several thinkers in the early seventeenth century, John Donne's analogies between colonial maps and the bodies of his female lovers being one example. Donne's work has been widely commented upon. His poem "To his Mistris Going to Bed" has the following lines: "Licence my roving hands, and let them goe/ Behind, before, above, between, below./ Oh my America, my new found lande . . ." Some readings of the poem emphasize colonialist desire: "It is impossible to get away from the idea," Edwards concludes (1997: 82), "that appropriation, domination, and the demand for exclusive rights are equally involved in both 'discoveries' – of a woman, and of America."

Some genomes are more equal. . .

The analogy of the mapping of the human genome and the colonial enterprise draws attention to the issue of genomic inequalities in the global context. The Human Genome Project sought to establish human universals by analyzing all the genetic material of a few individuals. Likewise, Celera's project was based on a few blood and sperm samples, including those of its director, Venter. While the international genome project was in full swing, a related project, the Human Genome Diversity Project (HGDP), was planned to explore human differences and history by sampling fragments of the genome from many individuals in a number of populations across the globe. For Luigi Luca Cavalli-Sforza, an instigator of the project and a leading population geneticist (see Stone and Lurquin 2005), the primary aim of the project was to sample the genomes of indigenous populations in order to archive human genetic diversity. "The populations that can tell us the most about our evolutionary past," Cavalli-Sforza and colleagues argued, are "far from airports and modern laboratories," "those that have been isolated for some time . . . often surrounded by geographical barriers" (1991: 490). The potential gains of the project, medical and intellectual, were said to be immense: "By an intense scrutiny of human diversity, we will make enormous leaps in our grasp of human origins, evolution, prehistory, and potential" (1991: 491). There was a sense of urgency, of a need to act swiftly before indigenous populations merged with their neighbors, "destroying irrevocably the information needed to reconstruct our evolutionary history" (1991: 490). Two recent monographs discuss the emergence and the fate of the Diversity Project in detail (M'charek 2005, Reardon 2005), situating it both in the laboratory and in the wider academic and social context, and illuminating the scientific and political difficulties encountered as well as the role played by anthropologists.

The HGDP was to begin in 1994. That year Moore wrote, in a paper that usefully explored the premises and implications of the project: "Within a decade, if all goes well, anthropologists will be deluged with genetic, linguistic, archeological, and cultural data generated by the Human Genome Diversity Project" (1994: 925). All, however, did not go well. Soon the project encountered a number of problems. Most important was the organized opposition from indigenous groups. The World Council of Indigenous Peoples dubbed it the "Vampire Project," accusing the scientists involved in it of "biopiracy" and, potentially, "scientific racism." The project, as Hayden observes, "is caught up in a geneticization of (endangered) cultural identity that serves as both a strategic appeal to urgency and a scientific and political Achilles' heel" (1998: 180). Attempting to respond to some of the bioethical critique leveled at the HGDP and, more generally, human genetic research among marginal groups, the organizers developed the concept of "group consent" (see Brodwin 2005). Such an idea, however, not only naturalized "ethnic" units and boundaries, it also seemed to paternalistically undermine the rights of the autonomous individual which were invariably applied at the time in most Euro-American contexts. Considerable efforts were organized to salvage the project in the face of political opposition. Although it lost much of its momentum, work continued. According to L. Luca Cavalli-Sforza

Africans
1 Bantu
2 Mandenka
3 Yoruba
4 San
5 Mbuti pygmy
6 Biaka
7 Mozabite

Europeans
8 Orcadian
9 Adygei
10 Russian
11 Basque
12 French
13 North Italian
14 Sardinian
15 Tuscan

Western Asian
16 Bedouin
17 Druze
18 Palestinian

**Central and
Southern Asians**
19 Balochi
20 Brahui
21 Makrani
22 Sindhi
23 Pathan
24 Burusho
25 Hazara
26 Uygur
27 Kalash

Eastern Asian
28 Han (S. China)
29 Han (N. China)
30 Dai
31 Daur
32 Hezhen
33 Lahu
34 Miao
35 Oroqen
36 She
37 Tujia
38 Tu
39 Xibo
40 Yi
41 Mongola
42 Naxi
43 Cambodian
44 Japanese
45 Yakut

Oceanians
46 Melanesian
47 Papuan

Native Americans
48 Karitiana
49 Surui
50 Colombian
51 Maya
52 Pima

FIGURE 6.2 Populations included in the Human Genome Diversity Project Collection (after Cavalli-Sforza 2005)

(2005: 334), located at the Centre d'Etude du Polymorphisme Humain (CEPH) in France, the collection currently consists of 1,064 cell lines from 52 populations around the world (see Figure 6.2). Much of the work that was planned by the HGDP has also been addressed by small and independent groups of scientists (some of whom were among the proposed participants of the project). Indeed, research into genetic differences among groups is thriving.

One recent spin-off from the HGDP is the Genographic Project introduced in 2005, a collaborative effort of the National Geographic Society, the IBM Corporation, and the Waitt Family Foundation. In this case there is no medical goal, only the attempt to trace the lineages of the individuals sampled and the migration routes of the human species. The project appeals to anybody interested in tracing his or her "haplogroup," charting lineages and ancestral routes back to a single African ancestor who lived some 60,000 years ago. Thus, the National Geographic Society is selling kits that allow anyone to take a cheek swab, post it to a laboratory in Arizona, and then to track the relevant personal information derived from the sample through a website. In doing so, it invites "individuals all over the world to be sort of associate researchers" (National Geographic News 2005). The project hopes to collect more than 100,000 DNA samples from throughout the world, emphasizing "indigenous identities" threatened by "being lost as more and more people move from their ancestral villages." Drawing upon the popular fascination with roots and ancestors, the Genographic Project aims to create a "virtual museum of human history." While somewhat akin to many of the genealogical databases available on the web, this database is less interactive in the sense that people cannot alter the information they have submitted but obviously far deeper in terms of the number of generations covered. The principles of the Genographic Project are somewhat similar to those of an earlier project conceived by geneticist Sykes (2001) that appealed to people of European descent with the promise, in return for a fee, to trace their roots to a particular ancient clan or cluster, represented by one of the "Seven Daughters of Eve," named Ursula, Xenia, Helena, Velda, Tara, Katrine, and Jasmine.

A much more important indirect product of the Diversity Project, and a direct product of the Human Genome Project, is the International Haplotype Map Project. Launched in 2001, the project seeks to establish common patterns of DNA sequence variation in the human genome by studying ninety samples from a US Utah population with Northern and Western European ancestry, ninety from Yoruba people in Ibadan, forty-five from Japanese in Tokyo, and forty-five from Han Chinese in Beijing. Keeping in mind the troubles encountered by the Diversity Project when confronted by indigenous groups, the organizers of the HapMap Project attempt to steer clear of confrontation by engaging in public consultation, allowing for the possibility that there are "culturally specific risks that may not be evident to outsiders" (The International HapMap Consortium 2003: 792). In the beginning, potential users were required to sign a web-based "click-wrap license" to the effect that they would not prevent others from using the HapMap data, in response to concern that third parties might seek patents on them. Later, in 2004, this license was no longer required and all data were released without restriction into the public domain (International HapMap Consortium 2005: 1317).

Given a history of hierarchy and domination, and the resultant risk of stigmatization and discrimination, biomedical projects among "native" groups can easily get into deep ethnopolitical trouble. Disenfranchised groups are likely to fear that human genetics is just one more tool for domination. Indeed, as we will see in Chapter 7, "population" studies can easily slip into a racial mode. One of the risks in genetic studies among people who have a history of being subject to discrimination is that, because of their association with such people, some diseases may receive low priority in funding for treatment and prevention. Genetic research on Native American populations is particularly sensitive. One recent case of confrontation is that of the Havasupai in Arizona who have one of the highest incidences of type 2 diabetes anywhere in the world. A project by a team from Arizona State University who planned to study the case soon ran into difficulty (Dalton 2004). Following its sampling of blood in the Havasupai reservation, the project spawned lawsuits claiming $75 million in damages filed by local people. Inflamed by personal differences and academic competition among the scientists involved, the project collapsed under claims about the violation of both civil rights and intellectual property rights. As a result, there is a moratorium on biomedical research in the Havasupai reservation.

One of the contested issues associated with genetic studies is that of the potential redefinition of origins and citizenship; the results of genetic studies may violate received notions of origins, sometimes even challenging established definitions of who counts as a "true native." Genetic studies of the skeletal remains of earlier generations can be no less sensitive than blood sampling among living people. Thus, in 1991 there was a storm of controversy around the excavations of the so-called "Negro Burying Ground" in New York City containing the remains of descendants of the slave trade, 408 people from as early as 1712. There were a number of concerns, about the benefits of the excavations to the black community, ethics, monitoring, and respect for the deceased. The excavations, whose main aim was to provide information on genetic origins, health, and nutritional stresses, went ahead after intensive community consultation and involvement (Kittles and Royal 2003). Native American groups, not least those that have been enriched by gambling revenues, are now in a position to assert their legal rights. With a shift in the balance of power, there are proposals for Native American gene banks controlled and monitored by the tribes themselves, providing the people involved with ownership of the products that might be derived from studies of their genetic characteristics and gene–environmental interactions.

Clearly, the global genome is riddled with divisions, inequalities, misunderstandings, and conflicts of interest. Sickle cell disease, for instance, which is less common in Europe and North America than in many other contexts, receives relatively little funding, much less than the far less common cystic fibrosis. As Thorsteinsdottir and colleagues point out (2004) in their study of health biotechnology in Brazil, China, Cuba, Egypt, India, South Africa, and South Korea, the notion of "health biotechnology" is usually raised in association with research-intensive Euro-American universities, not in connection with poor people in developing countries. A rough estimate suggests that between eighty and ninety projects have been planned or established on the global scene, mostly in Europe and North America, with none in South America. Médicins Sans Frontières estimates that between 1975 and 1999 only 15 new drugs were developed for tropical diseases, while 179 new drugs were developed for cardiovascular diseases. And yet many new medicines are tested in the developing world, in order to cut the costs involved and to speed up the trials. The situation is unlikely to improve significantly for indigenous groups and the developing countries unless they strengthen their own biomedical research and industry (Sunder Rajan 2005). To attempt to redress the global balance in health and human well-being, the US-based organization CPTech has suggested an international treaty modeled along the lines of the Kyoto protocol on climate change. The treaty would oblige states signing it to invest a certain percentage of their GDP in globally relevant medical research. This would challenge current patent legislation which provides temporary monopoly rights to the holder to reward innovation.

The rise and fall of the South Korean World Stem Cell Hub headed by Hwang Woo-Suk, one of the biggest ethical scandals in bioscience in recent years, illustrates the fierce international competition in scientific and ethical leadership, the global dealing in virtue. Over a period of a few years, Hwang and his colleagues published impressive articles in key journals in the field reporting remarkable advances in cloning and human stem-cell research. Hailed in both local and international media as the frontline in stem-cell research, their project was heavily funded by the South Korean government. Hwang quickly became a national hero who had his fame engraved on a Korean postage stamp that celebrated his scientific achievements, the Korean "dream" it represented, and the "miracles" it promised in terms of new avenues in biomedicine, including the reversal of spinal cord damage and the prevention, through *in utero* transplantation, of genetic disorders. Hwang took pride in the efficiency and ethics of his laboratory team, the Korean "cloning factory," underlining Korean diligence and Buddhist notions of reincarnation. With an article in *Science* in the spring of 2005 which described the creation of eleven patient-specific cell lines he seemed to firmly establish South Korean leadership. A few months later, however, the Korean dream collapsed. Hwang had to apologize for massive fraud and misconduct and

Science retracted the article. Not only were the cell lines crude fakes, Hwang had committed flagrant ethical violations in guaranteeing egg donations for his research, 242 eggs from 16 "volunteers" (some of whom were his staff), an incredible "success" given the medical risks and the potential complications involved.

While Hwang's fall from grace was probably inevitable, given the flaws in his ethics and practices, it was no doubt accelerated by the Euro-American perception that Korea and, more generally, the Far East were emerging as threatening biotech tigers on a global scale. The geopolitical competition was played out partly through the big journals in the field. Rumor has it that Hwang first submitted his *Science* paper to *Nature* which rejected it, presumably on the grounds of signals from whistle-blowers under growing pressure to tame the tiger before it became too powerful. *Nature* had its way. In this case, the Western bioethical gaze was focused on the Orient and its biomedical otherness. The battle on genetic databases, in contrast, as we have seen, has been largely an internal, Occidental squabble. The South Korean case not only illuminates the intense global competition in biomedicine, it also invites critical thinking on several other aspects of the new genetics, in particular the spectacular tendencies of the biotech industry (the investing in lofty promises and genohype), the limits of peer review, and the problems of governance (see, for instance, Gottweis and Triendl 2006).

Another interesting case, that of Nobel Laureate C. Gajdusek and his transactions with Western medical staff and the New Guinea Highlands Fore, in particular their big men, underlines the rearticulation of the local and the global in the contest over human biological resources. In the 1950s and 1960s, Gajdusek circulated Fore blood and brains in a communitarian fashion within the reward system of science, for the advancement of the study of "possessing kuru," a condition variously diagnosed as the result of a slow virus, adjustment disorder, or sorcery. Later on, however, in the 1990s, Gajdusek became a patent-holder, participating in the commodification of human cells. Anderson (2000) concludes his comparison of the big men of New Guinea and the big men of science along the following lines:

we need to develop more locally specific models of the scientific exchange of gifts and commodities, to consider further the social life and moral weight of scientific things, and to document the cultural differentiation of scientific artifacts, rather than generalize about the global economy of science. But an emphasis on local knowledge should not be taken to deny the importance of global structures and systems. Instead, it challenges us to try to understand global science as a series of local economic accomplishments. (Anderson 2000: 735–736)

While during the latter half of the twentieth century, biomedicine established new kinds of properties in persons and personal information, and ongoing developments in biotechnology and bioinformatics continue to open up new biological and social worlds, each case represents a particular articulation of the global and the local. The relations between the local and the global are often fraught with tension, competition, and mistrust, but there is also plenty of scope for mutual collaboration. Thus, the kind of work carried out by deCODE genetics benefits from the mappings of the human genome projects and likewise deCODE has contributed with its own mapping efforts. One of the successes of the company is its high-resolution recombination map of the human genome constructed by examining Icelandic families (Kong *et al.* 2002). Described as "the gold standard for researchers and mapmakers alike" (Roberts 2005: 19), this map increased about five times the resolution of the earlier "Marsfield map." This underlines the interdependence of individual projects and more general developments.

"Fictitious" commodities?

Long ago, Polanyi (1944) made a distinction between "fictitious" and "true" commodities. According to him, true commodities are those that are produced for exchange and use through labor, while fictitious commodities are not produced but are bought and sold as if this were the case. Thus, things such as land and water and even labor itself are partitioned into commodities and ascribed an "artificial" exchange value. Theoretical criticism of commodification often draws upon the medieval European "house view" of profit, money, and the market, a view formulated by Thomas Aquinas and the Schoolmen, and later developed by Marx, Simmel, and several other social theorists. Following a similar path, modern critics of the process of commodification often argue that market approaches violate egalitarian sensibilities and communitarian notions of stewardship and responsibility. Resistance to commodification is commonly manifest as a condemnation of profit-oriented motives, laden with metaphors of danger, greed, and immorality. The concept of the ideal or perfect society, the ground from which such critique is projected, and its antithesis have taken many forms in the genealogy of Western scholarship. All of these forms assume, as Berlin points out (1989: 120), a Golden Age when "men were innocent, happy, virtuous, peaceful, free, where everything was harmonious," followed by some kind of catastrophe – "the flood, man's first disobedience, original sin, the crime of Prometheus, the discovery of agriculture and metallurgy, primitive accumulation, and the like." And, we may add, the new genetics.

Recent developments in medical technology and molecular biology have clearly opened up new possibilities for the fragmenting and marketing of body parts (Waldby and Mitchell 2006), raising strong public objections and pressing ethical debates. Munzer (1994) explores the "uneasy case" against recognizing property rights in human organs, tissues, fluids, cells, and genetic material; for some, somatic commodification is inhuman and degrading, an offence against personhood and dignity, but for others it represents a humanitarian effort in that it increases the supply of body parts and, therefore, saves lives. Significantly, the notion of human organic materials as commodities is more problematic in some cases than in others. Thus, different kinds of organ transplants may invite different kinds of ethical debates and property regimes (Waldby 2002). Given the gender differences of human bodies, men and women are not subjected to exactly the same concepts and regulations. This does not, however, as Sharp points out (2000: 293), fully explain the prevailing gender bias in the anthropological literature on human commodification. Women tend to emerge as specialized targets of commodification, due to the reproductive potential of the female body. While commodified male virility is also an object of desire and reproduction, it has been less carefully problematized in anthropology: "When set against discussions of women's bodies . . . far less concern is voiced, for example, over the military use of soldiers' bodies, or the commercial status of sperm donation" (2000: 294). Women's bodies, Sharp concludes, are privileged, making men almost invisible in the literature.

While resistance to the commodification of the body has escalated with new opportunities for extracting and marketing body material and information, it is not a new phenomenon. Thus, Immanuel Kant flatly asserted that a man "is not entitled to sell a limb, not even one of his teeth"; "a person cannot be a property and so cannot be a thing which can be owned, for it is impossible to be a person and a thing, the proprietor and the property" (quoted in Munzer 1994: 275). In nineteenth-century America, there was strong opposition to the marketing of human life in the form of life insurance, benefits from life insurance being regarded as "dirty money." Resistance to "betting" with one's life against insurance companies, Zelizer suggests, "introduced structural sources of strain and ambivalence" (1992: 287). The ethnography provides a number of reports on "greedy" people who make their fortunes by stealing other people's blood; see, for instance, Weiss (1996) on the Haya of Tanzania.

One of the important issues in theoretical debates on the "fictitious" commodification of human body material and information is that of alienation and self-ownership. Many people who have birthmarks on their body have them surgically removed, either for aesthetic reasons or to avoid imminent or potential malignant growth, the threat of melanoma. Surgery of this kind, a kind of tattooing in reverse, is now a growing industry in many contexts. Those who use this service often later on miss the marks that have disappeared. Interestingly, Sigurðardóttir (personal communication), the artist who made the Birthmark series discussed in Chapter 2, has repeatedly been approached by people who plan to have birthmarks removed from their bodies, wanting to have them photographed and "mapped" before the operation as if they are hanging on to or celebrating an essential, integral part of themselves. Perhaps this underlines the idea that the microcosms of the body somehow represent the whole, the person and his or her identity, much like genetic fingerprints. Perhaps it also suggests persistent notions of self-ownership. Because for humans everywhere the body is both the locus and agent of experience (Csordas 1994), it is often represented as "sacred space" resisting invasion, extraction, commodification, and ownership (Scheper-Hughes 2000).

It was Hugo Grotius who developed the concept of self-ownership that provided the foundation for the classic Lockean conception of property rights. Grotius argued that the free use of life and limbs was a basic right that could not be infringed without injustice, a notion that proved effective in justifying the "freedom" of the high seas and European colonization. The application of the labor theory of property, however, is not as straightforward as it may sound. For one thing, it does not necessarily follow from the notion of "self-ownership" that we each own the genetic information found in our cells: "Ownership of a token does not entail ownership of a type. In other words, I may own a copy of *The Sun Also Rises* (a token), but this does not mean that I own the intangible work (the plot, characters, theme, and style – or types)" (Moore 2000: 107). Also, the notion of self-ownership itself need not be taken for granted. Generally people are not allowed to sell their organs, although some body parts may be sold, including hair and blood (sperm and ova in some contexts).

Recent developments, indeed, have thrown the notion of self-ownership into disarray, raising new questions about the nature of the human subject. Increasingly, the limits of self-ownership are being contested as biomedicine develops new techniques for fragmenting, preserving, and engineering the body, some of which are spawned by the Human Genome Project (Tierney 1999). An interesting and well-documented case is the 1990 *Moore* vs. *Regents of California* which focused on the ownership of cell lines (see, for instance, Boyle 1996). In this case, a patient claimed that his physicians had taken tissue from him and created an immortal cell line of huge financial value. The California Supreme Court concluded that the extracted tissue and the cell line were not something to which the patient could claim property rights. By then the researchers had already patented the cell line they had invented. Such cases foreshadowed debates on the legal status of DNA. In 1995, Oregon became the first US state to declare DNA the property of the individual; the Oregon Genetic Privacy Act specifically states that an individual's genetic information is "the property of the individual" (see Everett 2003).

Property, it is often pointed out (see, for instance, Hann 1998), has more to do with relations than with the essence of things, establishing bonds and boundaries within communities of potential property holders. The way in which one mixes one's labor, however, with a thing must depend partly on the nature of the thing itself. As Rose has argued (1994: 269),

property doctrine often takes at least some of its shape from the material characteristics of the "things" over which property rights are claimed ... [T]he physical characteristics of the resource frame the kinds of actions that human beings can take toward a given resource, and these in turn frame the "jural relations" that people construct about their mutual uses and forbearances with respect to the resource.

For Rose, property is an unstable phenomenon, established and maintained by successful speech acts, through rhetoric and persuasion. As a result, the visual clues available to competing claimants are important for establishing property rights. In the case of whaling, perhaps, the property issue is relatively straightforward. Whales are conspicuous, tangible objects – some, indeed, are the largest organisms on earth – and, after all, the process of chasing them, from the moment of sighting to the point of capture, is highly transparent and obvious to competing users if not the entire community of whalers. While whales and body parts are radically different things, the frequent suggestion that the "newness" of contemporary medical technology leaves us culturally unprepared to deal with the implications of the fragmenting of the human body may well be an exaggeration. In medieval Europe, as Rabinow points out, there were intense, learned debates over "what would happen to fingernails discarded over the course of a lifetime on the day of judgment. Which ones would the resurrected body have?" (1996a: 147).

The issue of the human genome remains legally complex and unsettled. It is complicated by substantial cultural differences across the globe, the problem of comparing and translating different notions of the boundary between individual and society, personhood, law, and ownership. While some policy-making bodies, including UNESCO, treat the human genome in a symbolic sense as the heritage of humanity, inviting the idea of international stewardship of the genome to avoid potential abuse, there is no legal foundation for such a "common heritage" concept. Despite the growing social and legal fragmentation of the family in the current age, an approach emphasizing the "familial" nature of human genetic material seems to be gaining acceptance in Western societies (Knoppers 1999: 23–24). Many legal traditions do not consistently recognize outright property rights in human bodies and persons. Organs have been typically exchanged within the framework of what has been called rather euphemistically the "gift." Biomedical information, however, does not fit easily into the legal tradition of the body (Greely 1998: 488).

The new genetics has brought with it a host of new candidates for commodification, including human cellular material and bioinformatic bits: genes, cell lines, DNA sequences, the human genome, medical records, and genealogies. Genealogies are subjected to somewhat different rules of access and privacy, depending on case and context. Some North American Indian tribes, for instance, tend to regard parentage as a private matter and, as a result, treat genealogies as highly confidential, an attitude that is radically different from that of most Icelanders. Moreover, as Brown points out (2003: 32), where genealogies are the key to tribal member- ship the information they provide is a hotly contested resource. As to the legal fight on the "Book of Icelanders," the critical issue under Icelandic law was the extent to which the new electronic database was the result of original, independent work or the "reproduction" of earlier texts.[1] Property, indeed, is a common issue in the information age, the core of what Boyle refers to as "author talk" (1996: 177). Similar questions have been raised by a series of legal cases on the European front involving, for instance, geographical maps in digital form (Iceland), telephone direc- tories on CD-ROM (Germany), and the linking of news pages on the web (Denmark). The contest over what counts as property, and on what grounds, is obviously played out in specific contexts with local concepts and histories. In every case, however, the opinion of the European Court has been consulted before the national legal authority has issued its final judgment.

Classical property categories, then, have been put under increasing strain. The collapse of the distinction between products of nature and products of human labour, partly as a result of the new genetics and the mapping of human chromosomes, has invited new questions. As genetic raw material is increasingly turned into a text, should it be patentable? Thus, Brown asks, "should the inherited sequence of nucleic acids that makes us who we are in physical terms be assigned to corporations as a monopoly for a limited period of time?" (2003: 102). To unpack the

---

[1] Many Icelandic scribes and collectors have mixed their labor with family histories through the centuries. This rich local tradition established and developed during the Middle Ages has now been adopted and enhanced by the powerful tools of computers and modern informatics. Icelandic law, enacted in 2000 in accordance with a European order of 1996, protects authorship of collections of independent works, whether in the format of books or digital files. According to the laws, the protection of authorship is conditioned on contributions to the works in question in terms of financial commitment and contributions.

intellectual freight of classical property discourse and to illuminate the complex functions and uses of property in different contexts, it seems useful to return to the early metaphor of property as a "bundle of rights" (von Benda-Beckmann, von Benda-Beckmann, and Wiber 2006). Thus, a series of rights can be bundled in a single property object and, moreover, a single social unit or legal persona – say, an individual, a family, a biotech company, a tribe, or a nation – can hold different kinds of property. Rather than, however, try to establish what property "is" or to define universal types of property – a perennial issue for legal theorists, courts, and legislators – anthropologists should focus on the ethnographic description and analysis of the "work" the property concept does, asking "how this concept works, who uses it, for what purposes, and with what effects" (Humphrey and Verdery 2004: 2).

While in most if not all contexts some kind of distinction is being made between what Polanyi (1944) called "true" and "fictitious" commodities, the dividing line is subject to redefinition and deconstruction in the course of political and ethical contests. Property concepts are both constituting and constitutive of the moral landscapes in which they are embedded. The new genetics, in fact, has brought a series of interesting examples of the refashioning of moral landscapes. One example is the way in which the notions of intellectual and cultural property have been expanded in response to encroachment by biomedical and pharmaceutical industries; under threats of biopiracy, monopoly and discrimination, genealogies and ethnobiological knowledge have sometimes been taken out of the public domain and redefined as "property." Another example is the impact of legal battles on "patenting DNA." Attempts to patent DNA with the launching of the Human Genome Project were often met with the public understanding that "persons" were being "patented" much like commodities, as a result of which "the 'Human Genome' is now widely conceived of as a common human creation and resource, where before the legal claims were made, it would not have entered ordinary perceptions in this way" (Hirsch 2004: 179).

One of the characteristics of the genome era is the fragmenting and marketing of body material and information. Genes, it may be argued, will be "the currency of the future" (see Nelkin and Andrew 1998). Increasingly, a "common wealth" of records, medical and genealogical, is being transformed into commercial property, much like distant lands and seas during the colonial era. These developments, which are trans-national and occurring at an exponential rate, have taken place in a social environment where the partnership of science and the market is by many considered to be the most efficient means of advancing knowledge and human well-being (Titmuss 1997, Starr 1998). Medical records, genealogies, and information on the genetic characteristics of individuals and entire populations may be quickly absorbed into the marketplace where they are exchanged in the form of commodities. As a result, the ownership of information has become a contested issue. The organization of collective memory through the use of computers, as Connerton notes (1989: 1), "is not merely a technical matter but one directly bearing on legitimation, the question of the control and ownership of information being the crucial issue."

Historically, many of the key issues in the theoretical debate about common property were fleshed out in the context of fisheries; hence, the generic relevance of Melville's reference to "fast fish." Fishing stocks and biomedical information, however, are different kinds of resources. In most places, fishing stocks are overused, sometimes by the logic of the so-called "tragedy of the commons." In the case of biomedical records, in contrast, the escalation of "effort" does not threaten the "carrying capacity" of the resource. Restrictions of access obviously limit the scope and capacity for prestige and financial gain, but biomedical records are immortal resources, no matter how one exploits them, as long as medical services operate. To the extent that genes and genomes represent property, they are examples of *intellectual* or *cultural* property, more like the whaler's knowledge of sea currents and animal behaviour and migrations than captured bodies of whales. Much intellectual and cultural property is best regarded as "limited common property" (LCP) in Rose's definition of the term (2004), being neither completely public nor completely private. With too much or overdeveloped property rights, biomedical resources may be subjected to a "tragedy of *anti*commons" (Heller and Eisenberg 1998); the resource, in other words, may be *underused* as a result of too many "owners" blocking each other. This was evident in both the genome war and the debate on the Icelandic Health Sector Database. In the latter case, territorial resistance within the local medical professions who tended to see themselves as *de facto* owners of medical records, partly explains the collapse of the genetic databases.

Rose and Novas suggest (2004: 452) the concept of "political economy of hope" to capture the ways in which life itself is "increasingly locked into an economy for the generation of wealth," in the context of "suffering, privation, and inequity." While biopiracy and corporate power pose continuous threats in the modern world, fear of them should not blind one to the possibilities of reconciling individualistic and communitarian enterprises in human genetics research. The high stakes involved – human well-being and the prevention and curing of common diseases – demand some kind of resolution. In many areas of intellectual property, including biomedicine, there are trade-offs between the promises of privatization and patenting, on the one hand, and, on the other, the risks of anti-commons. Too much "rights talk," as Brown remarks for debates about cultural property, can be counter-productive, undermining social peace: "progress will be built on small victories, innovative local solutions, and frequent compromise" (2003: 252). The main issue is how to allocate access to the "resource" through some form of licensing, shared ownership, or public trust, maintaining at the same time public ownership of the resource and requesting reasonable rewards to the community. The solution in each case will depend upon context – upon culture, politics, and history.

Perhaps, paraphrasing McCay (1995), one should speak of the "romance" of a complex constellation of commons and anticommons in the domain of the new genetics, as key contestants in legal debates about the control of body material and information – the individual citizen, the family, the private sector (biomedical companies), the medical professions, and nation states – negotiate and establish new property regimes. The metaphor of romance, McCay argues, is a realistic literary metaphor for many commons regimes, allowing for some degree of future hope, in a world with contesting perspectives, conflicting interests, and unexpected turns. In romance, she suggests (1995: 110), "conflict drives the narrative and is not overcome ... Romance implies ... complex development of character, situation, and plot and hinges upon the tension of not knowing what the outcome will be, but hoping for the best."

SEVEN

Human variation

Some of the scholars participating in the formation of the Human Genome Diversity Project assumed that the sampling of humans for the purpose of studying global genetic variability was relatively straightforward (see Marks 2002). Such an assumption is seriously flawed. Not only does sampling necessarily raise complex ethical and political questions about consent and fairness (Choudhury and Knapp 2005), but procedures of sampling themselves may also affect statistical results and their interpretation. This chapter explores the significance of the new genetics for the understanding of human history and diversity, focusing on the relevance of genetic research for discussions of race, the invention of community, and the implications of the notion of insular populations. Despite its sampling flaws, I will argue, in its selection of human populations, the Diversity Project has indirectly generated critical and innovative research on perceptual bias and the effects of sampling strategies. Assuming in advance an island model of diversity – and, by implication, particular categories of "populations" and "races" – may lead to sampling from the extremes of continental landmasses, which, in turn, generates results that reify the cultural notions about essences and boundaries assumed at the outset. While the new genetics, I suggest, has shifted the conceptual ground for discussions of human variation, the notion of racial difference is repeatedly reinvented along familiar lines, sometimes both unexpectedly and unwittingly. Racial discourse keeps being used in both innovative and problematic ways by the privileged as well as the underprivileged, for securing or denying citizenship and for gaining or restricting access to power and resources. A critical reassessment of the issues of sampling, populations, and so-called historical isolates has potentially profound implications for the understanding of genetic practice, biopolitics, health care, and race.

There are signs that race is firmly back on the agenda. In anthropology, the race concept and its history have recently been subject to some rethinking; see, for instance, a special 2003 issue of the *American Anthropologist* (especially, Caspari 2003). And in genetics and biomedicine there is a strong demand for an increase in the attention paid to racial differences. Risch *et al.* suggest (2002), for instance, that an understanding of racial differences is critical for dealing with race-specific disease and that a "color-blind" or non-recognition approach would be harmful for everybody, including racial minorities, in the long run:

Every race ethnic has its own collection of clinical priorities based on differing prevalence of disease . . . Taking advantage of . . . diversity in the scientific study of disease to gain understanding helps all of those afflicted. Ignoring our differences, even if with the best of intentions, will ultimately lead to the disservice of those who are in the minority. (Risch *et al.* 2002: 11)

The application of racial categories along genetic lines into medical research has led to the development of several "ethnic" drugs and, possibly, ethnically targeted biological weapons. In 2003, the National Human Genome Center at Howard University in Washington, DC, an historically "black" university, convened a workshop on "Human Genome Variation and 'Race'" which underlined the search for personalized, genetic and "racial" medicine. By now, at least twenty-nine medicines are claimed to have differences in efficacy among racial or ethnic groups (Tate and Goldstein 2004: S34), including BiDil which has been presented as a "race-specific" treatment for heart failure. In June 2005, the US Food and Drug Administration approved BiDil for use for about 750,000 self-identified

African Americans. Interestingly, given the notion of "ignoring our differences" (Risch *et al.* 2002) referred to above, the clinical trials involved seem not to have addressed the question as to whether BiDil might work better in African Americans than in others and, if so, why this would be the case. How are we to understand these developments?

The insular body: clades, races, and clines

The issues of race and human variation have long and winding histories in several fields of scholarship, including anthropology (see, for instance, Brace 2005). Some scholars have suggested race must be downplayed or ignored whatever the biological facts, since racial thinking violates an ethos of egalitarianism. In the cultural anthropology of Boas, developed partly in a battle with eugenics early last century, race was at least partly a biological fact. "Whites" and "Negroes," in particular, Boas suggested, were different: "The Whites, with their light skin, straight or wavy hair and light nose, are a race set off clearly from the Negroes with their dark skin, frizzly hair and flat nose. In regard to these traits the two races are fundamentally distinct" (1940: 4). In Boas's view, however, racial differences were far less marked than was commonly assumed. Rather than continue the racial politics of the day, which would inevitably lead to interracial struggle, he suggested, it would be better to "try to recognize the conditions that lead to the fundamental antagonisms that trouble us" (1940: 17).

Another argument has surfaced from time to time suggesting that race does not deserve any serious discussion or application since it is simply a social construction without any biological significance. Interestingly, such an argument gained substantial support with the development of the new genetics. Summing up the evidence, Templeton concludes (1999) that the genetic data is consistent and conclusive. First, he suggests, human races do not exist under the traditional concept of subspecies since the level of differentiation is well below the usual threshold applied to establish races in non-human species. Moreover, the representation of human "races" as branches on an intraspecific population tree is genetically indefensible, even when the time scale is represented as being at 100,000 years ago. Interestingly, there is a significant disparity between phenotypical characterization of races and molecular genetic data. Thus, Melanesians and Africans who share features such as dark skin and hair texture (features often used in racial classification) have almost maximal genetic divergence. Moreover, Europeans are closer to both Africans and Melanesians in terms of molecular markers than are Africans to Melanesians; "blacks," then, can hardly be said to represent a single branch on the evolutionary tree.

As molecular biology took off in the 1960s, it redefined the meaning of the visible and the physical. Biologists were able to consign conspicuous physical human traits, apparently visible to everyone, to the realm of folk accounts, reversing earlier notions about a one-to-one correspondence between phenotype and genotype (see Reardon 2005: ch. 3). "Obvious" phenotypic traits such as skin color were now seen as surface differences providing trivial if not misleading information about the deeper realities of the human body, hiding the fundamental similarities revealed by scientific expertise. Race, then, was only a façade, the tip of an iceberg saturated with the confounding debris of human history. Population genetics, however, did not remove race for good from the scientific agenda. Rather, in effect, it established a new *genetic* definition of race, a definition based on populationist terms. The notion of population, in fact, a central notion in many accounts of human diversity, is a highly problematic construct that deserves some discussion.

One of the basic models or approaches in genetic studies of human variability is that of the "island model" of insular populations. This model, as Wright outlined it in formalistic terms, assumes "a population subdivided into random breeding islands with populations of size N of which the proportion *m* consists of immigrants that may be considered a random sample of the species" (1969: 291). One model alternative to the island model is that of "isolation by distance" in a continuum:

Differentiation arises from the balance between the tendency toward local fixation by inbreeding and the swamping effect of dispersion. The most important unit is that of "neighbourhood," with an effective size, *N*, which is that of the total population from which the parents of an individual may be considered as if drawn at random. (Wright 1969: 487)

Although the terms "local fixation" and "neighborhood" may suggest boundaries, the model of isolation by distance assumes gradients in space rather than sharp breaks or discontinuities. Wright nicely captures the dimensions and complexities of continuity with the help of geographic metaphors:

There may be significant differentiation only along a single line, as in a chain of islands, a long narrow mountain valley, or the shore line of a lake or sea. There may be branching as in a river system, or differentiation in all directions as in an archipelago, a forest, a prairie, or a large body of water. (Wright 1969: 290)

Why should the choice of a model make a difference? Because it has important implications for research design, the interpretation of results, and the understanding of human differences. There is a tendency in the literature on humans to take the island model for granted and to sample from presumed isolated "populations" at the extremes of continental landmasses. Thus, some studies using DNA polymorphism have suggested that human genetic diversity is organized in continental *clades* (from the Greek *clados* for "branch"), the result of a history of sharp population separations (see Cavalli-Sforza 2005). It may, however, make more sense to pay attention to gradual variations in space, focusing on the gradients of *clines* (from the Greek *klinein* for "to lean"). While insular models of clades may be more simple to deal with mathematically than clines (Wright 1969: 290), this hardly accounts for the general fascination with insular populations in the literature. Part of the reason relates to the popularity of tree-like visualization and representation. Cavalli-Sforza, who himself has published a number of phylogenies that reportedly show the branching events that have separated human groups through evolutionary history, recognizes (2005: 339) that the construction of trees tends to force population data into clades, echoing Klapisch-Zuber's argument (1991, 2000) about the rhetoric and historicity of pedigrees.

Another reason for the popularity of insular thinking has to do with *a priori* notions of what counts as a population and of how to collect samples (Moore 1994). A recent study by Serre and Pääbo (2004) of the possible influence of research design in human genetics illustrates the point. Serre and Pääbo began by systematically comparing the effects of two different sampling strategies roughly representing the island model on the one hand, and, on the other hand, the model of isolation by distance. One of the datasets they used was based on published studies of specific populations, while the other was based on "neighbourhood," in Wright's sense, assembling individuals selected "such that their geographic distribution around the world approximates the subdivision of the human population as a whole and includes areas where Africa, Asia, and Europe meet" (Serre and Pääbo 2004: 1680).[1] Given their approach, *detecting patterns rather than assuming them*, the individual analyzed can belong to one or more "inferred populations" depending on his or her "coefficients of ancestry." Serre and Pääbo concluded from this exercise that the population-based method of sampling resulted in a view that suggests two discrete continental units of diversity, Africans and non-Africans. In other words, sampling geographically disconnected populations from different continents reinforced views of human genetic diversity that emphasized discrete units. In contrast, in the case of the other dataset, no

---

[1] Using a program ("STRUCTURE") that operates on genotype data from individuals and *infers* populations to which the individuals are assigned, they explored the genotype data involved (in technical terms, from twenty unlinked autosomal microsatellites).

such genetic subdivision was found to exist: all individuals were estimated to be "40 percent–50 percent admixed between two inferred populations, and no qualitative differences between Africans and non-Africans can be detected" (Serre and Pääbo 2004: 1680). While the sampling study was based on fairly limited data (few markers and few individuals), it was nevertheless suggestive.

Intrigued by their results, Serre and Pääbo undertook to reanalyze more extensive data from the CEPH cell line panel developed by the Human Genome Diversity Project. An earlier study of the CEPH panel (Rosenberg *et al.* 2002) found strong evidence of continental clustering, again inferring populations on the basis of patterns in genotype information. Assuming only three inferred populations, the researchers were able to assign Africans to one population, Native Americans and people from East Asia to another, and people from Europe and Central Asia to a third population. On the other hand, the pattern was unstable and ambiguous. For some of the individuals in the sample, the coefficients of ancestry changed significantly when the computer was instructed to increase the number of inferred populations beyond three; some individuals, then, were reassigned to a new cluster each time the rules of the game were changed, that is, when the number of inferred populations was altered. How many clusters should one assume, then, and on what grounds? Is race, after all, simply a matter of taste or preference, the number of cells one would like to see in a classificatory scheme?

In order to provide a more robust representation of human genetic diversity, to maximize the geographic distribution of samples, and to avoid the invention of substructures, Serre and Pääbo analyzed subsamples from the CEPH panel, equalizing the number of individuals per population. The results were radically different from those of Rosenberg and colleagues. With better coverage of the geographical distribution of humans across continents, Serre and Pääbo concluded, "the human gene pool no longer appears to be composed of discrete clusters" (Serre and Pääbo 2004: 1682). Most people were found to be highly admixed between two or three inferred populations and, moreover, three major geographical gradients became apparent, within Africa, in Eurasia, and in the Americas. Interestingly, then, given these results, the Diversity Project may contain the seeds of its own rebuttal, generating arguments against its own selective and insular approach to population studies. In their response to Serre and Pääbo, expanding their earlier dataset, Rosenberg and colleagues seem to qualify their earlier position, suggesting that human genetic diversity consists of clines of variation, maintaining nevertheless the position that diversity also consists of "clusters" which appear repeatable and robust. Small discontinuous jumps in genetic distance "across oceans, the Himalayas, and the Sahara" provide "clusters that correspond to geographic regions" (Rosenberg *et al.* 2005: 668). Cavalli-Sforza suggests, on the other hand, (2005: 339) that the article by Serre and Pääbo invites rethinking of the Diversity Project's approach, "whether the HGDP should focus in the future on individuals as the unit of sampling, or whether the emphasis should remain on sampling populations."

Geneticists sometimes base their analyses on samples from fellow scientists, their students and co-workers – and themselves; thus, Venter sampled his own DNA for his human genome project. Nevertheless, they tend to advocate a highly modernist approach, assuming a radical separation of the observer and the observed. Interestingly, given the modernist perspective, human genetic reasoning sometimes reveals a surprising and ironic post-modern twist; faithful to an island model of diversity, geneticists sometimes invent in their data the islands of their imagination. It may be tempting to conclude that the issue of sampling in human genetic research, much like the issues of "race" and "ethnicity," is hopelessly trapped in social constructions, body politics, and ideological discourse. This would, however, be an overstatement. Some approaches do a better job at representing human diversity than others. While the jury is still out, the model of gradual variation and isolation by distance, seems to more adequately represent global human genetic diversity than the model of major genetic discontinuities.

Some molecular biologists have been strangely resistant to this train of thought and the evidence it has accumulated. For one thing, as previously argued, there is a tendency to take for granted that genetic data on real human populations adequately fit an island model. Often, insularity has simply been assumed at the outset, resulting in circular reasoning about similarities and differences. Moreover, there is a tendency to present human "races" as evolutionary lineages, as distinct branches on a tree. Even when observed genetic differences have been shown to reflect gene flow between groups – where "treeness" constraints, by definition, do not apply – some researchers uncritically apply computer programs that by default presuppose that genetic distance data can be presented in terms of a branching tree (see Templeton 1999: 639). Failing to statistically test for treeness, they reify the evolutionary trajectories assumed at the outset.

One sign of resistance to the critique of the assumptions of islands and lineages within molecular biology is the tendency to invoke "admixture" events when needed. In order to salvage the model of purity when accounting for the complexities of genetic data, for instance when accounting for the disparity between the "racial" traits of dark skin and hair texture, on the one hand, and, on the other hand, molecular data for Africans, Europeans, and Melanesians, some scholars continue to treat human races as separate evolutionary lineages with the qualification that races were "purer" in the past, before admixture. The results of molecular genetics do not substantiate the claim about purity in the past (Cavalli-Sforza *et al.* 1996). Such an assumption is a byproduct of cladistic models based on the premise that each entity (population, race, or language) has only one parent. In the tree-like cladograms that they engender, the branches of the tree necessarily get progressively fewer as one approaches the trunk of the tree, the founder. Of course, in most cases other parent entities have been around at the same time, but cladistic models have nothing to say about them. As a result, cladistics necessarily conveys an image of purity in the past.

Some philosophers have been no less resistant than molecular biologists to the heavy theoretical critique that has been mounted against insular notions of population and race and the growing negative empirical evidence available. Thus Andreasen argues that biological races exist as clades or monophyletic groups: "they are ancestor-descendant sequences of breeding populations, or groups of such sequences, that share a common origin" (1998: 214). Interestingly, keeping in mind the analyses just discussed of data from the Diversity Project, Andreasen maintains that a biological conception of race along these lines is an objective construct, independent of the classifying activities of humans. Gannett suggests that Andreasen's position is "typical of the uncritical stance that philosophers of science assume vis-à-vis the scientific discipline whose conceptual foundations are of interest to them," adding that "other humanists, and social theorists need to look more warily on the deference they have shown to biologists over the past number of decades on questions concerning race" (Gannett 2004: 324).

Hunting and gathering genes

During the preparation of the Human Genome Diversity Project, there was considerable disagreement about how to define the units of analysis, a critical starting point for the project. Some of the organizers favored the sampling of selected "populations," while others opted for sampling within evenly spaced geographic grids. Critics of the grid approach worried about the intrusion of "outside" elements. One anonymous population geneticist observed:

sampling now in a grid fashion . . . regardless of what you know . . . if you go through the middle of Zimbabwe, or some other sort of thing, and you just sample randomly, you may pick up a tourist from Ohio. I mean, you know, if you just drop a dart down. (Quoted in Reardon 2005: 77)

The alternative strategy of sampling individuals from populations was no less problematic. How are population boundaries established? Where does one population start and another one end? Some scholars, including Renfrew (1992) and L. Luca Cavalli-Sforza (Cavalli-Sforza and Cavalli-Sforza 1998), suggest that language differences provide a useful heuristic solution to demarcating populations, assuming a fairly good fit between language, culture, and physical type (see Figure 7.1), a notion that is highly problematic.

It is interesting in this context to examine the extent to which different notions and procedures of sampling are applied in the genetic study of humans and other organisms. Are there different procedures for exploring variation across space and, if so, is anything wrong with that? The fruit fly provides an interesting contrast, given the extensive literature on it (see, for example Kohler 1994) and its historic role in the development of genome research, establishing the hegemony of genetics in modern biology. Gannett and Griesemer (2004b) provide an intriguing account of different practices and histories in genetic work on *Homo sapiens*, on the one hand, and, on the other, fruit flies. The evolution and migration history of *Homo sapiens*, they argue, is addressed at the level of groups while work on fruit flies tends to focus on individuals and chromosomes: "there is little serious attempt to fix group boundaries based on the evidence available" (Gannett and Griesemer 2004b: 166). Overall, Gannett and Griesemer suggest, there is a striking contrast between "mapping people and mapping flies":

> *D. pseudoobscura* populations are composed of whatever flies reside in an area at the time they are sampled, for example, those flies that congregate at a particular feeding station. The ABO blood group maps, in contrast, are based on the agglutination reactions of only those individuals whom investigators consider as indigenous, that is, "in situ" prior to European colonization. (2004b: 167)

There are obvious and important differences between flies and humans as objects of genetic and historical research. Possibly, researchers would approach *D. pseudoobscura* in a similar fashion if they had access to

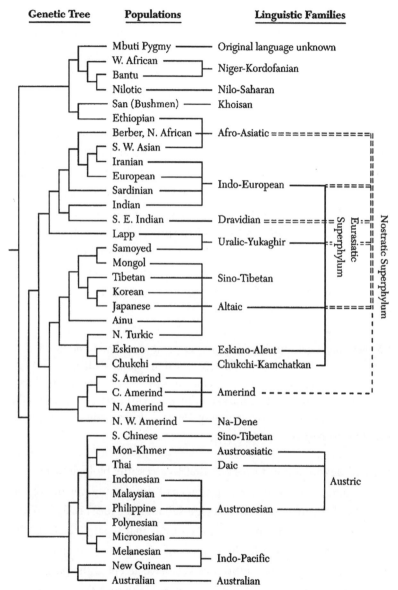

FIGURE 7.1 An attempt to match language groups with biological taxa based on gene frequency (from Moore 1994)

comparable historical and archeological information about them. And perhaps studies of chimpanzees might be more revealing than flies about our anthropocentric biases. Nevertheless, the contrast between the sampling of flies and humans is striking. Flies, unlike humans, are not assumed to constitute "indigenous" communities.

Hunter-gatherer populations have been appointed a special place in many studies in population genetics and biological anthropology. The highly influential volume *Man the Hunter* (Lee and deVore 1968), the result of the first international conference on hunting and gathering societies, helped to establish a paradigm wherein contemporary hunter-gatherers became cultural and biological representatives of our Paleolithic ancestors, supposedly less affected by the processes of history that transformed non-hunter-gatherers. Significantly, the subtitle of the volume refers to "a single, crucial stage of human development – man's once universal hunting way of life." As Washburn and Lancaster succinctly put it:

In a very real sense our intellect, interests, emotions, and basic social life – all are evolutionary products of the success of the hunting adaptation. When anthropologists speak of the unity of mankind, they are stating that the selective pressures of the hunting and gathering way of life were so similar and the result so successful that populations of *Homo sapiens* are still fundamentally the same everywhere. (1968: 293)

Lee and deVore go on to suggest that to assert the biological unity of humankind is "to affirm the importance of the hunting way of life," to claim that "the main selection pressures that forged the species were the same. The biology, psychology, and customs that separate us from the apes – all these we owe to the hunters of time past" (Lee and deVore 1968: 303). By and large, anthropologists have accepted the perspective established by the Man the Hunter conference, although the unified (and gendered) notion of the hunter has been modified and challenged on ethnographic, comparative, and theoretical grounds (see, for instance,

Panter-Brick, Layton and Rowley-Conwy 2001). In the standard view, the essential, common characteristics of humans (such as bipedalism and the capacity for language) were inscribed in the genome during the hunting and gathering "stage," representing the biological foundations on which cultural differences rest.

Interpretations of the genetic history of African hunter-gatherers, in particular of the !Kung San, Pygmies, and Hadza, reveal an intriguing discourse about the age of genes and populations. Genetic data from hunter-gatherer populations are often introduced to present contemporary hunter-gatherers as timeless representatives of a universal human prehistory. Thus, apparently isolated indigenous groups are considered to be a "window into the past," offering "a unique glimpse into the gene pool of our ancestors who lived thousands of years ago" (Roberts 1991: 1614). In the words of Chen *et al.*:

[T]he Biaka Pygmies of sublineage β may be one of the oldest distinct African populations and, hence, one of the oldest human populations in the world... The Vasikela Kung sublineage α may be the other truly ancient African mtDNA cluster . . . [I]t is positioned at the deepest root of the African phylogenetic tree, suggesting that the Kung San became differentiated very early during human radiation. (2000: 1372)

Similarly, Cavalli-Sforza and Cavalli-Sforza suggest that the hunter-gatherer population structure is particularly interesting since it provides "precious information on the evolution of the human species and the differences between ourselves and our recent ancestors, who also fall into the category of modern humans" (1998: 26). This suggests that hunter-gatherer populations are older than other populations, living relics of early Neolithic hunter-gatherer groups.

In fact, there are no valid grounds for regarding the genetic lineages of hunter-gatherers as more ancient than those of any other population. Every organism is an unfinished project subject to the emergent processes of a developmental system and, as a result, it doesn't make much sense to speak of biological universals and baselines (Ingold 2000). The hunter-gatherer of the contemporary world is part of a developmental system partly of his or her own design, not a representative of a Paleolithic regime. In addition, the evidence does not support the idea that hunter-gatherers have maintained an ancient way of life, isolated from food-producing populations. Much recent archeological and social anthropological evidence suggests there has been persistent contact between foragers and neighboring populations. As Solway and Lee point out, "the time depth of contact with non-hunters has increased from a few centuries to a millennium or more" (1990: 110). Evolutionary psychologists are particularly vulnerable to the idea that contemporary hunter-gatherers adequately represent the ancient past, suggesting, for instance, that the choice of female sexual partners and body shapes among male hunters and gatherers reflect the Pleistocene legacy (see Orgel, Urla, and Swedlund 2005). Such speculations nicely illustrate Sahlins's argument (1977) about the ethnocentric imposition of particular modern ideas upon human biological essence, the isomorphism between biological accounts and cultural frameworks.

Despite heavy critique of the approach, methodology, and assumptions of the Diversity Project, some of the key geneticists involved keep referring to "populations of anthropological interest – that is, those that were in place before the great diasporas started in the fifteenth and sixteenth centuries, when navigation of the ocean became possible" (Cavalli-Sforza 2005: 334). Perhaps anthropologists themselves are to blame for such a narrow definition of the "study of humans." The implicit assumption is that "indigenous" populations, in particular hunter-gatherers, were outside history – "in place," in Cavalli-Sforza's words – before European colonialism. The case of the Inuit of the Arctic, one of the blind spots in the collection of the Diversity Project, is interesting in this context. In the course of history, Inuit groups have identified themselves with a series of ethnonyms whose boundaries and definitions have continually changed. Yet, one of the longstanding clichés of northern explorers and scholars of various kinds presented Inuit groupings in terms of a fixed cultural mosaic mapped on the geography of the Arctic. Presented as the remnants of the Stone Age, isolated in a harsh environment to which they had adapted through millennia by ingenious techniques, the Inuit were often assumed to have been the only people who occupied the Arctic to which they had adapted as skillfully as polar bears (see McGhee 2005).

In line with this static view, several Arctic explorers of the nineteenth and twentieth centuries proudly announced the discovery of Inuit who had never before seen a European. Thus the anthropologist-explorer Vilhjalmur Stefansson claimed in 1912 to have discovered an isolated group of Copper Inuit on Victoria Island. He had spent four years in the Canadian Arctic searching for the Copper Inuit, a tribe reported to look more European than other "Eskimos" (Pálsson 2005). Stefansson and his contemporaries appear to have discounted the possibility that the Inuit could have migrated long distances and encountered "other" people on their journeys. At the time in question it was generally accepted that the Inuit had for centuries lived in isolated groups in practically the same location. Westerners, on the other hand, had traveled about, "discovering" Inuit and bringing them into contact with history and the outside world. These conceptions were clearly colored by colonial perspectives that still persist today under a new disguise. It is interesting to note that oral traditions among the Inuit of northwestern Canada tell of their ancestors journeying to the east, to territories of foreign peoples.

It seems clear from archeological excavations (McGhee 2005) that Inuit societies have been subjected to extensive change, with frequent "ethnic" intermixing and regrouping. In addition, research on the genetic history of Inuit (Helgason *et al.* 2006) shows that migration in the Arctic during the past 1,000 years or so has been complex and quite extensive. The ancestors of the people we now know as the Inuit arrived in Arctic Canada about 1,000 years ago, encountering people they called Tunit, in all probability the descendants of so-called Palaeo-Eskimos who had expanded from Beringia along the northern Alaskan and Canadian coastlines about

4,500 years ago, into the Canadian Arctic archipelago and ultimately, via Ellesmere Island, into Greenland. In a few generations, their descendants would explore the Arctic. Their ways of life developed in contrast with the evolving global context since the thirteenth century when they migrated into the eastern Arctic in order to trade with Europeans.

Imagined genetic communities

There are many ways of telling stories, tracking time, and accounting for origins (Powers 2005). The clash of histories brings us to the implications of the new genetics for the ways in which people imagine ancestry and relatedness. Native Americans do not always agree with archeological and genetic narratives about the crossing of the Bering Strait. Thus, Brody tells the story of a woman from a Cree community, a doctoral student at an American university. In her view, the idea that people originally came as immigrants from Asia sounded absurd; "in place after place," she said, "the first people arose where they now live. There had been no immigration, but an emergence; not an arrival from elsewhere, but a transformation from an ancient, prehuman time" (Brody 2000: 113).

The "molecular clock" hypothesis introduced in the early 1960s, according to which nucleotide or amino acid substitutions occur at a constant rate, has been hailed as a powerful avenue for assigning reliable dates to the divergence of ancestral sequences and for drawing phylogenic trees. Anthropological studies of human genetic history, as a result, are likely to increase in number during the coming years and decades. No doubt, such studies will have implications for the politics of identity and difference. Some nation states and groups may encourage and take political advantage of genetic studies that show they diverge from neighboring populations. Often genetic divergence is taken to indicate "ancientness" and an aboriginal status. In some cases, however, individuals or groups refuse to provide DNA samples for such studies. Inevitably, the geneticists and biological anthropologists involved must engage with complex ethics and politics of difference (Lock 1999). The Diversity Project, indeed, raised pressing questions of identity, power relations between experts and non-experts, and allocation of resources (see Brodwin 2005). At a conference in 1996 a spokesperson for the project stated, apparently in the heat of a debate, "We are going to tell these people who they really are!," to which a Native American activist angrily responded: "I know who I really am. Shall I tell you who *you* really are?" (see Marks 2002: 355). Such exchanges did not facilitate mutual understanding between observers and observed.

Despite the tensions and conflicts involved in research on human genetic variation, narratives from genetic studies are increasingly finding their way into the public domain. Thus, the contemporary media and literature are full of references to the new genetics. One humorous example is the following dialogue from McCall's novel *Morality for Beautiful Girls*:

"We all came from the same small group of ancestors. Dr. Leakey has proved that."
Mma Ramotswe was thoughtful. "So we are all brothers and sisters, in a sense?"
"We are," said Mma Makutsi. "We are all the same people. Eskimos, Russians, Nigerians. They are the same as us. Same blood. Same DNA."
"DNA?" asked Mma Ramotswe. "What is that?"
"It is something which god used to make people," explained Mma Makutsi. "We are all made up of DNA and water."
Mma Ramotswe considered the implications of these revelations for a moment. She had no views on Eskimos and Russians, but Nigerians were a different matter. But Mma Makutsi was right, she reflected: if universal brotherhood – and sisterhood – meant anything, it would have to embrace the Nigerians as well.
"If people knew this," she said, "if they knew that we were all from the same family, would they be kinder to one another, do you think?" (2001: 12–13)

An interesting BBC documentary "Motherland: A Genetic Journey" (2003) explores the roots of British African-Caribbeans through DNA analysis, drawing upon the fact that the majority of the African-Caribbean community in Britain are descended from the millions of Africans taken from their families and homes to work on the Caribbean sugar plantations during the slave trade. The aim of the genetic study on which the film is based was to see whether genetics could reconnect individuals to contemporary population groups. In order to do so, the researchers involved took DNA samples by means of cheek cell swabs from 229 volunteers selected from a sample of Britons who had four African-Caribbean grandparents. The film follows several Britons during their search for African ancestors, documenting their emotional journeys to their relatives and their responses to the DNA results, in particular their sense of identity. One person in the study, a woman from Bristol, was able to track down African relatives living on a small island off the coast of Cameroon. Another woman experienced an historic meeting with her blood relatives in Equatorial Guinea. While some of the DNA results were comforting, others were unsettling. Thus, a Peterborough schoolteacher was disappointed to find her roots in Jamaica and to discover that a significant proportion of her ancestry was European. The study revealed that more than one in four British African-Caribbeans have white male ancestry on their direct fatherline, underlining the extent to which female African slaves were made pregnant by male European slave-owners.

Sometimes referred to as "recreational genomics," such exercises may have important political implications, securing access to health services, casino money, or citizenship, and, possibly, undermining existing schemes meant to compensate those truly disadvantaged because of race. As Glick Schiller suggests, the popular reference in many contexts to genetic relatedness should not be dismissed simply as naïve essentialism: "It is important to understand why disempowered people embrace in their struggles forms of 'strategic essentialism,' including metaphors of blood" (2005: 306). The notion of "race" has a whole range of somewhat contradictory meanings that vary with context and speaker. Emerging in many contexts throughout the world, communities of relatedness based on genetic testing represent a revitalization of biological metaphors to mark belonging beyond established political boundaries, signaling the growth of what Glick Schiller calls "long-distance nationalism." Transnational political projects to build a state or an ethnic community thus increasingly draw upon notions of biological belonging informed by genetic testing.

In a society that tends to establish familial "truth" in terms of biology, trans-racial adoptions seem to raise existential questions about roots, substance, and identity similar to those of the descendants of the slave trade. This is underlined in Patton's (2000) study of adoption in the United States. In this context, being white functions as being unmarked; blackness, in contrast, is an unmistakable signature, a birthmark. One of the people Patton interviewed, a white woman adopted into a white family, commented that at the time she was adopted there was a tendency to "pick babies that would fit in physically with the family that was adopting them"; for her it meant the "absence of a *birthmark* – made it kind of easy . . . to just be transplanted into another family or another surrounding and not having anyone know" (Patton 2000: 19; *emphasis in the original*). Patton, herself an adoptee, reflects on what it means to have unknown, "alien" origins:

The lack of information about our birth families often translates into frustration that we have no family medical history, no (known) biological ancestors, no (biologically based) physical resemblance with our families, and no sense of physical connection to our parents or knowledge of our birth. We know we have "alien" origins that guide our bodily development with biological, genetic maps sketched in indecipherable codes. (2000: 171)

For Patton, however, the popular notion of "roots" is too restrictive and one-dimensional when applied to the construction of personal identity; instead she suggests (2000: 18) the more flexible metaphor of roads, paths, and diasporic histories.

Genetics are likely to play an increasingly important role for notions of identity and relatedness in the future (see, for instance, Santos and Maio 2004). This poses an important problem for those involved in biological research into human history – namely, how to avoid triggering unwarranted discourse about identity when discussing such studies in the public domain (Pálsson and Helgason 2003). Anthropologists and geneticists must reflect on the contexts in which their research is embedded and explore the potential implications of their work as their statements and findings enter public discourse through academic conferences, publications, and the mass media. Genetic-historical research, of course, is necessarily situated in time and context. Inevitably, researchers are faced with what linguists have referred to as the "observer's paradox"; they arrive on the scene to record things as they are (language, myth, identity, etc.), but their mere presence unavoidably shapes the course of events and, therefore, their representation. Even when researchers shun making statements about identities and relatedness, both when in the field and later, the mere fact that they are sampling DNA in an attempt to map genetic histories unavoidably gets people talking about who they are and where they come from.

In this respect, however, there is no fundamental difference between studying genetic history, on the one hand, and archeology, language, and heritage, on the other. Clifford observes for the Alaskan context that while Native and non-Native scholars have not always been on speaking terms, in some contexts they usefully collaborate in documenting and sustaining heritage: "While they do not transcend long-standing inequalities or resolve struggles for cultural authority, they at least demonstrate that Natives and anthropologists, openly recognizing a fraught common history, need not paint themselves into corners" (2004: 23). The same can be said for students of genetic history. Some form of collaborative discourse ethics seems essential.

It is one thing, of course, to explore genetic histories and quite another to tell people "who they really are." The responses to genetic analyses are likely to depend on a host of factors, including how people construct personhood, genetics, and relatedness. The Iñupiat of Alaska represent a particularly interesting case. Bodenhorn (2000) has discussed their ideas about personal names, marriage, families, and relatedness, based on her recent ethnographic fieldwork in Barrow and the surrounding area, emphasizing that her intent is not to unearth past customs but primarily to show how the Iñupiat of today form connections with one another and how they discuss family relations. One of the people interviewed by Bodenhorn spoke as follows concerning a person who had been mentioned: "He used to be my relative." For the Iñupiat, family connections are changeable and flexible, just like other social connections. When asked to translate words such as "family" to their native language, they often have difficulty, as this is a complicated matter. Individual persons, families, and family connections are constantly being formed, through adoption, naming, and everyday practical activities.

Adoption was and still is very common among Iñupiat. In some Alaskan villages up to 40 percent of children are adopted. The reasons given by people for adoption vary greatly. Some say simply that they "wanted" a child, others say they only had boys and wished to have a girl, and still others say that they had too many children and felt it was natural to share them with others. Sometimes the child him or herself is said to have "chosen" to be adopted. This is not merely an *ex post facto* justification, as one might perhaps suspect, since sometimes children are in fact allowed to decide whether they are to be adopted and, in such cases, by whom. Seldom if ever do they make reference to a blood relationship. Family connections are thus by no means a given, but rather the result of exchanges and discussions where the child's views are significant. Biology is almost beside the point. Sometimes children who have been placed in the temporary custody of neighbors or friends are eventually adopted. Perhaps one could speak of serial adoption. Among the Iñupiat, relatedness is generally regarded as the result of people's efforts. A man who has genetically fathered a child is not its "real" father unless he establishes this right by his actions, by looking after the child following its entry into the world. Maintaining paternity is a continuous and demanding task, not something which is determined once and for all; the same is true of the maternal role and all family connections. This is why it is possible to say that people "used to be" related. The word employed by the Iñupiat for "family," *ilya*, simply means "addition."

The complex social network which moulds an Inuk's person is to a considerable extent interlinked through personal names. This seems to pertain rather widely for most Inuit (Nuttall 2000). Names imply certain personality traits that are passed from one generation to another, traits that are reincarnated with each new generation. Friends and acquaintances give each other names as children and later in life. A person's character is thus more determined by the names he or she is given than by the parents' DNA. Hyperactivity and disobedience in children are sometimes explained by the fact that they have too many names. Children acquire the status of citizens at a very early age, as is evidenced by their rights with regard to adoption. Outsiders are often surprised at the way Inuit allow very young children to determine their own actions and to make important decisions concerning their lives. Sometimes children are said to determine when they are born and what gender they will be; "the Inuit foetus has the power to select the preferred sex according to an already deep memory of family history" (O'Neil and Leyland Kaufert 1995: 61). Given such cultural conceptions of personhood and relatedness, the Inuit are less likely than many others to redefine who they are on the basis of studies of genetic history. For them, individual identity and relatedness are not genetic matters. Nevertheless, genetic studies may have their impact in the long run here as elsewhere. While such studies are unlikely to influence the system of naming or to redefine parenthood, they may affect existing notions of Inuit ethnicity.

The label "Inuit," one may note, is a matter of some debate among people normally referred to as "Inuit." While traditionally the term referred to "people," to living beings inhabiting a certain place, it has increasingly been adopted in the Arctic as an ethnonym. Ingold suggests that the term *inuit* provides a clear example of the implication of the genealogical model for hunter-gatherer self-perception:

In the past to be a person, an *inuk*, meant to be alive, to inhabit a certain place, and to undergo growth and development within a nexus of social relations. The plural form, *inuit*, referred to "existence", or the "state of being animate" . . . Since the early 1970s, however, *inuit* has been explicitly adopted as an ethnonym to be applied on the basis of common descent from a putatively aboriginal population. To be an *inuk*, then, is no longer to occupy a particular subject position *vis-à-vis* others, but to belong as a member of a more inclusive genealogically defined category. (Ingold 2000: 427, n. 15)

A similar transformation has occurred in the case of the Alaskan Yup'ik (Fienup-Riordan 2000: 167). Broadly speaking, the growing emphases on common descent seem to be chiefly the result of complex political processes involving Fourth World ethnopolitics in the context of globalization. The redefinition of what it means to be an Iñupiak, an Inuk, or a Yup'ik is one aspect of the advance of modernity through which key notions of self and society are increasingly being revised.

Lost tribes: black Jews and blond Eskimos

Anthropologists have for a long time been fascinated with "discoveries" of tribes previously unknown to the West, a nostalgia nowadays echoed by the Diversity Project and similar projects. Newly discovered tribes keep being presented as evidence of past history, of "lost worlds" that need to be described and placed on the map before they become the victims of modernity and disappear from the scene. The paradox of such a "myth model," Kirsch suggests (1997: 59), "is that lost tribes cannot be considered in isolation" (1997: 58). Being "lost" necessarily presupposes someone who is interested in "discovery." The Tasaday, a foraging community on Mindanao Island in the Philippines, are probably the best contemporary example of the fascination with lost tribes. Another interesting episode in the literature on lost tribes is the fuss surrounding "Blond Eskimos" during the first half of the last century.

On September 9, 1912, the headline of the *Seattle Times* ran as follows: "American Explorer Discovers Lost Tribe of Whites, Descendants of Leif Erikssen." The explorer, the anthropologist Stefansson, was reported to have discovered "white people" among the Copper Inuit "purely of Norwegian origin." Stefansson later remarked that similar reports from what is now the Canadian Arctic had a long history (see Pálsson 2005). This was in the heyday of racial typologies. The idea of blondness had become potentially explosive, charged with the rhetoric of eugenic movements. When Stefansson returned from the field, the media reported that his discovery was the equivalent of finding the lost generations of Israel.

One reason why many people, including Stefansson, found the story about the "lost tribes of whites" attractive has to do with an old Greenlandic mystery involving a colony of Norsemen. From the tenth century onwards, Norse sailors established settlements in Greenland. These settlements expanded over the years to a population of 2,000–3,000. By 1450 they had been completely abandoned, but for many years this fact remained unknown in Europe. The fate of the colony posed a strange puzzle that has never been adequately explained, although it seems that one of the main reasons for its collapse had to do with climatic change and a shortened growing season. Stefansson argued that the Copper Inuit and the Norse might have intermixed, as a result of which the Inuit had passed on European phenotypic traits – blond genes or, in the jargon of the day, white blood. Reflecting on the debate over the Blond Eskimos later in his life, Stefansson observed that beyond all other strange reports that had come out of the Arctic, the public seemed most interested in those that concerned the "Blond" Eskimos. Originally he claimed that out of a thousand people he had met he had seen ten or more who had blue eyes, but the media reported that he had discovered nothing less than a Blond race. The Blond Eskimo story in its journalistic form was too good to die. Responses to the story varied, though, from one place to another. The Church of England in Canada decided to launch a campaign to convert "Stefansson's Blond Eskimos." After all, it assumed, they were among the lost children of European civilization.

The Inuit of Cambridge Bay on Victoria Island have little or no interest in identifying with blonds, Europeans, or the lost tribes of Israel, partly because demonstrating their genetic "impurity" might undermine their claims for land settlement under the Nunavut agreement and more broadly their political status as indigenous people. The case of the Lemba of South Africa is another matter. The Lemba are a small group that has recently been identified as "Black Jews." In the wake of genetic studies which suggest that they are of Middle Eastern origin, the media have shown extreme interest in them, much like in the case of the Blond Eskimo almost a century earlier. Reports about the "Jewishness" of these otherwise Bantu-looking people are not new. Time and again ethnographers and explorers have concluded that the Lemba show phenotypic traits (including lighter skin and "Jewish" noses) that testify to their Middle Eastern background. While such reports, as Parfitt points out (2003: 114), were an "endemic part of the colonial enterprise," psychologically extending the domain of colonial powers, they were welcomed by the Lemba. Genetic studies indicate that the Lemba male line substantially originates outside Africa although their reported Jewish ancestry remains contested. These studies have buttressed the sense of Jewishness among the Lemba, leading to a new form of Judaism which celebrates Hebrew, Jewish holidays, and orthodox Jewish law. The Lemba, who have for long maintained that in spite of their blackness they are "white people," now point to genetic studies as evidence for shared physicality with the white Jewish elite of South African cities.

The media fanfare accompanying stories of European traits such as fair skin among aboriginal groups in the Canadian Arctic and South Africa is not simply antiquated thinking; rather, it is an extreme illustration of a racial essentialism that one needs to watch for continually in reports on genetic work. A recent hoax on the imminent disappearance of the blond gene illustrates the point. On September 27, 2002, several British newspapers reported a genetic study indicating that blonds would become extinct within 200 years. The reports varied, but the general argument ran as follows: The World Health Organization had carried out a study – "a blond-shell study," as *The Daily Star* of London put it – suggesting that since blondness was caused by a recessive gene it was bound to disappear. Moreover, since dyed blonds were more attractive to men who choose them as partners over true blonds, too few people would carry the gene for blonds to last beyond the next two centuries. So-called bottle blonds, then, were partly to blame for the disappearance of natural ones. The *Sun* and the *Express* reported that blonds would survive longest in Scandinavia, where they are most concentrated, and the last true blond would probably be born in Finland. The respectable BBC reported that "a study by experts in Germany suggests people with blonde hair are an endangered species and will become extinct by 2202" (see *BBC News World Edition*, September 27, 2002). The same day the report was repeated on the ABC News program "Good Morning America." The host on the show began the story by saying:

There's a study from the World Health Organization, this is for real, that blonds are an endangered species. Women and men with blond hair, eyebrows and blue eyes, natural blonds, they say will vanish from the face of the earth within 200 years, because it is not as strong a gene as brunettes. (See Altman 2002)

The day after the story was covered by CNN.

None of these media reported any details about the German "experts," or the scientists allegedly working for WHO. While these media uncritically reported the story about the disappearing blonds, some remained sceptical. The Associated Press, for instance, said that while it had considered running the story, it decided not to after talking to the WHO. When interviewed about details, WHO officials said that WHO neither commissioned nor published any research on the future of the blond gene. Apparently the story originated in a report run by a German news agency quoting an article published in a local women's magazine two years earlier. As a result of the report, the press office of WHO in Geneva fielded nearly forty calls asking for the alleged study. Meanwhile there was an embarrassing silence about a real statement WHO had produced: "We put out a press statement on the health situation in Palestine on the same day. And comparatively we had very few calls on that, which was quite pathetic, really" (see *The Globe and Mail* 2002).

Why many of the London tabloids, the BBC, and several NBC-TV affiliates were driven to participate in the hoax, reporting an imaginary study predicting the demise of naturally blond hair, remains open to question. The idea of blondness has a long and complex history in the West. Western narratives about blondness, typically in the context of "race," tend to portray this heritable trait both as desirable and as representing some kind of essence of European identity. With recent advances in reproductive technology, the sperm and ova of blond people have become valuable marketable commodities. An American sperm bank, Scandinavian Cryobank based in Seattle, specializes in worldwide delivery of donor sperm from "blond" Scandinavians (Scandinavian Cryobank 2003). Advertisements on the web for egg donors have similarly offered bonuses for blonds.

Race, as we have seen, remains a contested issue, despite (or because of) the new genetics. The fusion of racial profiling and personalized medicine necessarily invites debates on perceptions, politics, and the role of environmental factors in the development of common diseases (see, for instance, Kahn 2003, Kittles and Royal 2003). One of the key issues underlying these debates, much like those surrounding the Diversity Project, is that of the concept of population. Attempts to abandon the term "race" seem futile as long as it keeps being replaced by equivalent euphemisms that are based on the same assumptions about ancestry, isolates, and cladistics. Kittles and Weiss suggest that while dendograms or tree-diagrams are useful visual aids for presenting data, "it is easy to lapse into accepting the populations thus portrayed as taxonomic rather than merely statistical spatial spot-sampling units, and equating these population samples to colloquially defined races as if the latter have some kind of biological reality" (2003: 37). They add that "careful geneticists know that if we had more geographically comprehensive samples, human genetic variation is actually characterized by clines (spatial gradients) of allele frequency rather than categorical variation between populations, and the pattern varies among genes . . ." Interestingly, those who advocate returning to the issue of race on the basis of the "primary" continent of origin (Risch *et al.* 2003: 3) tend to emphasize an "objective" scientific perspective that radically separates fact from fiction, nature from culture, and the observer from the observed, failing to recognize the embeddedness and circularity of their own reasoning. Circularity and subjectivity seem to be inevitable travel companions in the sampling and exploration of human diversity. Sampling cannot possibly take place without a subjective judgment about how to proceed.

The notion of the insular body discussed above is no less pervasive in modern medicine than in human genetics. Martin has explored its circulation and use in modern immunology. Drawing upon several kinds of evidence – mass media articles, textbooks, fieldwork in a university department, and in-depth interviews – she poses the key question: "are there powerful links between the particular metaphors chosen to describe the body scientifically and features of our contemporary society that are related to gender, class, and race?" (1990: 422). Often, she suggests, discourses on immunology present the boundary between the body (self) and the external world (non-self) as rigid and absolute, in contrast to the relatively fluid internal boundaries within the body. One of the key metaphors involved in the reinforcing of boundaries is that of the human body as an island enmeshed in an ocean inhabited by ruthless aggressors. As one author had it (cited in Martin 1990: 411), ·

The immune system evolved because we live in a sea of microbes . . . The human body provides an ideal habitat for them and they try to break in . . . When immune defenders encounter cells or organisms carrying molecules that say "foreign," the immune troops move quickly to eliminate intruders.[2] (Schindler 1988: 1)

While such a metaphorical language is, no doubt, a useful pedagogical device for introducing newcomers to the world of immunology, it has another rationale as well, an epidemiology of its own. Its contagiousness, as Martin indicates (1990: 414), has much to do with the fact that its images of bodily identities "relate in complex ways to social forces pervasive in our time," namely those of the nation state. The imagined cell, in a sense, is a conceptual microcosm of the imagined community of the nation state, an image focused on boundaries, information, differences, alien languages, control, and hierarchy. The science of immunology developed along with the concept of the immune system in the 1960s. Its key metaphor was that of "the body at war." Martin speculates that "one kind of ideological work such images might do is to make violent destruction seem ordinary and part of the necessity of daily life" (1990: 417). Assuming a relationship between immunological representations of cellular processes and the state of the national body, and given the growing discourse on international terrorism with the 9/11 attacks on the Twin Towers of New York City, one might expect to witness an even more violent and treacherous language than before. The seed of a terrorizing immunological discourse was already around at the time of Martin's writing. Treichler suggests, as Martin observes (1990: 423), that the AIDS virus is a "spy's spy, capable of any deception . . . a terrorist's terrorist, an Abu Nidal of viruses" (Treichler 1987: 282).

---

[2] Another metaphor that dominates accounts of the immune system, Martin suggests, is that of the body as police state. Thus, every cell in the body is said to be equipped with "proof of identity" or "identity papers" which guard it against the body's own police force.

As we have seen, research on genetic variability necessarily involves pragmatic concerns that direct the researchers' choices about where to assemble data and how to analyze them and interpret the results. "These choices and the values that inform them," as Gannett and Griesemer emphasize (2004a: 167), "direct the writing of the history of human evolution, a history that, unlike for flies, is written by, for, and about those for whom there exists an interest in such a history." Humans not only leave a variety of signatures in the historical record – in language, customs, and archeological remains – long after they are gone; they also usually have firm ideas about both their identities and social history which are bound to somehow affect the ways in which we study genetic history. While genetic sampling cannot possibly take place without some prior notion about how the empirical world is structured and how to go about studying it, some notions work better than others. It is essential to ask why certain judgments are made rather than others and how they inform the research process from beginning to end. The organizers of the HapMap emphasize that while selecting a single population might offer simplicity, it obviously cannot be representative and, conversely, while grid-sampling is representative of current worldwide distribution it is not practical. Any choice of DNA samples, they point out, represents a pragmatic "compromise": "The project chose to include DNA samples based on well-known patterns of allele frequencies across populations, reflecting historical genetic diversity" (International HapMap Consortium 2005: 1316). Rather than assume that populations are genuine biological objects with fixed boundaries that only need to be discovered, it seems to make more sense to conclude that populations are pragmatically constituted in line with the interests of the researchers in question.

EIGHT

Conclusion

Early last century, Franz Boas remarked that in a few decades physical anthropology and social anthropology had "drifted more and more apart": "This seems unavoidable on account of the difference in subject matter . . ." (Boas 1940: 172). "Nevertheless," he added, "some method must be found, if the important borderland between the two is not to be neglected – much to the detriment of either." While the subdisciplines have perhaps continued to drift apart, the new genetics has created a new borderland which Boas could not possibly have anticipated. Inevitably, with its visualization, mapping, and manipulation of the universe within, it provides an "obligatory point of passage," in Latour's sense (1988), a node through which the study of humans, much like many other disciplines, is bound to move – perhaps even more so than other disciplines. The popular dualistic view that underpins an academic division of labor that allocates human universals to the realm of biology and human differences to the realm of social and cultural anthropology fails to adequately reflect actual research agendas within these fields; social and cultural anthropology has always expressed considerable interest in human universals and, conversely, physical and biological anthropology have remained committed to the exploration of differences among contemporary human populations, focusing on skeletal morphology and blood types.

Anthropology and the New Genetics

In preceding chapters, I have suggested that while anthropology seems destined to pass through the node represented by the new genetics, a development that is already on full course, this poses both challenges and potential diversions or dangers. Some of the latter relate to anthropology's past, its politics of difference, its reification of cultures and populations (and, more recently, genomes), its ethics of "sampling" and research, and its tendency to lapse into a sectarian subdisciplinary mode. Just as biological anthropologists (and human geneticists) have sometimes failed to critically examine their assumptions about "populations" and "races," social and cultural anthropologists have sometimes too easily dismissed the implications of genetic studies on the grounds that they are trivial and uninteresting or, in any case, simply social constructions. The challenge for anthropology is to critically engage with ongoing developments rather than shy away from them, to draw upon and rethink the discipline's comparative and historical knowledge and its understanding of the species, in an effort to seriously make sense of the implications of the new genetics for what it means to be human (and post-human) in the modern age. Perhaps, as a starting point, the term "genomic anthropology" should be adopted, to denote a hybrid and broadly defined field that overcomes the longstanding fissure between "social" and "biological" perspectives. Such a concept seems to allow for a more holistic perspective than is normally associated with the labels of "genetic" and "biological" anthropology, avoiding at the same time the reductionisms often seen to be implicit in them.

The analyses of the new genetics and the biopolitics they represent are bound to have profound implications for human well-being and the general understanding, and reshaping, of the human condition. Moving from one context to another – from the "dry fog" surrounding the Icelandic Health Sector Database to the deCODE laboratory and the larger world of biotechnology and human genetics – my discussion has addressed a number of related issues: the tension between gene centrism and epigenetics, efforts to map the human genome, the uses of family histories, the rhetoric, construction, and design of genetic assemblages, the politics of bioethics, the appropriation and commodification of the human genome, and the charting of "race," human genetic differences, history, and evolution. In the remainder of this chapter I highlight the general arguments of previous chapters, focusing at the same time on some interrelated themes in the rethinking of anthropology in the wake of the new genetics: the nature/society divide and the relevance of substance for the construction of identity and relatedness, diverse projects of mapping, and, finally, the reading of bodily inscriptions.

The substance of substance

The distinction between nature and society is central to both modern science and modernist culture (Descola and Pálsson 1996). Not only has it been reinforced by a rigid academic division of labor and massive institutional structures, it also tends to be "engraved" in the financial and spatial organization of universities and campuses, in their architecture, layout, and budgets. In many places, anthropology itself remains firmly divided along this axis. While criticism of the modernist project and its separation of nature and society has been fuelled by recent developments, including the advances of the new, it is not a brand new phenomenon. Wagner argued in an important and somewhat neglected paper from a different, "semiotic" perspective that the distinction between the environment and the environed was an arbitrary one, fixed for the sake of analysis:

Positivistic epistemology has generally favoured the notion of "levels" in the sense that the cultural is said to be an "abstraction from" nature – a replication of its "orders" via human artifice . . . The arbitration of this limit, forging a literalistic culture that continually separates itself from a figurative nature that continually encompasses it, is the key to the "environment" problem. In fact . . . the distinction is itself non-locatable . . . nature is as much abstraction from culture as the cultural is an abstraction from nature. (Wagner 1977: 395–396)

Wagner's conclusion has a clear postmodern twist. In his view, nature and semiotics are so "completely and mutually continent of one another . . . that no boundary of any sort can be established between them" (1977: 409). This implies, he argues, "that the Cartesian duality is at once completely insoluble and largely irrelevant."

No doubt, the dualism of nature and society was highly convenient in the sense that it made room for social scientific approaches within academies and universities traditionally dominated by natural science. If dualistic programmes in the human sciences were primarily reactions to the hegemony of biological reductionism, what, we may wonder, will be the consequences if the nature/society dualism is suppressed? Is it necessary, perhaps, given the power struggle within universities and bureaucracies, to staunchly defend a well-demarcated social scientific camp? Surely, budgets are important, but I don't think that stubborn adherence to the dualisms of the past is a realistic defense strategy. In recent years, the distinction itself between nature and society has increasingly been subject to critical discussion in several fields, including anthropology. And there are good grounds for second thoughts.

One of the reasons for the critique of the nature/society dualism is the recognition that humanity has an embodied physicality that, by definition, naturalizes it. One theoretical avenue for addressing this is the phenomenology of embodiment recently developed by Csordas (1994) and some others. This is an important part of what I earlier referred to as "anthropology completely at home." A related perspective is the relational view of personhood. The notion of the natural, autonomous person – after nature, in Strathern's sense (1992) – is a fairly recent and, in fact, an ethnocentric invention. In many contexts, the individual is seen as a social being even before birth, wrapped up in a complex net of connections with his or her fellow citizens. As Carsten remarks for the Malay (1995: 235), bodies are "simultaneously bounded and porous. In some respects it seems hard to say where one person stops and another begins." Anthropological writings on the Inuit, as we have seen, suggest similar notions of personhood. Some historians have claimed that conceptions of Northern Europeans in the Middle Ages were not so very different; people were regarded as being integrally joined both to one another and to the country in which they lived (Gurevich 1992). The notion of intercorporeality is sometimes introduced to underline such "dividual" notions of conflated selves. Bird-David suggests, however, that behind some of the theoretical discussion of intercorporeality there "clearly lurks a 'methodological individualism' of sorts and a market perspective" (2004: 326) in that the bounded individual is still the unit of observation and analysis. Her exploration of the imagery of embodiment and illness among the Nayaka of India highlights the local notion of "joined beings," a notion that extends beyond the Cartesian idea of the autonomous self, the family, and the community, "to an open-ended web of local connections which is granted without being fully known. It expresses Nayaka concern with an irreducible plurality constructed as 'relatives' that transcends classes and boundaries, both human and non-human" (Bird-David 2004: 337). The logic of Nayaka thinking, Bird-David argues, "expresses a kind of intercorporeality that is almost tantamount to transcorporeality" (2004: 337).

The relational perspective on personhood is echoed in the feminist argument that neo-classical economics deals with a "mushroom man," an autonomous agent alienated from context and history and suddenly brought to full maturity like a mushroom (Nelson 1995). The mushroom metaphor may nevertheless be useful for highlighting sociality and connectedness (Ingold 2000: ch. 8); mushrooms, like trees, are connected by subterranean networks of fibers that are central to their being although they may not be visible to most spectators. Surprising as it may seem, mushrooms convey a rhizomic image of relatedness in stark contrast to the cladistics of the phylogeny of trees and the mosaic of cultures.

A further reason for the growing discontent with dualistic notions is that modern humans are presented with a "nature" very different from that experienced by earlier generations. The new genetics and its technological wings, biotechnology and genetic engineering, have revolutionized our capacity to analyze and alter DNA material, raising new and fundamental questions as to what constitutes "nature" and "life itself" (Rheinberger 1995); organisms are engineered and manufactured according to human designs and for human purposes. Nature is increasingly turned into an artifact of consumer choice, through a radical extension of the Foucauldian notion of the care of the self. Human nature, then, must be a fleeting category.

Conceptions of personhood, individuality, kinship, and society are in many contexts undergoing radical change, in part due to the impact of biomedicine on people's lives through innovations such as artificial insemination, surrogate motherhood, genetic engineering, tissue transfer, and organ transplants. The conceptual collapse of nature and culture with the new genetics is nicely captured in Rabinow's notion of biosociality:

In the future, the new genetics will cease to be a biological metaphor for modern society and will become instead a circulation network of identity terms and restriction loci, around which and through which a truly new type of autoproduction will emerge, which I call "biosociality." (1996: 99)

In a recent commentary on the concept of biosociality, Hacking suggests (2006: 81) that while Rabinow may have invented it partly as a joke, to challenge the biological determinism of the "sociobiology" fashionable at the time, the new genetics and its associated developments "is fuelling fascination with this concept." Indeed, since it was written, Rabinow's essay on biosociality has generated extensive discussion in the humanities and the social sciences. While biosociality, no doubt, has been taken into several different avenues, one of these avenues is the ways in which the concept might serve to underline the post-disciplinary nature of contemporary science and, possibly, to realign the "social" and the "biological."

It seems as if the indigenous people of the High Arctic and several other contexts, who were long considered to belong to the Stone Age, have had premonitions of some of the consequences of the new genetics. For them the flexible, (post)-modern self – a self which is relational, contradictory, multi-faceted, and continuously developing – is nothing new, only old wine in new bottles.

Despite the conflation of nature and culture in an age characterized by biosociality, current gene talk often assumes the autonomy of genes and the primacy of genealogical relations. Personhood is seen to emerge at the encounter of lines of "descent," usually with the vertical passing on of substance from one generation to another. Whatever the form, the end result of phylogenetic geometries is usually to underline deterministic and essentialist classification, what is "in the genes." "Heredity," as Canguilhem put it (1989: 280), "is the modern name of substance." Not only is relatedness and identity frequently reduced to genetic connections and genome properties, genetic discourse acquires an authoritative status in discussions of human similarities and differences. While the new genetics is often consulted to refute the concept of "race" and the gene talk on which it is based, such consulting has an ironic touch: "The irony that these concerted efforts to refute racism might well reproduce it stems from the nature of geneticists' claims; implicit in the very conviction that genetics can refute the logic of racism is an assumption about the authority of genetics . . . to establish definitive terms of relatedness" (Wald 1992: 704).

Although the gene is a central element in both biological theory and public discourse, it is by no means clear what it entails. For Rheinberger the gene belongs to a class of heuristic and fuzzy "boundary objects," scientific objects that cannot be assigned a precise and codified meaning. The epistemological take-home lesson, he argues, of his analysis of the use and meaning of the concept, is a disappointing message for non-deconstructivists: "A gene is a gene is a gene" (2000: 235). In his view, however, the usefulness of boundary objects does not rest with our ability to define them from the outset: "indeed it can be rather counterproductive, to try to sharpen the conceptual boundaries of vaguely bounded research objects while in operation" (Rheinberger 2000: 221). Despite the uncertainty surrounding the definition of the gene, the successes of molecular biology have produced a powerful discourse that presents the "blueprints" of life as being encoded in DNA molecules and genomes. One of the important implications of the new genetics is the powerful metaphor of the "book of life."

What do people mean when they speak of human genome research in terms of deciphering and editing the codes of the "book of life" and what are the implications of such a metaphor for human life and self-understanding? Inevitably, the focus on codes and messages brought about by the new genetics has resulted in a shift in the way people talk about health, care for the body, and human responsibility. Canguilhem observes that the terms anomaly and lesion, originally borrowed from the language of morphological pathology, have now been incorporated into the language of information theory which presents sickness as genetic and enzymatic misunderstanding: "To be sick is to have been made false . . ." (1989: 276). As a result, he suggests, disease is no longer seen to be a matter of individual responsibility but an original flaw in genetic message: "There is then no ill will behind the ill fate. To be sick is to be bad, not as a bad boy but as poor land. Disease is no longer related to individual responsibility" (Canguilhem 1989: 278). This is true, but only up to a point. While the main *cause* of disease is often seen as being beyond human influence, a matter of genetic disposition, knowledge of family histories and genetics increasingly informs people's responses to health risks. Exploring the ways in which people experience the new genetics and how they respond to perceived health threats, partly through the formation of virtual community, is an important task for anthropology.

Given the emphasis on texts and codes, genetics and literary criticism have much in common. Wald suggests (1992: 681) that geneticists are near kin of literary critics in that they eagerly acknowledge, much like textual experts, the mutability of their "texts." The textual resemblance between biology and the humanities is neither superficial nor coincidental. Biology, genetics, linguistics, anthropology, and related fields mutually collaborated in the development of theories of communication at the middle of the last century. Structuralists, among them Claude Lévi-Strauss and Roman Jakobson, suggested that the minimal units of mythologies and languages, mythemes and phonemes, should not be seen as things in themselves but have to be understood in terms of relational systems, much like the elements of the genetic code. During a famous televised debate in Paris in 1967, Jakobson, Lévi-Strauss, and biologist Françoise Jacob, were all "fascinated by the striking isomorphisms between the code of language and molecular code which were revealed in this discussion" (Jakobson, cited in Kay 2000: 307).

Recent theoretical developments in biology have questioned the classic argument of Mendel and Darwin that organisms are autonomous objects dictated by genes and selective pressures. An emerging, alternative model emphasizes that the organism is empowered to shape its own development, the *subject* of evolutionary forces. The dialogic vocabulary of co-evolution seems to be emerging in the place of mechanical Newtonian notions. Any distinction between inside and outside (and, by extension, between nature and society) seems beside the point. Such a shift in perspective from the dualism of genes and environments to developmental processes and epigenetic systems entails redefining the concept of adaptation introduced into biology in the nineteenth century. There is an interesting resemblance between such a perspective and the critical perspective of the Nayaka which Bird-David describes as "almost tantamount to transcorporeality" (2004: 337). Whereas the new genetics focuses on the world within, voyaging into the cell, the Nayaka and other developmental systems theorists do the opposite, focusing on "joined beings" and the embeddedness of the web of life. In anthropology, such a view has been forcefully argued and developed by Ingold who argues that capacities are "constituted within developmental systems, rather than carried with the genes as a biological endowment" (2000: 385). Once this is realized, he suggests, "we can begin to see how the dichotomies between biology and culture, and between evolution and history, can be dispensed with."

Maps and trees

As the ancient notion of the "book of life" was redefined in terms of the hieroglyphics of genetic messages, new forms of biological citizenship, biopower, and governmentality developed. The mapping of the human body became a central enterprise in academe, government, and industry, focusing on the genetics and distribution of disease and the identification and management of troubled bodies and populations. Foucault's work *The Birth of the Clinic* anticipates some of these developments through its emphasis on the "spatialization" of bodies and disease. Philo's "geographical reading" of the *Clinic* suggests that "littered with explicit references to geography, space, spatialization, regionalism and the like" it focuses on "very tangible worldly geographies" (Philo 2000: 17). Genetic databases along the lines discussed in previous chapters became one of the important developments by the turn of the century. In each case, the structure of the database and the public perception of it have been informed by what I have referred to as moral landscape, by context, history, and culture. National projects that combine genetic information, family histories, and medical records represent, I have argued, the extension of the mapping process, a significant part of biomedicalization.

Bioethics, too, has its own moral landscapes that are subject to historical, globalizing change. In the past decade or so, bioethics seems to have taken a communitarian turn, shifting from the perspective of the autonomous individual and the heavy reliance on informed consent which it has advocated in the recent past to a more social and holistic perspective, emphasizing the principles of reciprocity, mutuality, solidarity, citizenry, and universality. Knoppers and Chadwick suggest that a new "participatory approach" has emerged as a result of the growing influence of social science on ethics and the reinterpretation of the concept of "expertise" in genetic ethics. "There might not," they conclude, "and cannot, be universal norms in bioethics, as emerging ethical norms are as 'epigenetic' as the science they circumscribe" (2005: 78). Thus the principle of informed consent which was at the center of the storm around genetic databases early on has given way to a broader participatory approach. One example is a recent statement by the National Council for Ethics in Germany emphasizing broad consent ("waivers") and the useful role of biobank trustees or curators (Nationaler Ethikrat 2004), a significant "ethical" turn in a context usually obsessed with restricting all kinds of assemblies involving body parts – with good reason, keeping in mind the depressing lessons of Third Reich eugenics.

A critical issue in any discussion of the implications of the new genetics for current anthropology is what to make of rapidly accumulating molecular genetic data on human differences. One of the products of the new genetics is the development of "race-specific" drugs. The list of "promising" drugs is likely to rapidly expand, despite the critique that some of them at least are not tested across ethnic lines and the health problems in question may be the result of gene–environment interactions. Somewhat surprisingly, a study by deCODE genetics, a company that has usually focused on a single and relatively homogeneous population, may be contributing to the development of "ethnic" drugs. The study in question indicates that a particular haplotype (HapK) of the LTA4H gene presents a modest risk of myocardial infarction in both Icelanders and European Americans and a threefold greater risk in African Americans.[1]

As we have seen, the idea of insular populations has had a strong hold on the imagination of many of those writing on human diversity. The

---

[1] The report concludes that the HapK haplotype is very rare in Africa and that its occurrence in African Americans is due to European admixture: "Interactions with other genetic or environmental risk factors that are more common in African Americans are likely to account for the greater relative risk conferred by HapK in this group" (Helgadottir et al. 2005).

same can be said for the issue of "race." The twin concepts of race and population, indeed, inevitably invoke similar theoretical and method-ological concerns and concepts, including those of maps and trees. Thus, Templeton raises the central question: "Are human populations genet-ically different from one another in such a fashion as to constitute either sharply genetically differentiated populations or distinct lineages of humanity?" (1999: 633). Templeton emphasizes that if one is to apply the term "race" in this context, the issue of what counts as a "sharply" differentiated and "distinct" lineage needs to be addressed with the same explicit criteria that are applied in genetic studies of evolutionary sublin-eages and speciation in the non-human world. A contrast in standards similar to that observed for those mapping people and others mapping flies would, indeed, justify the conclusion that race is a social construction. Race, I suggest, is no less problematic than before, despite its rethinking in the wake of the new genetics.

Many students of human diversity, including Renfrew (1992), L. Luca Cavalli-Sforza (Cavalli-Sforza and Cavalli-Sforza 1998), and Mace, Holden, and Shennan (2005), insist that the histories and geographies of genes, cultures, and languages are similar if not identical since they have coevolved in a phylogenetic fashion in the course of time within the same ethnos. As several scholars have shown (see, for instance, Moore 1994), this is a highly dubious assertion. Keeping in mind the growing genetic evidence on human diversity, the failure of the data to reflect the constraints of treeness, and the flaws of models of islands and clades, it makes sense to assume an alternative model for the species, a more or less permanent state of hybridity or creolization. To describe such a state as permanent "admixture" is to miss the point. In their discus-sion of the axiom of bounded and pure populations prevalent in human genetics, Kittles and Weiss seem unnecessarily cautious: "Does the very use of the term admixed," they ask, "imply (falsely) the existence of some prior, pure, and distinct ancestral populations?" (2003: 44). In fact, it would be more to the point to speak of genome rhizomics as the general rule with an occasional, temporary "split" in the course of time.

The idea of insular genomes often underlined in human genetics, the Human Genome Diversity Project, and related projects, has its parallel in the idea of cultural islands represented by the Human Relations Area Files (HRAF), a Cold War effort to map and archive global cultural diversity. The HRAF project drew upon the established anthropological idea that each culture is a bounded and stable unit, to be studied through ethnographic fieldwork and "translated" for a larger audience. Just as genetic sampling for the purpose of studying human diversity has emphasized geographic extremes, ignoring the borderlands, the study of cultural diversity has focused on the extreme pieces of the cultural mosaic of the globe. Despite heavy critique, the notion of the cultural mosaic has remained resilient, sometimes reappearing rather unexpectedly under the banner of cultural critique. An alternative perspective would emphasize the fleeting and rhizomic nature of the cultural world: "We are interested less in establishing a dialogic relation between geographically distinct societies than in exploring the processes of *production* of difference in a world of culturally, socially, and economically interconnected and interdependent spaces" (Inda and Rosaldo 2002: 72). Given the island model of cultural critique, the Human Relations Area Files, and the Human Genome Diversity Project, contact zones between cultures and populations tend to disappear from sight.

An alternative rhizomic approach to language, culture, and genomics is provided by the perspective of ethnogenesis, one of the anthropological challenges to cladistic models. Ethnographic analogy, Moore suggests (1994), shows that genes quickly flow to neighboring groups through intermarriage which precludes the idea that ethnic groups can be characterized as exclusively possessing one definitive genetic structure at any one time. The ethnogenetic perspective, in contrast to the cladistic model, suggests that interaction across ethnic and cultural boundaries has continually ensured hybridization of cultures and languages and, as a result, languages, cultures, and physical types are no more complex now than in the past. Fuzzy and unstable boundaries are the rule, not the exception. The branching tree, therefore, is an inadequate metaphor. One reason why ethnographers have often failed to notice the fuzziness and transformations of relatedness when in the field is that periodic ethnogenetic episodes are widely spaced in time. Moreover, informants often imagine their community to be more bounded, stable, and pure than it really is.

Anthropologists have increasingly challenged the notion of insular worlds. The persistent attempt to identify "cultures" and "peoples" as pieces in a geographic mosaic, it is argued, has more to do with the eyes of the anthropological observer than any ethnographic realities on the ground. Ethnographic maps that profess to show the spatial distribution of peoples and cultures across the world present space as a neutral grid on which cultural differences are inscribed. In doing so, they obscure the Orientalist notions and the power differentials on which the maps are based. Space is central in the mapping enterprise, but at the same time it seems to disappear from analytical purview. Gupta and Ferguson suggest that with the recent reshuffling of spatial relations and imagery in postmodernity, space has not become irrelevant, rather it has been reterritorialized. For them, it is important to "interrogate" the mapmakers, to go beyond "naturalized conceptions of spatialized 'cultures' and to explore instead the production of difference within common, shared, and connected spaces – 'the San,' for instance, not as 'a people,' 'native' to the desert, but as a historically constituted and depropertied category systematically relegated to the desert" (Gupta and Ferguson 1997: 74). The same can be said for the Inuit of the High Arctic. Inuit history is just as rhizomic as the mighty Mackenzie Delta in which some of them live, with its endless splitting and recombining of channels of water – creeks, swamps, and rivers – on its long journey through northwest Canada to the Beaufort Sea.

How deep is the skin?

The skin is an important site for theoretical inscription. In medical discourse, it is often presented as the largest organ of the body, charged with central physiological, regulating, and perceptual functions. For some social theorists, in contrast, informed by Michel Foucault and Jacques Derrida, the skin is an important canvas for recordings of various kinds, an archeological record with a series of temporal layers of social memory (Gell 1993, Schildkrout 2004). Some of these inscriptions are deliberate, in particular, tattoos. For instance, in pre-European times Hawaiian tattoos were an important genealogical device, a kind of bar code for both identification and protection. Other inscriptions are less intentional (scars and wrinkles of aging, disease, drudgery, and accidents). For some theorists, a whole range of scholars informed by phenomenology, psychoanalysis, and feminist theory (Ahmed and Stacey 2001), the skin embodies lived social experience, the construction of self and other, and the intercorporeality of human touch – of bodies open to, and communicating with, other bodies and the environment in which they are embedded.

If the skin is packed with social memory, "dermography" (from the Greek "derma," skin) is ethnography, the "writing" of a way of life embodied in the skin. No wonder, perhaps, that we consult the skin as an (auto)biographical source of information, as a kind of visual curriculum vitae saturated with details about the body's identity and its encounter with the world throughout the life course. This is not to say that such a description is necessarily accurate. The skin diplomatically mediates fact and fiction in the politics of the body; it is "the body's ambassador" in the sense that "it represents the interface between inside and outside. . . ." (Stacey 1997: 84). For some scholars, to focus on the skin is to succumb to visualism and appearance; thus Waldby (2002) criticizes Weiss's notion (1999) of intercorporeality for placing too much emphasis on the specular skin. For others, however, the skin signifies connectivity. Bird-David observes that for the Nayaka the skin, above all, presents an opportunity to "stay in touch": "If in some Euro-American images the skin binds and isolates 'the body' from the 'outside'; in local experience equally at least it also, and equally, *connects* bodies" (Bird-David 2004: 334). The tactile notion is underlined in Nayaka conceptions of illness. Illness, it is assumed, does not so much suggest that there is something wrong "within the body"; rather, there is something wrong in the "touch" with other beings, human and non-human.

In Fanon's book, *Black Skin, White Masks* (1967), a classic work on racial politics and the phenomenology of identity, the skin is rendered literally as a giant birthmark, with no space for anything else other than "color," blackness or whiteness. For Fanon, such a birthmark was unmistakable and of great consequence for the bearer – a "stain" that went "as deep as life itself," to borrow from Hawthorne's story about the scientist bothered by a birthmark on the cheek of his wife (1959: 229). As Fanon put it, "[a]ll birds of prey are black" (1967: 191). While skin color is a birthmark of great significance in many contexts, it is not unambiguous. Baylis, a Canadian philosopher, reflects on her own racial identity: "my mother is from Barbados (my father is from England). I have a white face; and truth be told, a white body too. The fact is, however, that I am Black. How do I know? My mother told me so" (Baylis 2003: 143). Drawing upon her own experience, she emphasizes that racial identity is not a matter of DNA but of the world in which we live and the narratives we tell each other: "Building a black identity is hard work when you are white" (Baylis 2003: 144). Building a white identity is equally hard work when you are black, as the case of musician Michael Jackson illustrates. Jackson's case, which entailed repeated, costly and, no doubt, painful cosmetic surgery, is symptomatic of the flexible post-modern body. Prosser observes that the vicissitudes of the inheritance of race in skin color show that "skin's memory is as much a fabrication of what didn't happen as a record of what did": "the fact that we continue to invest the legibility of identity in the skin in spite of knowing its unreliability suggests skin to be a fantasmatic surface, a canvas for what we wish were true – or for what we cannot acknowledge to be true. Skin's memory is burdened with the unconscious" (2001: 52).

The fact that bodily identities (including those of race and gender) are increasingly subject to biomedical manipulation of the skin should not be taken to suggest that prior to the postmodern era or late modernity the skin was seen to be a stable "natural" marker of identity. Thus, it would be wrong to assume that in the past birthmarks were unambiguously regarded as signatures given from "the start," independent of human activity. Indeed, notions of the agents of creation are bound by time and culture. Interestingly, some Jewish scholars seem to suggest that humans are capable of taking part in the creative acts of God, possibly acts of birthmarking (Wahrman 2002). Circumcision, which is sometimes regarded as a birthmark, as if somehow taking place "prior to life," is usually seen as an activity performed by the family or the community. The Biblical story of Genesis (25: 25–26) tells of the birth of Isaac's and Rebekah's twin boys, one of whom was Esau who seems to have been born with a giant hairy torso nevus marking him for life. While, apparently, Esau was destined for bad fate due to his birthmark (he was cheated by his twin brother Jacob and lost his birthright), the meaning of the birthmark is not unambiguous in Jewish and Christian scholarship. Definitions of the *timing* of birth and birthmarking are also context dependent. According to the Malay worldview, another reminder of the relativity of the concept of "birth," the child belongs to a set of "birth siblings," along with the placenta, whose existence precedes birth (Carsten 1995: 226). This sibling relationship establishes itself in the womb and continues to influence a person's life until death. For the Malay, human bodily substance and identity are continually in the making, not something with which the Malays are provided simply at the point of delivery. In the Jewish tradition, one may add, there are many narratives about people being born circumcised. Usually being born circumcised was seen as a sign of blessing.

While fingerprints provide much less information on personal history than tattoos and other markings of the skin, as they usually remain more or less unchanged from birth to death, they are powerful marks of identity. This is underlined in the notion of "DNA fingerprints." To explore the usefulness of fingerprints for tracing ancestry, Francis Galton undertook a kind of human diversity project with a small sample of what he took to be English, Welsh, Jewish, Negro, and Basque fingerprints; "it seemed reasonable to expect to find racial differences in finger marks" (1892: 193). Attentive to the nature and details of his data, however, he was forced to conclude in the negative: "it may emphatically be said that there is no *peculiar* pattern which characterizes persons of any of the above races" (1892: 192–193). It was pointless, Galton added in disappointment, to pursue the subject, "except in the case of the Hill tribes of India and a few other peculiarly diverse races, for the chance of discovering some characteristic and perhaps a more monkey-like pattern" (1892: 18). Galton's reference to the "more monkey-like," of course, underlined the eugenic idea that races were not just clearly bounded and different populations but represented some kind of ladder or scale, some human races being closer than others to "lower" primates and the rest of the animal kingdom.[2]

One of the potential advantages of fingerprints, on the other hand, was that, much like the terrain nowadays explored by students of hereditary material, they could be used as a means of personal identification, along with "moles or birth-marks" which were "almost always . . . serving for identification, on the body of every one . . ." (Galton 1892: 163). This fact was swiftly employed in forensic work; each set of fingerprints, Galton emphasized, "differentiates the person who made it, throughout

[2] By the end of the nineteenth century, a number of scientists were following Galton's early lead, studying the fingerprint patterns of epileptics, criminals, and mental patients. The results were invariably frustrating as they failed to establish heredity. The last article on the issue that was published in the eugenic journal *Biometrika* appeared in 1924. Cole suggests (1999: 160) that the declining interest in fingerprints was the result of the rediscovery of Mendelian genetics.

the whole of his life, from all the rest of mankind" (1892: 4). Interestingly, Galton both pioneered the practice of police fingerprinting for individual identification and the theory of correlation and regression extensively used for biopolitical purposes in all kinds of population studies, in establishing the birthmarks of national bodies.

Written only two years after the publication of Galton's book, Mark Twain's novel *Pudd'nhead Wilson* testifies to the early fascination with fingerprints in Euro-American popular culture. Focusing on the use of fingerprints in the detection of a horrible crime, it offers perceptive and humorous observations on the reading of the "natal autographs" of the skin, what they imply for people's lives, their potentials, and their limits, as if foretelling the modern enthrallment with DNA fingerprints. One of the characters in the story, Tom, is scornful of such "scientifics":

"But look here, Dave," said Tom, "you used to tell people's fortunes, too, when you took their finger marks." Dave's just an all-round genius – a genius of the first water, gentlemen; a great scientist running to seed here in this village, a prophet with the kind of honor that prophets generally get at home – for here they don't give shucks for his scientifics, and they call his skull a notion factory – "Hey, Dave, ain't it so?" But never mind, he'll make his mark someday – finger mark, you know, he-he! But really, you want to let him take a shy at your palms once . . . Why, he'll read your wrinkles as easy as a book, and not only tell you fifty or sixty things that's going to happen to you, but fifty or sixty thousand that ain't. (Twain 1997: 135)

Despite warnings by some fingerprint enthusiasts, including Faults who originally brought the issue to his attention, Galton overemphasized the value of fingerprints for personal identification. So-called "latent fingerprints," small distorted fingerprint fragments detected at crime scenes and routinely used in criminal cases, seem to be far less reliable than normally assumed by both the courts and the public. Based on demonstrating points of similarity, a given minimum number of "ridge characteristics" (between twelve and thirty, depending on national standards), the method of identifying latent fingerprints turns out to be a highly subjective one, with an embarrassing amount of error and disagreement. Moreover, the central idea that no two people possess identical sets of fingerprints remains a matter of faith. Recent analyses indicate that fingerprint forensics is a ritualistic exercise more akin to religion than science, a matter of "divine following" and "cultish demeanor" (Ashbaugh, quoted in Epstein 2002: 645). Summing up the evidence, Epstein concludes (2002: 657) that the so-called "science of fingerprints," a science that for almost a century has assumed absolute certainty of identifications leading to a great number of convictions and imprisonments, is "nothing but a myth"; the picture that has emerged is "of poorly trained law enforcement fingerprint examiners making extremely subjective determinations without the benefit of any uniform standards, and in the absence of any testing to validate the fundamental premises upon which the field is based."

With the use of recombinant DNA technology in forensics, Galton's project of linking the individual to a population has been resumed on a vast scale. Since 1984, DNA profiles have routinely been used as critical evidence in a great number of criminal cases. DNA forensics, however, is more a "question of types" (Rabinow 1996a: 123) than individual identities, involving standardization of procedures, group definitions, and probability estimates. Deciding which population is the most likely candidate for "matching" a DNA sample in a criminal case in fact invites complex genetic, probabilistic, and legal debates on definitions, sampling, and number of markers, about strategies of inclusion and exclusion.[3]

---

[3] An illuminating example is a recent murder case in the Netherlands analyzed by M'charek (2005). Here, both the victim and the immediate suspects were Turkish and much of the buzz in the legal and public representation of the case had strong "racial" undertones. Establishing the "matching likelihood number", a statistical test for individualization in criminal litigation, turned out to be a complex and protracted matter involving a series of contested definitions of "population." Thus, the population issue was variously seen as a matter of family names, laboratory routines, genetic proximity, racial similarities, national boundaries, and the number of genetic markers applied: "These different versions do not add up to produce an integral picture of population. They are not pieces that can complete a puzzle" (M'charek 2005: 47).

The issue of establishing the relevant population cannot be settled in any absolute manner since it necessarily involved negotiations about techniques, materials, and practices. "Race," then, is an unstable property in modern forensics, no less unstable than the racial descriptions in the travel accounts of colonial observers (Magubane 2003: 101); the "obvious" aspects of bodies and populations selected for observation and commentary are the result of opportunistic definitions which may change from one context to another.

In DNA forensics, then, the "truth" about race remains just as elusive as before. Nevertheless, there is a growing industry of DNA identification that assumes that racial and ethnic identities are encoded in the biological identity cards of our genes. Activated in 1998, the US CODIS (Combined DNA Index Systems) now contains several indices, including the Convicted Offender Index, the Victims Index, the Forensic Index, the Unidentified Persons Index, the Missing Persons Index, and the Close Biological Relatives Index. Rabinow suggested a few years ago (1996a: 126) that while "there will be finer and finer grids linking subethnic groups down to particular breeding populations, and no doubt a more sophisticated probabilistic statistics to do this," going back to where early eugenics gave up (back to "Galton's regret") would be the right way to go: "Perhaps some researchers should keep their data banks open for the possibility of looking for and discovering individual genetic variation. Perhaps the genes for fingerprints – so individualizing – would be the place to start looking" (Rabinow 1996a: 127). This would mean working with thousands of distinctive alleles unrelated to race, paving the way to truly personalized forensics. Such a proposal no longer sounds that futuristic. Brookes points out (2001: 515) that someday it may "come to be that each of us will carry genetic ID cards that define our individual genomes. Then one's genome will be nothing more that [*sic.*] another 'phenotype' to be collected by the clinicians and interpreted by the epidemiologists!"

Indeed, the fast reading of DNA and the public exposure of personal biomarkers is no longer science fiction. Along with colleagues at

Harvard University, Church has launched what he calls the Personal Genome Project, in an attempt to explore the wider implications of a truly personalized medicine (Church 2006). Church reasons that the new kind of information acquired through personal genomics necessarily prompts worries about potential misuse by, for instance law-enforcement agencies and insurance companies, In order to "test the waters," to try to anticipate the implications, he and his colleagues are making their own genome and phenome data publicly available and recruiting volunteers to do the same. This will include full genome sequences, medical records, as well as a host of other kinds of personal data, all of which will be put on the Worldwide Web so that anyone can explore them and test his or her hypotheses. While such an exposure of highly personal data may prove to be a useful educational exercise – learning-by-doing, an interesting diversion in the body pragmatics of the genome era – at the same time it both illuminates and escalates the erosion of privacy and the fusion of the personal and the public whose implications it claims to establish and to explore.

Given the conflation of genotype and phenotype, perhaps one can expect a revival of the ancient Greek tradition of physiognomy (from *gnome*, "judgment," and *physio*, from "physical appearance"), the attempt to draw inferences about "inner" character from "outward" appearance. One development along these lines is the attempt to manufacture "race specific" or "ethnic" drugs on the basis of information derived from genetic ID cards. Such attempts seem to imply debates and problems similar to those of DNA forensics and population genetics, given the *ad hoc* and pragmatic nature of any notion of "population." In one futuristic perspective, drawing upon these developments and resonating with the idea of genetic ID Cards, physicians are less and less likely to actually see their patients; the exploration of a patient's DNA sequence, presumably through an on-line database, would be the main basis on which treatment would be recommended, functioning as a proxy "visit." This would represent a fundamental rethinking of medical practice, a striking contrast to earlier rules of the game that emphasized physical presence – a close, tactual encounter between physician and patient. At some point in the early history of professional medicine, the patient would live with the physician, under the same roof, while treatment was going on. With proxy visits and genetically informed, personalized treatment, there might not be any physical contact at all.

Studies of the genetics of common diseases have made important advances in recent years, demonstrating correlations between biomarkers and health risks. No doubt, as a result, personalized medicine is likely to be one of the fruitful developments of the biomedical industry in the near future. On the other hand, some of the lofty promises of the new genetics have clearly failed to materialize. The cargo just hasn't arrived. Genetic determinism has also been challenged by important theoretical arguments. Consequently, simplistic determinisms are giving way to more complex models, including those of epigenetics and developmental systems. But while the genotype may have limited *explanatory* power in research on health and disease and genes do not tell people who they are, traces of DNA provide important information in both forensic and historical research, sometimes providing the only clues available to key moments in the archeology of the developmental systems involved, much like comparative linguistics and the material remains of ancient human settlements. Thus, a comparison of the mtDNA and Y chromosomes of people from throughout the world provides important clues about where and when social groups united and separated. Indeed, biological anthropology has thrown a new light on human evolution, history, and migration.

Our bodies and the ways in which we talk about them are sometimes presented as separate "houses of being." Their natures and relationships are interpreted in many ways, phenomenological, realist, structuralist, and constructivist, to name a few. While the contours, properties, and processes of the body have been variously presented through history, depending on culture, time, and context, the body is not necessarily more stable than the discourses applied to it. As Gell observes (1995: 253), neither language nor the body offers stability: "language is one function of the body. But there is no 'absolute' body . . . the body is a locality, an ambience, and a certain perceptual regime imposed by that ambience and inculcated over a lifetime." Some kind of distinction between bodily structure and surface, between inside and outside, is fairly common, but rarely if ever is it straightforward. Strathern points out (2004: 10) with reference to a Papua New Guinea example that the issue of where to locate the body surface is far from simple:

The inside of a Mekeo person's body includes or encompasses an outside. The digestive tract and abdomen is not regarded as the innermost part of a person but, to the contrary, as a passage connected to the outside world, which makes it an appropriate repository of food: The tract is part of the outside that is inside the body.

As a result of recent technological and scientific developments that have allowed for the visualization and mapping of genes, a more radical conflation of inside/outside has taken place. Now, with the powerful perspectives and tools of the new genetics our field of vision has been enormously expanded. Not only has it become possible to zoom in on minute details, in the process the meaning of both phenotype and genotype have changed. Before the arrival of molecular biology, the scientific description and understanding of human differences was heavily reliant on phenotypic traits such as skin color. The exploration of human differences, however, is no longer limited to visualization. At the same time, the underlying and hitherto invisible genotype is being rendered visible as a phenotype – as a fingerprint or a birthmark.

References

Abbot, Alison. 2000. "Manhattan versus Reykjavik," *Nature* 406: 340–342.

— 2004. "Icelandic Database Shelved as Court Judges in Peril," *Nature* 429: 118.

Agamben, Giorgio. 1995. *Homo Sacer: Sovereign Power and Bare Life*. Trans. Daniel Heller-Roazen. Stanford: Stanford University Press.

Ahmed, Sara and Jackie Stacey. 2001. "Introduction: Dermographies," in Sara Ahmed and Jackie Stacey (eds.), *Thinking Through the Skin*. London: Routledge.

Almarsdóttir, Anna Birna, Janine Morgall Traulsen, and Ingunn Björnsdóttir. 2004. "'We Don't Have That Many Secrets': The Lay Perspective on Privacy and Genetic Data," in Garðar Árnason, Salvör Nordal, and Vilhjálmur Árnason (eds.), *Blood and Data: Ethical, Legal and Social Aspects of Human Genetic Databases*. Reykjavík: University of Iceland Press and Centre for Ethics.

Altman, L. K. 2002. "Stop Those Presses! Blonds, It Seems, Will Survive After All." *The New York Times*, 2 October.

Andersen, Bogi, Einar Arnason, and Skuli Sigurdsson. 1999. "Kafkaesque Ethics for Postmodern Vikings?," *British Medical Journal* 23 August. www.bmj.com/cgi/eletters/319/7207/441.

Anderson, W. 2000. "The Possession of Kuru: Medical Science and Biocolonial Exchange," *Comparative Studies in Society and History* 42: 713–744.

Andreasen, Robin O. 1998. "A New Perspective on the Race Debate," *British Journal for the Philosophy of Science* 49: 199–225.

Appadurai, Arjun. 1986. "Introduction: Commodities and the Politics of Value," in A. Appadurai (ed.), *The Social Life of Things: Commodities in Cultural Perspective*. Cambridge: Cambridge University Press.

— 1988. "Introduction: Place and Voice in Anthropological Theory," *Cultural Anthropology* 3(1): 16–20.

— 1991. "Global Ethnoscapes: Notes and Queries for a Transnational Anthropology," in Richard G. Fox (ed.), *Recapturing Anthropology: Working in the Present*. New Mexico: School of American Research Press.

References

Asad, Talal (ed.). 1973. *Anthropology and the Colonial Encounter*. London: Ithaca Press.

Atran, Scott. 1990. *Cognitive Foundations of Natural History*. Cambridge: Cambridge University Press.

Árnason, Arnar and Bob Simpson. 2003. "Refractions through Culture: The New Genomics in Iceland," *Ethnos* 68(4): 533–553.

Árnason, Einar. 2003. "Genetic Heterogeneity of Icelanders," *Annals of Human Genetics* 67: 5–16.

Árnason, Einar, H. Sigurgíslason, and E. Benedikz. 2000. "Genetic Homogeneity of Icelanders: Fact or Fiction?," *Nature Genetics* 25: 373–374.

Árnason, Vilhjálmur and Garðar Árnason. 2004. "Informed Democratic Consent?," *TRAMES* 8(1/2): 164–177.

Bakhtin, Michael. 1986. *Speech Genres and Other Late Essays*. Ed. C. Emerson and M. Holquist, trans. V. W. McGee. Austin: University of Texas Press.

Balmer, B. 1996. "Managing Mapping in the Human Genome Project," *Social Studies of Science* 26: 531–574.

Bamford, Sandra. 2004. "Conceiving Relatedness: Non-substantial Relations among the Kamea of Papua New Guinea," *Journal of the Royal Anthropological Institute* 19(2): 287, 306.

Barbujani, Guido and David B. Goldstein. 2004. "Africans and Asians Abroad: Genetic Diversity in Europe," *Annual Review of Genomics and Human Genetics* 5: 119–150.

Baylis, Françoise. 2003. "Black as Me: Narrative Identity," *Developing World Bioethics* 3(2): 142–150.

BBC News World Edition. 2002. http://news.bbc.co.uk/2/hi/health/2284783.stm. September 27.

Beer, G. 1986. "'The Face of Nature': Anthropometric Elements in the Language of *The Origin of Species*," in L. J. Jordanova (ed.), *The Languages of Nature: Critical Essays on Science and Literature*. London: Free Association Books.

Berlin, Isaiah. 1989. *Against the Current: Essays in the History of Ideas*. Oxford: Clarendon Press.

Bestard, Joan. 2004. "Kinship and the New Genetics: The Changing Meaning of Biogenetic Substance," *Social Anthropology* 12(3): 253–263.

Bibeau, Gilles. 2004. *Le Québec transgénique: Science, marché, humanité*. Quebec: Boréal.

Biddle, Jennifer. 2001. "Inscribing Identity: Skin as Country in the Central Desert," in S. Ahmed and J. Stacey (eds.), *Thinking Through the Skin*. London: Routledge.

Bird-David, Nurit. 2004. "Illness-Images and Joined Beings: A Critical/Nayaka Perspective on Intercorporeality," *Social Anthropology* 12(3): 325–339.

Boas, Franz. 1940. *Race, Language and Culture*. New York: Macmillan Company.

References

Bodenhorn, Barbara. 2000. "'He Used to Be My Relative': Exploring the Bases of Relatedness among the Iñupiat of Northern Alaska," in Janet Carsten (ed.), *Cultures of Relatedness: New Approaches to the Study of Kinship*. Cambridge: Cambridge University Press.

The Book of Icelanders, www.islendingabok.is.

Bouquet, Mary. 1996. "Family Trees and Their Affinity: The Visual Imperative of the Genealogical Diagram," *Journal of the Royal Anthropological Institute (incorporating Man)* 2: 43–66.

    2000. "Figures of Relations: Reconnecting Kinship Studies and Museum Collections," in J. Carsten (ed.), *Cultures of Relatedness: New Approaches to the Study of Kinship*. Cambridge: Cambridge University Press.

Boyle, J. 1996. *Shamans, Software, and Spleens: Law and the Construction of Information Society*. Cambridge, MA: Harvard University Press.

Brace, C. Loring. 2005. *"RACE" Is a Four-Letter Word: The Genesis of the Concept*. New York: Oxford University Press.

Brodwin, Paul. 2005. "'Bioethics in Action' and Human Population Genetics Research," *Culture, Medicine and Psychiatry* 29: 145–178.

Brody, Hugh. 2000. *The Other Side of Eden: Hunter-Gatherers, Farmers, and the Shaping of the World*. Vancouver: Douglas & McIntyre.

Brookes, Anthony J. 2001. "Rethinking Genetic Strategies to Study Complex Diseases," *Trends in Molecular Medicine* 7(11): 512–516.

Brown, M. F. 2003. *Who Owns Native Culture?* Cambridge, MA: Harvard University Press.

Brown, Nik and Andrew Webster (eds.). 2004. *New Medical Technologies and Society: Reordering Life*. Cambridge: Polity.

Brown, T. A. 2002. *Genomes*, 2nd edn. Oxford: BIOS Scientific Publishers Ltd.

Busby, Helen. 2004. "UK Biobank: Social and Political Landscape," in Garðar Árnason, Salvör Nordal, and Vilhjálmur Árnason (eds.), *Blood and Data: Ethical, Legal and Social Aspects of Human Genetic Databases*. Reykjavík: University of Iceland Press & Centre for Ethics.

Cambon-Thomsen, A. 2004. "The Social and Ethical Issues of Post-genomic Human Biobanks," *Nature* 5: 866–873.

Canguilhem, Georges. 1989 [1966]. *The Normal and the Pathological*. With an Introduction by Michel Foucault. New York: Urzone Inc.

Carsten, Janet. 1995. "The Substance of Kinship and the Heat of the Hearth," *American Ethnologist* 22: 223–241.

    2004. *After Kinship*. Cambridge: Cambridge University Press.

Caspari, Rachel. 2003. "From Types to Populations: A Century of Race, Physical Anthropology, and the American Anthropological Association," *American Anthropologist* 105 (1): 65–76.

References

Casteret, Anne-Marie. 1992. *L'Affaire du sang*. Paris: La Découverte.

Cavalli-Sforza, L. Luca. 2005. "The Human Genome Diversity Project: Past, Present and Future," *Nature Reviews/Genetics* 6(April): 333–340.

Cavalli-Sforza, L. L. and F. Cavalli-Sforza. 1998. *The Great Human Diasporas: The History of Diversity and Evolution*. Cambridge, MA: Perseus Books.

Cavalli-Sforza, L. L., P. Menozzi, and A. Piazza. 1996. *The History and Geography of Human Genes*. Princeton: Princeton University Press.

Cavalli-Sforza, L. L., A. C. Wilson, C. R. Cantor, R. M. Cook-Deegan, and M.-C. King. 1991. "Call for a Worldwide Survey of Human Genetic Diversity: A Vanishing Opportunity for the Human Genome Project." *Genomics* 11: 490–491.

Chadwick, Ruth. 1999. "The Icelandic Database – Do Modern Times Need Modern Sagas?," *British Medical Journal* 319: 441–444.

Chen, Y. S., A. Olckers, T. G. Schurr, A. M. Kogelnik, K. Huoponen, and D. C. Wallace. 2000. "mtDNA Variation in the South African Kung and Khwe and their Genetic Relationships to Other African Populations," *American Journal of Human Genetics* 66(4): 1362–1383.

Cheng, Wan-Chiung and Wan-Ping Li. 2004. "A Study of the Ethical, Legal, and Social Aspects of the Chinese Genetic Database in Taiwan," in Garðar Árnason, Salvör Nordal, and Vilhjálmur Árnason (eds.), *Blood and Data: Ethical, Legal and Social Aspects of Human Genetic Databases*. Reykjavík: University of Iceland Press and Centre for Ethics.

Choudhury, Shormila Roy and Leslie A. Knapp. 2006. "A Review of International and UK-based Ethical Guidelines for Researchers Conducting Nontherapeutic Genetic Studies in Developing Countries," *European Journal of Human Genetics*. Online publication, 14: 9–16.

Church, George M. 2006. "Genomes for All," *Scientific American* (January): 33–40.

Clarke, A. E., L. Mamo, J. K. Shim, J. R. Fosket, and J. R. Fishman. 2003. "Biomedicalization: Technoscientific Transformations of Health, Illness and U.S. Biomedicine," *American Sociological Review* 68: 161–194.

Clifford, James. 2004. "Looking Several Ways: Anthropology and Native Heritage in Alaska," *Current Anthyropology* 45(1): 5–30.

Cole, Simon. 1999. "What Counts for Identity?: The Historical Origins of the Methodology of Latent Fingerprint Identification," *Science in Context* 12(1): 139–172.

Collier, Stephen J. and Aihwa Ong. 2005. "Global Assemblages, Anthropological Problems," in Aihwa Ong and Stephen J. Collier (eds.), *Global Assemblages: Technology, Politics, and Ethics as Anthropological Problems*. Malden, MA: Blackwell Publishing.

Condit, Celeste Michele. 1999. *The Meanings of the Gene: Public Debates about Human Heredity*. Madison: University of Wisconsin Press.

References

Connerton, Paul. 1989. *How Societies Remember*. Cambridge: Cambridge University Press.

Connor, Steven. 2004. *The Book of Skin*. Ithaca: Cornell University Press.

Corner, James. 1999. "The Agency of Mapping: Speculation, Critique and Invention," in D. Cosgrove (ed.), *Mappings*. London: Reaction Books.

Cosgrove, Denish. 1999. "Introduction: Mapping Meaning," in D. Cosgrove (ed.), *Mappings*. London: Reaction Books.

Crandall, Keith A. and Jennifer E. Buhay. 2004. "Genomic Databases and the Tree of Life," *Science* 306: 1144–1145.

Creager, Angela N. H. 2002. *The Life of a Virus: Tobacco Mosaic Virus as an Experimental Model, 1930–1965*. Chicago: University of Chicago Press.

Csordas, Thomas (ed.). 1994. *Embodiment and Experience: The Existential Ground of Culture and Self*. Cambridge: Cambridge University Press.

Dalton, Rex. 2004. "When Two Tribes Go to War," *Nature* 430 (29 July): 500–502.

Davies, Glyn. 1994. *A History of Money: From Ancient Times to the Present Day*. Cardiff: University of Wales Press.

Davis, Dona Lee and Dorothy I. Davis. In Press. "Dualing Memories: Twinship and the Disembodiment of Identity," in Peter Collins and Anselma Galinat (eds.), *Keeping an Open "I": Memory and Experience as Resources in Ethnography*. London and New York: Berghahn Press.

Deleuze, G. and F. Guattari. 1988. *A Thousand Plateaus: Capitalism and Schizophrenia*. London: Athlone Press.

Delsuc, Frédéric, Henner Brinkmann, and Hervé Philippe. 2005. "Phylogenomics and the Reconstruction of the Tree of Life," *Nature Reviews Genetics* 6 (May): 361–375.

Demarée, G. R. and Astrid E. J. Ogilvie. 2001. "Bons baisers d'Islande: Climatic, Environmental, and Human Dimensions Impacts of the Lakagígar Eruption (1783–1784) in Iceland," in P. D. Jones, A. E. J. Ogilvie, K. R. Briffa, and T. D. Davies (eds.), *History and Climate: Memories of the Future*. Dordrecht: Kluwer Academic/Plenum Publishers.

Descola, Philippe and Gísli Pálsson (eds.). 1996. *Nature and Society: Anthropological Perspectives*. London: Routledge.

Dezalay, Yves and Bryant Garth. 1996. *Dealing in Virtue: International Commercial Arbitration and the Construction of a Transnational Legal Order*. Chicago: University of Chicago Press.

1998. "Droits de l'homme et philanthropie hégémonique," *Actes de la recherche en sciences sociales* 121–122: 23–41.

Doolittle, W. Ford. 1999. "Phylogenetic Classification and the Universal Tree," *Science* 284: 2124–2128.

References

2000. "Uprooting the Tree of Life," *Scientific American* 282: 90–95.

Dumit, Joseph. 2004. *Picturing Personhood: Brain Scans and Biomedical Identity.* Princeton: Princeton University Press.

Dunn, Michael, Angela Terrill, Ger Reesink, Robert A. Foley, and Stephen C. Levinson. 2005. "Structural Phylogenetics and the Reconstruction of Ancient Language History," *Science* 309 (23 September): 2072–2075.

DV. 2003. "Ættarhöfðinginn" ("The Tribal Chief"). 13 February. Reykjavík.

Edwards, Philip. 1997. *Sea-Mark: The Metaphorical Voyage, Spencer to Milton.* Liverpool: Liverpool University Press.

Eggertsson, Kjartan. 2003. "Kári Stefánsson vegur að aðheiðri ættfræðinga" (Kári Stefánsson Attacks the Honor of Genealogists), *Morgunblaðið* January 28: 26. Reykjavík.

Enfield, N. J. 2005. "The Body as a Cognitive Artifact in Kinship Representations: Hand Gesture Diagrams by Speakers of Lao," *Current Anthropology* 46(1): 51–81.

Epstein, Robert. 2002. "Fingerprints Meet *Daubert*: The Myth of Fingerprint 'Science' Is Revealed," *Southern California Law Review* 75: 605–657.

Everett, Margaret. 2003. "The Social Life of Genes: Privacy, Property and the New Genetics," *Social Science & Medicine* 56: 53–65.

Fanon, Frantz. 1967. *Black Skin, White Masks.* Trans. Charles Lam Markman (from the French). New York: Grove Press, Inc.

Feeley-Harnik, Gillian. 2001. "The Ethnography of Creation: Lewis Henry Morgan and the American Beaver," in S. Franklin and S. McKinnon (eds.), *Relative Values: Reconfiguring Kinship Studies.* Durham, NC: Duke University Press.

Fernandez, James W. 1998. "Trees of Knowledge of Self and Other in Culture: On Models for the Moral Imagination," in Laura Rival (ed.), *The Social Life of Trees: Anthropological Perspectives on Tree Symbolism.* Oxford: Berg.

Fienup-Riordan, Ann. 2000. *Hunting Tradition in a Changing World: Yup'ik Lives in Alaska Today.* New Brunswick, NJ: Rutgers University Press.

Finkler, Kaja. 2000. *Experiencing the New Genetics: Family and Kinship on the New Medical Frontier.* Philadelphia: University of Pennsylvania Press.

Finnbogason, Guðmundur. 1922. "Mannkynbætur" ("Racial Improvement"). *Andvari* 47: 184–204. Reykjavík.

Fischer, M. M. J. 2003. *Emergent Forms of Life and the Anthropological Voice.* Durham, NC: Duke University Press.

Fortun, Michael. 2000. "Experiments in Ethnography and its Performance." Mannvernd web site, www.mannvernd.is.

Foucault, Michel. 1970. *The Order of Things.* London: Routledge.

1973. *The Birth of the Clinic: An Archaeology of Medical Perception.* Trans. A. M. Sheridan. London: Tavistock.

References

1994. "The Birth of Biopolitics," in *Foucault: Ethics, Subjectivity and Truth.* Paul Rabinow (ed.). Vol. I. New York: The New Press.

Franklin, Sarah and Margaret Lock. 2003. "Animation and Cessation: The Remaking of Life and Death," in Sarah Franklin and Margaret Lock (eds.), *Remaking Life and Death: Towards an Anthropology of the Biosciences.* Santa Fe: School of American Research Press.

Galton, Francis. 1892. *Finger Prints.* London: Macmillan and Co.

Gannett, Lisa. 2003. "Making Populations: Bounding Genes in Space and Time," *Philosophy of Science* 70: 989–1001.

2004. "The Reification of Biological Race," *British Journal of the Philosophy of Science* 55: 323–45.

Gannett, Lisa and James Griesemer. 2004a. "Classical Genetics and the Geography of Genes," in Hans-Jörg Rheinberger and Jean-Paul Gaudillière (eds.), *Classical Genetics Research and its Legacy: The Mapping Cultures of Twentieth-Century Genetics.* London: Routledge.

2004b. "The ABO Blood Groups: Mapping the History and Geography of Genes in *Homo sapiens*," in Hans-Jörg Rheinberger and Jean-Paul Gaudillière (eds.), *Classical Genetics Research and its Legacy: The Mapping Cultures of Twentieth-Century Genetics.* London: Routledge.

Gell, Alfred. 1993. *Wrapping in Images: Tattooing in Polynesia.* Oxford: Clarendon.

1995. "The Language of the Forest: Landscape and Phonological Iconism in Umeda," in Eric Hirsch and Michael O'Hanlon (eds.), *The Antropology of Landscape: Perspectives on Place and Space.* Oxford: Clarendon Press.

Genetic Isolates. 2005. www.geneticisolates.com.

GenomeWeb News. 2005. "NHGRI's Collins Says US Must Launch its Own Biobanking Project." www.genomeweb.com/articles/view.asp?Article=20051027132131. Accessed on 30 October.

Gibbon, Sarah. 2002. "Re-examining Geneticization: Family Trees in Breast Cancer Genetics," *Science as Culture* 11(4): 429–57.

Gillis, John R. 2004. *Islands of the Mind: How the Human Imagination Created the Atlantic World.* New York: Palgrave Macmillan.

Glick Schiller, Nina. 2005. "Blood and Belonging: Long-Distance Nationalism and the World Beyond," in Susan McKinnon and Sydel Silverman (eds.), *Complexities: Beyond Nature & Nurture.* Chicago: University of Chicago Press.

The Globe and Mail. 2002. www.globeandmail.com/servlet/ArticleNews/front/RTGAM/20021002/wblond1002/Front/homeBN/breakingnews). 2 October.

Godbout, Jacques T. 1998. *The World of the Gift.* In collaboration with Alain Caillé. Montreal and Kingston: McGill-Queen's University Press.

Gottweis, Herbert and Robert Triendl. 2006. "South Korean Policy Failure and the Hwang Debacle," *Nature Biotechnology* 24(2): 141–143.

References

Grant, Struan F. A. *et al.* 2006. "Variant of Transcription Factor 7-like 2 (*TCF7L2*) Confers Risk of Type 2 Diabetes," *Nature Genetics* 38: 320–323.

Greely, Henry T. 1998. "Legal, Ethical, and Social Issues in Human Genome Research," *Annual Reviews in Anthropology* 27: 473–502.

—— 2000. "Iceland's Plan for Genomics Research: Facts and Implications," *Jurimetrics* 40: 31–67.

Greenhalgh, Susan and Edwin A. Winckler. 2005. *Governing China's Population: From Leninist to Neoliberal Biopolitics.* Stanford: Stanford University Press.

Greinargerðum erfðafræðirannsóknir á Íslandi. 1974. ("Report on Genetic Research in Iceland"). Reykjavík: The Genetics Committee of the University of Iceland.

Grétarsdóttir Bender, Elín Klara. 2002. "Íslensk ættfræði" (Icelandic Genealogies). B.A. dissertation in anthropology. University of Iceland.

Griesemer, James R. 1999. "Reproduction and the Reproduction of Genetics," in P. Beurton, R. Falk, and H.-J. Rheinberger (eds.), *The Concept of the Gene in Development and Evolution.* Cambridge: Cambridge University Press.

Griffiths, Paul E. 2006. "The Fearless Vampire Conservator: Philip Kitcher, Genetic Determinism, and the Informational Gene," in Eva M. Neumann-Held and Christoph Rehmann-Sutter (eds.), *Genes in Development: Re-reading the Molecular Paradigm.* Durham, NC: Duke University Press.

Griffiths, P. E. and R. D. Gray. 1998. "Developmental Systems and Evolutionary Explanations," in David L. Hull and Michael Ruse (eds.), *The Philosophy of Biology.* Oxford: Oxford University Press.

Grubb, A. 1998. "'I, Me, Mine': Bodies, Parts and Property," *Medical Law International* 3: 299–317.

Gudmundsson, H., D. F. Gudbjartsson, A. Kong, H. Gudbjartsson, M. Frigge, J. R. Gulcher, and K. Stefánsson. 2000. "Inheritance of Human Longevity in Iceland," *European Journal of Human Genetics* 8: 743–749.

Gugerli, David. 2004. "Mapping: A Communicative Strategy," in J.-P. Gaudillière and H.-J. Rheinberger (eds.), *From Molecular Genetics to Genomics: The Mapping Cultures of Twentieth Century Genetics.* London: Routledge.

Gulcher, Jeffrey and Kári Stefánsson. 1998. "Population Genomics: Laying the Groundwork for Genetic Disease Modeling and Targeting," *Clinical Chemistry and Laboratory Medicine* 36: 532–537.

—— 2000. "The Icelandic Healthcare Database and Informed Consent," *New England Journal of Medicine* 342: 1827–1830.

Gulcher, Jeffrey, Augustine Kong, and Kári Stefánsson. 2001. "The Role of Linkage Studies for Common Diseases," *Current Opinion in Genetics and Development* 11: 264–267.

References

Guðmundsson, Einar Már. 2002. *Draumar á jörðu*. (Dreams on Earth). Reykjavík: Mál og menning.

Gupta, Akhil and James Ferguson. 1997. "Beyond 'Culture': Space, Identity, and the Politics of Difference," in Akhil Gupta and James Ferguson (eds.), *Anthropological Locations: Boundaries and Grounds of a Field Science*. Berkeley: University of California Press.

Gurevich, Aron. 1992. *Historical Anthropology of the Middle Ages*, J. Howlett (ed.), Cambridge: Polity Press.

Hacking, Ian. 1982. "Biopower and the Avalanche of Printed Numbers," *Humanities in Society* 5: 279–295.

_____ 2006. "Genetics, Biosocial Groups and the Future of Identity," *Daedalus* (Fall): 81–95.

Hakonarson, H. *et al.* 2005. "Effects of a 5-Lipoxygenase-Activating Protein Inhibitor on Biomarkers Associated with Risk of Myocardial Infarction: A Randomized Trial," *Journal of the American Medical Association* 293: 2245–2256.

Hamer, Dan. 2004. *The God Gene*. New York: Anchor Books.

Han, Sallie. *In press*. "Making Room for Daddy: Men's 'Belly Talk' in the Contemporary United States," in Tine T. Thomsen, Helene Goldberg, and Maruska La Cour Mosegaard (eds.), *The Second Sex in Reproduction: Men, Sexuality, and Masculinity*. Berkeley: University of California Press.

Hann, Chris M. (ed.). 1998. *Property Relations: Renewing the Anthropological Tradition*. Cambridge: Cambridge University Press.

Hanson, F. Allan. 2004. "The New Superorganic," *Current Anthropology* 45(4): 467–482.

Haraway, Donna. 1988. "Situated Knowledges: The Science Question in Feminism and the Privilege of Partial Perspective," *Feminist Studies* 14(3): 575–599.

_____ 2000. "Deanimations: Maps and Portraits of Life Itself," in A. Brah and A. E. Coombes (eds.), *Hybridity and its Discontents: Politics, Science, Culture*. London: Routledge.

Harðardóttir, Kristín E. 2002. "Þeim rennur blóðið til skyldunnar: Blóðgjafir Íslendinga í mannfræðilegu ljósi" (Blood and the "Obligation" to Give: Anthropological Perspectives on the Exchange of Blood in Iceland). MA Dissertation. Department of Anthropology, University of Iceland.

Hawthorne, Nathaniel. 1959 [1843]. "The Birthmark," in *The Complete Short Stories of Nathaniel Hawthorne*. New York: Doubleday and Company.

Hayden, Corinne P. 1998. "A Biodiversity Sampler for the Millennium," in Sarah Franklin and Helen Ragoné (eds.), *Reproducing Reproduction: Kinship, Power, and Tehnological Innovation*. Philadelphia: University of Pennsylvania Press.

Hayles, N. K. 1999. *How We Became Posthuman*. Chicago: University of Chicago Press.

References

Heidegger, Martin. 1977 [1927]. "The Question Concerning Technology," in Martin Heidegger, *Basic Writings*, David Farrell Krell (ed.). San Francisco: HarperCollins.

Heisler, Eva. 2004. "Of Landmarks and Birthmarks: On the Work of Katrín Sigurðardóttir." Unpublished paper.

Helgadottir, Anna *et al.* 2004. "The Gene Encoding 5-lipoxygenase Activating Protein Confers Risk of Myocardial Infarction and Stroke," *Nature Genetics* 36: 233–239.

    2006. "A Variant of the Gene Encoding Leukotriene A4 Hydrolase Confers Ethnically-Specific Risk of Myocardial Infarction," *Nature Genetics* 38: 68–74.

Helgason, Agnar. 2001. "The Ancestry and Genetic History of the Icelanders: An Analysis of MTDNA Sequences, Y Chromosome Haplotypes and Genealogy." Doctoral dissertation. Institute of Biological Anthropology, University of Oxford.

Helgason, A., G. Nicholson, K. Stefánsson, and P. Donnelly. 2003. "A Reassessment of Genetic Diversity in Icelanders: Strong Evidence from Multiple Loci Relative Homogeneity Caused by Genetic Drift," *Annals of Human Genetics* 67: 281–297.

Helgason, Agnar and Gísli Pálsson. 1997. "Contested Commodities: The Moral Landscape of Modernist Regimes," *Journal of the Royal Anthropological Institute (incorporating Man)* 3(3): 451–471.

Helgason, Agnar, Gísli Pálsson, Henning Sloth Pedersen, Emily Angulalik, Ellen Dröfn Gunnarsdóttir, Bryndís Yngvadóttir, and Kári Stefánsson. 2006. "mtDNA Variation in Inuit Populations of Greenland and Canada: Migration History and Population Structure in the Arctic," *American Journal of Physical Anthropology* 130: 123–134.

Helgason, A., S. Sigurdadóttir, J. R. Gulcher, R. Ward, and K. Stefánsson. 2000. "mtDNA and the Origin of the Icelanders: Deciphering Signals of Recent Population History," *American Journal of Human Genetics* 66: 999–1016.

Helgason, Agnar and Kári Stefánsson. 2003. "Erroneous Claims about the Impact of Mitochondrial DNA Sequence Database Errors," *American Journal of Human Genetics* 73: 974–975.

Helgason, A., B. Yngvadóttir, B. Hrafnkelsson, J. R. Gulcher, and K. Stefánsson. 2005. "An Icelandic Example of the Impact of Population Structure on Association Studies," *Nature Genetics* 37: 90–95.

Heller, M. A. and R. S. Eisenberg. 1998. "Can Patents Deter Innovation? The Anticommons in Biomedical Research," *Science* 280: 698–701.

Helmreich, Stefan. 2001. "Kinship in Hypertext: Transubstantiating Fatherhood and Information Flow in Artificial Life," in Sarah Franklin and Susan McKinnon (eds.), *Relative Values: Reconfiguring Kinship Studies*. Durham, NC: Duke University Press.

References

Herzfeld, Michael (ed.). 2001. *Anthropology: Theoretical Practice in Culture and Society*. Oxford: Blackwell.

Hirsch, Eric. 2004. "Boundaries of Creation: The Work of Credibility in Science and Ceremony," in Eric Hirsch and Marilyn Strathern (eds.), *Transactions and Creations: Property Debates and the Stimulus of Melanesia*. New York: Berghahn.

Hirsch, Eric and Michael O'Hanlon (eds.). 1995. *The Anthropology of Landscape: Perspectives on Place and Space*. Oxford: Clarendon Press.

Hirsch, Eric and Marilyn Strathern (eds.). 2004. *Transactions and Creations: Property Debates and the Stimulus of Melanesia*. New York: Berghahn.

Hoeyer, Klaus. 2004. "Ambiguous Gifts: Public Anxiety, Informed Consent and Biobanks," in Richard Tutton and Oonagh Corrigan (eds.), *Genetic Databases: Socio-Ethical Issues in the Collection and Use of DNA*. London: Routledge.

2005. "Studying Ethics as Policy: The Naming and Framing of Moral Problems in Genetic Research," *Current Anthropology* 46(Supplement): 71–90.

Hoeyer, Klaus, Bert-Ove Olofsson, Tom Mjörndal, and Niels Lynöe. 2005. "The Ethics of Research Using Biobanks," *Archives of Internal Medicine* 165 (10 Jan.): 97–100.

Humphrey, Caroline and Katherine Verdery. 2004. "Introduction: Raising Questions about Property," in Katherine Verdery and Caroline Humphrey (eds.), *Property in Question: Value Transformation in the Global Economy*. Oxford: Berg.

Hunt, Alan. 1999. *Governing Morals: A Social History of Moral Regulation*. Cambridge: Cambridge University Press.

Icelandic Parliament. 1998. Act on a Health Sector Database no. 139. http://eng. heilbrigdisraduneyti.is/laws-and-regulations/nr/659#allt.

2000. Act on the Protection of Privacy and the Treatment of Personal Information no. 77. www.althingi.is/lagas/nuna/2000077.html.

Inda, Jonathan Xavier 2005. "Analysis of the Modern: An Introduction," in Jonathan Xavier Inda (ed.), *Anthropologies of Modernity: Foucault, Governmentality, and Life Politics*. Oxford: Blackwell.

Inda, Jonathan Xavier and Renato Rosaldo. 2002. "Introduction: A World in Motion," in Jonathan Xavier Inda and Renato Rosaldo (eds.), *Anthropology of Globalization: A Reader*. Oxford: Blackwell.

Indriðason, Arnaldur. 2004 [2000]. *Jar City*. London: The Harvill Press.

Ingold, Tim. 2000. *The Perception of the Environment: Essays in Livelihood, Dwelling and Skill*. London: Routledge.

The International HapMap Consortium. 2003. "The International HapMap Project," *Nature* 426: 789–796.

2005. "A Haplotype Map of the Human Genome," *Nature* 437: 1299–1320.

International Human Genome Sequencing Consortium. 2004. "Finishing the Eucromatic Sequence of the Human Genome," *Nature* 431(21 October): 931–945.

References

Jablonka, Eva and Marion J. Lamb. 2005. *Evolution in Four Dimensions: Genetic, Epigenetic, Behavioral, and Symbolic Variation in the History of Life.* Cambridge, MA: MIT Press.

Jasanoff, Sheila (ed.). 2004. *States of Knowledge: The Co-Production of Science and Social Order.* London: Routledge.

Jiayou, Chu *et al.* 1998. "Genetic Relationships of Populations in China," *Proceedings of the National Academy of Sciences of the USA* 95(20): 11763–11768.

Johnson, Kirk. 2004. "By Accident, Utah Is Proving an Ideal Genetic Laboratory," *The New York Times.* July 31.

Jones, C. A. and P. Galison (eds.). 1998. *Picturing Science, Producing Art.* New York: Routledge.

Jones, O. and P. Cloke. 2002. *Tree Cultures: The Place of Trees and Trees in their Place.* Oxford: Berg.

Joralemon, D. 1995. "Organ Wars: The Battle for Body Parts," *Medical Anthropological Quarterly* 9(3): 335–356.

Kahn, Jonathan. 2003. "Getting the Numbers Right: Statistical Mischief and Racial Profiling in Heart Failure," *Perspectives in Biology and Medicine* 46(4): 473–483.

Kay, Lily E. 2000. *Who Wrote the Book of Life? A History of the Genetic Code.* Stanford: Stanford University Press.

Kaye, Jane and Paul Martin. 2000. "Safeguards for Research Using Large-scale DNA Collections," *British Medical Journal* 321(4): 1146–1149.

Keller, C. M. and J. D. Keller. 1996. *Cognition and Tool Use: The Blacksmith at Work.* Cambridge: Cambridge University Press.

Keller, Evelyn Fox. 1996. "The Biological Gaze," in George Robertson, Melinda Mash, Lisa Tickner, Jon Bird, Barry Curtis, and Tim Putnam (eds.), *Future Natural: Nature, Science, Culture.* London: Routledge.

2000. *The Century of the Gene.* Cambridge, MA: Harvard University Press.

Kirsch, Stuart. 1997. "Lost Tribes: Indigenous People and the Social Imaginary," *Anthropological Quarterly* 70(2): 58–67.

Kittles, Rick and Charmaine Royal. 2003. "The Genetics of African Americans: Implications for Disease Gene Mapping and Identity," in A. Goodman, D. Heath, and S. Lindee (eds.), *Genetic Nature/Culture.* Los Angeles: University of California Press.

Kittles, Rick A. and Kenneth M. Weiss. 2003. "Race, Ancestry, and Genes: Implications for Defining Disease Risk," *Annual Review of Genomics and Human Genetics* 4: 33–67.

Klapisch-Zuber, Christian. 1991. "The Genesis of the Family Tree," *I Tatti Studies: Essays in the Renaissance* 4(1): 105–129.

2000. *L'Ombre des ancêtres: Essai sur l'imaginaire médiéval de la parenté*. Paris: Fayard.

Kleinman, Arthur. 1995. *Writing at the Margin: Discourse between Anthropology and Medicine*. Berkeley: University of California Press.

Klug, Aaron. 2004. "The Discovery of the Double Helix," in Torsten Krude (ed.), *DNA: Changing Science and Society*. Cambridge: Cambridge University Press.

Knoppers, Bartha Maria. 1999. "Status, Sale and Patenting of Human Genetic Material: An International Survey," *Nature Genetics* 22: 23–26.

Knoppers, Bartha Maria and Ruth Chadwick. 2005. "Human Genetic Research: Emerging Trends in Ethics," *Nature Reviews Genetics* 6 (January): 75–79.

Knorr-Cetina, Karin. 1999. *Epistemic Cultures: How the Sciences Make Knowledge*. Cambridge, MA: Harvard University Press.

Kohler, Robert E. 1994. *Lords of the Fly: Drosophila Genetics and the Experimental Life*. Chicago: University of Chicago Press.

Kong, A. *et al*. 2002. "A High-resolution Recombination Map of the Human Genome," *Nature Genetics* 31: 241–247.

Korts, Kulliki. 2004. "Becoming Masters of Our Genes: Public Acceptance of the Estonian Genome Project," in Garðar Árnason, Salvör Nordal, and Vilhjálmur Árnason (eds.), *Blood and Data: Ethical, Legal and Social Aspects of Human Genetic Databases*. Reykjavík: University of Iceland Press and Centre for Ethics.

Krude, Torsten (ed.). 2004. *DNA: Changing Science and Society*. Cambridge: Cambridge University Press.

Laqueur, Thomas W. 2001. "'From Generation to Generation': Imagining Connectedness in the Age of Reproductive Technologies," in Paul E. Brodwin (ed.), *Biotechnology and Culture: Bodies, Anxieties, Ethics*. Bloomington: Indiana University Press.

Latour, Bruno. 1987. *Science in Action: How to Follow Scientists and Engineers through Society*. Cambridge, MA: Harvard University Press.

1988. *The Pasteurization of France*. Translated by Alan Sheridan and John Law. Cambridge, MA: Harvard University Press.

1999. *Pandora's Hope: Essays on the Reality of Science Studies*. Cambridge, MA: Harvard University Press.

Laxness, Halldór Kiljan. 1962 [1943]. "Mannlíf á spjaldskrá" (Indexing Human Life) in Halldór Kiljan Laxness, *Sjálfsagðir hlutir: Ritgerðir*. Reykjavík: Helgafell.

Leatherman, Thomas and Alan Goodman. 2005. "Context and Complexity in Human Biological Research," in Susan McKinnon and Sydel Silverman (eds.), *Complexities: Beyond Nature & Nurture*. Chicago: University of Chicago Press.

References

Lee, Richard B. and Irven deVore (eds.). 1968. *Man the Hunter: The First Intensive Survey of a Single, Crucial Stage of Human Development: Man's Once Universal Hunting Way of Life*. Chicago: Aldine Publishing.

Lemonick, Michael D. 2006. "The Iceland Experiment: How a Tiny Island Nation Captured the Lead in the Genetic Revolution," *Time*, February 20: 50–51.

Lewontin, Richard. 1995. "Genes, Environment, and Organisms," in R. B. Silvers (ed.), *Hidden Histories of Science*. New York: New York Review Books.

———. 1999. "People Are Not Commodities," *The New York Times*. January 23.

Lindenbaum, Shirley and Margaret Lock (eds.). 1993. *Knowledge, Power, and Practice: The Anthropology of Medicine and Everyday Life*. Berkeley: University of California Press.

Linton, Ralph. 1955. *The Tree of Culture*. New York: Knopf.

Lock, Margaret. 1999. "Genetic Diversity and the Politics of Difference," *Chicago-Kent Law Review* 75: 83–111.

———. 2005. "Eclipse of the Gene and the Return of Divination," *Current Anthropology* 46 (Supplement): 47–70.

Löwy, Ilana. 1996. *Between Bench and Bedside: Science, Healing, and Interleukin-2 in a Cancer Ward*. Cambridge, MA: Harvard University Press.

Lyotard, Jean-François. 1984. *The Postmodern Condition: A Report on Knowledge*. Translated from the French by Geoff Bennington and Brian Massumi. Minneapolis: University of Minnesota Press.

Mace, Ruth, Clare J. Holden, and Stephen Shennan (eds.). 2005. *The Evolution of Cultural Diversity: A Phylogenetic Approach*. London: UCL Press.

Maddox, Brenda 2002. *Rosalind Franklin: The Dark Lady of DNA*. New York: Harper-Collins.

Magubane, Zine. 2003. "Simians, Savages, Skulls, and Sex: Science and Colonial Militarism in Nineteenth-Century South Africa," in Donald S. Moore, Jake Kosek, and Anand Pandin (eds.), *Race, Nature, and the Politics of Difference*. Durham, NC: Duke University Press.

Marcus, George E. 1998. *Ethnography Through Thick and Thin*. Princeton: Princeton University Press.

Marks, Jonathan. 2001. "'We're Going to Tell These People Who They Really Are': Science and Relatedness," in S. Franklin and S. McKinnon (eds.), *Relative Values: Reconfiguring Kinship Studies*. Durham, NC: Duke University Press.

———. 2002. *What It Means to Be 98% Chimpanzee: Apes, People, and Their Genes*. Berkeley: University of California Press.

———. 2005. "Your Body, My Property: The Problem of Colonial Genetics in a Postcolonial World," in Lynn Maskell and Peter Pelts (eds.), *Embedding Ethics*. Oxford: Berg.

References

Marsden, Wendy. 2004. "Analyzing Multiple Discourses in the Establishment of Genetic Databases," in Garðar Árnason, Salvör Nordal, and Vilhjálmur Árnason (eds.), *Blood and Data: Ethical, Legal and Social Aspects of Human Genetic Databases*. Reykjavík: University of Iceland Press and Centre for Ethics.

Martin, Emily. 1989. *The Woman in the Body: A Cultural Analysis of Reproduction*. Boston: Beacon Press.

——— 1990. "Toward an Anthropology of Immunology: The Body as Nation State," *Medical Anthropology Quarterly* 44: 410–426.

——— 1992. "The End of the Body?," *American Ethnologist* 19: 121–140.

Maskell, Lynn and Peter Pelts (eds.). 2005. *Embedding Ethics*. Oxford: Berg.

McCall Smith, Alexander. 2001. *Morality for Beautiful Girls*. New York: Anchor Books.

McCay, Bonnie M. 1995. "Common and Private Concerns," *Advances in Human Ecology* 4: 89–116.

McCloskey, D. N. 1993. "Some Consequences of a Conjective Economics," in M. Ferber and J. A. Nelson (eds.), *Beyond Economic Man: Feminist Theory and Economics*. Chicago and London: University of Chicago Press.

McEwen, Jean E. 1997. "DNA Data Banks," in Mark A. Rothstein (ed.), *Genetic Secrets: Protecting Privacy and Confidentiality in the Genetic Era*. New Haven: Yale University Press.

McGhee, Robert. 2005. *The Last Imaginary Place: A Human History of the Arctic World*. Ottawa: Canadian Museum of Civilization.

M'charek, Amade. 2005. *The Human Genome Diversity Project: An Ethnography of Scientific Practice*. Cambridge: Cambridge University Press.

Melville, Herman. 1962 [1851]. *Moby Dick*. New York: Macmillan Company.

Mills, Antonia. 2004. "Rebirth and Identity: Three Gitkasan Cases of Pierced-Ear Birthmarks," in Antonia Mills and Richard Slobotin (eds.), *Amerindian Rebirth: Reincarnation Belief among North American Indians and Inuit*. Toronto: University of Toronto Press.

Moore, A. D. 2000. "Owning Genetic Information and Gene Enhancement Techniques: Why Privacy and Property Rights May Undermine Social Control of the Human Genome," *Bioethics* 14(2): 97–119.

Moore, Donald S., Jake Kosek, and Anand Pandian (eds.). 2003. *Race, Nature, and the Politics of Difference*. Durham, NC: Duke University Press.

Moore, John M. 1994. "Putting Anthropology Back Together Again: The Ethnogenetic Critique of Cladistic Theory," *American Anthropologist* 96(4): 925–948.

Moretti, Franco. 2005. *Graphs, Maps, Trees: Abstract Models for a Literary Theory*. London: Verso.

Morgunblaðið. 1998–2000. Reykjavík.

References

2002. "Lýsing ÍE á þróun gagnasafnsins er rétt" (deCODE's Description of the Development of the Database is Correct). September 25. Reykjavík.

2003. "Ljóstraðupp um hliðarspor í Íslendingabók" (Disclosures on Illegitimacy in the Book of Icelanders). March 15. Reykjavík.

Motherland: A Genetic Journey. 2003. Takeaway Media Production for BBC TWO, directed by Archie Baron and produced by Tabitha Jackson.

Mumford, Lewis. 1962 [1934]. *Technics and Civilization.* San Diego: Harcourt Brace and Company.

Munzer, Stephen A. 1994. "An Uneasy Case against Property Rights in Body Parts," in Ellen Frankel Paul, Fred D. Miller, Jr., and Jeffrey Paul (eds.), *Property Rights.* Cambridge: Cambridge University Press.

Nationaler Ethikrat. 2004. *Biobanken für die Forschung Stellungnahme.* Berlin: Nationaler Ethikrat.

Nature. 1999. "Sweden Sets Ethical Standards for Use of Genetic 'Biobanks'." 400: 3.

2000. October, 407: 395.

2003. "A Vision for the Future of Genomics Research." 422: 835–847.

2004. "When Two Tribes Go To War," News Feature. 430(29 July): 500–502.

Nelkin, Dorothy and Lori Andrews. 1998. "Homo Economicus: Commercialization of Body Tissue in the Age of Biotechnology," *Hastings Report* 20(5): 30–39.

Nelkin, Dorothy and M. Susan Lindee. 1995. *The DNA Mystique: The Gene as a Cultural Icon.* New York: W. H. Freeman and Company.

Nelson, Julie A. 1995. "Feminism and Economics," *Journal of Economic Perspectives* 9: 131–148.

Neumann-Held, Eva M. and Christoph Rehmann-Sutter. 2006. "Introduction," in Eva M. Neumann-Held and Christoph Rehmann-Sutter (eds.), *Genes in Development: Re-reading the Molecular Paradigm.* Durham, NC: Duke University Press.

Nuttall, Mark. 2000. "Choosing Kin: Sharing and Subsistence in a Greenlandic Hunting Community," in Peter P. Schweitzer (ed.), *Dividends of Kinship: Meanings and the Uses of Social Relatedness.* London: Routledge.

O'Donnell, Christopher J. 2005. "Translating the Human Genome Project into Prevention of Myocardial Infarction and Stroke: Getting Close?" *Journal of the American Medical Association* 293: 2277–2279.

O'Neil, John D. and Patricia Leyland Kaufert. 1995. "Sex Determination and the Inuit Struggle for Birthrighting Rights in Northern Canada," in F. D. Ginsburg and R. Rapp (eds.), *Conceiving the New World Order.* Berkeley: University of California Press.

Õnnepalu, Tõnu. 2000. *Border State.* Evanston, IL: Northwestern University Press.

References

Orgel, Mary, Jacqueline Urla, and Alan Swedlund. 2005. "Surveying a Cultural 'Waistland': Some Biological Poetics and Politics of the Female Body," in Susan McKinnon and Sydel Silverman (eds.), *Complexities: Beyond Nature & Nurture*. Chicago: University of Chicago Press.

Orr, J. E. 1996. *Talking About Machines: An Ethnography of a Modern Job*. Ithaca: Cornell University Press.

Our Inheritance, Our Future: Realising the Potential of Genetics in the NHS. 2003. www.doh.gov.uk/genetics/whitepaper.htm.

Oyama, Susan. 2000 [1985]. *The Ontogeny of Information: Developmental Systems and Evolution*, 2nd edn. Durham, NC: Duke University Press.

Pálsson, Gísli. 2002. "The Life of Family Trees and the Book of Icelanders," *Medical Anthropology* 21(3–4): 337–367.

2004. "Decoding Relatedness and Disease: The Icelandic Biogenetic Project," in Jean-Paul Gaudillière and Hans-Jörg Rheinberger (eds), *From Molecular Genetics to Genomics: The Mapping Cultures of Twentieth-Century Genetics*. London: Routledge.

2005. *Travelling Passions: The Hidden Life of Vilhjalmur Stefansson*. Winnipeg and Hanover, NH: University of Manitoba Press and University Press of New England.

2006. "Appropriating Family Trees: Genealogies in the Age of Genetics," in Franz von Benda-Beckmann, Keebet Benda-Beckmann, and Melanie G. Wiber (eds.), *Changing Properties of Property*. New York: Berghahn Books.

2007. "The Rise and Fall of a Biobank: The Case of Iceland," in Herbert Gottweis and Alan Peterson (eds.), *Monitoring Bodies*. London: Routledge.

Pálsson, Gísli and Kristín E. Harðardóttir. 2002. "For Whom the Cell Tolls: Debates About Biomedicine," *Current Anthropology* 43(2): 271–301.

Pálsson, Gísli and Agnar Helgason. 2003. "Blonds, Lost and Found: Representations of Genes, Identity, and History," *Developing World Bioethics* 3(2): 159–169.

Pálsson, Gísli and Paul Rabinow. 1999. "Iceland: The Case of a National Human Genome Project," *Anthropology Today* 15(5): 14–18.

2005. "The Iceland Controversy: Reflections on the Trans-national Market of Civic Virtue," in Aihwa Ong and Stephen J. Collier (eds.), *Global Assemblages: Technology, Politics, and Ethics as Anthropological Problems*. Malden, MA: Blackwell Publishing.

Palsson, Bernhard and Snorri Thorgeirsson. 1999. "Decoding developments in Iceland," *Nature Biotechnology* 17 (May): 407.

Panter-Brick, C., R. H. Layton, and P. Rowley-Conwy (eds.). 2001. *Hunter-Gatherers: An Interdisciplinary Perspective*. Cambridge: Cambridge University Press.

References

Parfitt, Tudor. 2003. "Constructing Black Jews: Genetic Tests and the Lemba: The 'Black Jews' of South Africa," *Developing World Bioethics* 3(2): 112–118.

Paster, Gail Kern. 1997. "Nervous Tension: Networks of Blood and Spirit in the Early Modern Body," in David Hillman and Carla Mazzio (eds.), *The Body in Parts: Fantasies of Corporeality in Early Modern Europe*. New York: Routledge.

Patton, Sandra. 2000. *BirthMarks: Transnational Adoption in Contemporary America*. New York: New York University Press.

Pelts, Peter. 2005. "'Where There Aren't No Ten Commandments': Redefining Ethics During the *Darkness in El Dorado* Scandal," in Lynn Maskell and Peter Pelts (eds.), *Embedding Ethics*. Oxford: Berg.

Philo, Chris 2000. "'The Birth of the Clinic': An Unknown Work of Medical Geography," *Area* 32(1): 11–20.

Polanyi, Karl. 1944. *The Great Transformation*. Boston: The Beacon Press.

Polanyi, Michael. 1958. *Personal Knowledge: Towards a Post-critical Philosophy*. Chicago: University of Chicago Press.

Powers, Thomas. 2005. "The Indians' Own Story," *New York Review of Books*. April 7: 73–77.

Prainsack, Barbara. 2006. "Biobanks in Israel" (unpublished paper).

Prainsack, Barbara and Gil Siegal. 2006. "The Rise of Genetic Couplehood? A Comparative View of Premarital Genetic Testing," *BioSocieties* 1: 17–36.

Prainsack, Barbara and Tim D. Spector. 2006. "Twins: A Cloning Experience," *Social Science and Medicine* 63(10): 2739–2752.

Prosser, Jay. 2001. "Skin Memories," in Sarah Ahmed and Jackie Stacey (eds.), *Thinking Through the Skin*. London: Routledge.

Rabinow, Paul. 1996a. *Essays on the Anthropology of Reason*. Princeton: Princeton University Press.

1996b. *Making PCR: A Story of Biotechnology*. Chicago: University of Chicago Press.

1999. *French DNA: Trouble in Purgatory*. Chicago: University of Chicago Press.

Rader, Karen A. 1999. "Of Mice, Medicine, and Genetics: C. C. Little's Creation of the Inbred Laboratory Mouse, 1909–1918," *Studies in History and Philosophy of Biological and Biomedical Sciences* 30(3): 310–343.

Radin, M. J. 1996. *Contested Commodities*. Cambridge, MA.: Harvard University Press.

Reardon, Jennifer. 2005. *Race to the Finish: Identity and Governance in an Age of Genomics*. Princeton: Princeton University Press.

Renfrew, Colin. 1992. "Archaeology, Genetics, and Linguistic Diversity," *Man (Journal of the Royal Anthropological Institute)*, 27(3): 445–478.

Restrepo, Eduardo and Arturo Escobar. 2005. "'Other Anthropologies and Anthropology Otherwise': Steps to a World Anthropologies Framework," *Critique of Anthropology* 25(2): 99–129.

Rheinberger, Hans-Jörg. 1995. "Beyond Nature and Culture: A Note on Medicine in the Age of Molecular Biology," *Science in Context* 8(1): 249–263.

1997. *Towards a History of Epistemic Things: Synthesizing Proteins in the Test Tube.* Stanford: Stanford University Press.

2000. "Gene Concepts," in P. Beurton, R. Falk, and H.-J. Rheinberger (eds.), *The Concept of the Gene in Development and Evolution.* Cambridge: Cambridge University Press.

Risch, N. 2000. "Searching for Genetic Determinants in the New Millennium," *Nature* 405: 847–856.

Risch, N., E. Burchard, E. Ziv, and H. Tang. 2002. "Categorization of Humans in Biomedical Research: Genes, Race and Disease," *Genome Biology* 3(7): 1–12.

Rival, Laura. 1998. "Trees, from Symbols of Life and Regeneration to Political Artifacts," in L. Rival (ed.), *The Social Life of Trees: Anthropological Perspectives on Tree Symbolism.* Oxford: Berg.

Roberts, Josh P. 2005. "Genetic Cartography," *The Scientist*, January 31: 18–19.

Roberts, L. 1991. "A Genetic Survey of Vanishing Peoples," *Science* 252: 1614–1617.

Rose, Carole M. 1994. *Property and Persuasion: Essays on the History, Theory, and Rhetoric of Ownership.* Boulder: Westview Press.

2004. "Economic Claims and the Challenges of New Property," in Katherine Verdery and Caroline Humphrey (eds.), *Property in Question: Value Transformation in the Global Economy.* Oxford: Berg.

Rose, Hilary. 2003. "The Commodification of Virtual Reality: The Icelandic Health Sector Database," in A. Goodman, D. Heath, and S. Lindee (eds.), *Genetic Nature/Culture.* Los Angeles: University of California Press.

Rose, Nikolas and Carlos Novas. 2005. "Biological Citizenship," in Aihwa Ong and Stephen J. Collier (eds.), *Global Assemblages: Technology, Politics, and Ethics as Anthropological Problems.* Malden, MA: Blackwell Publishing.

Rosenberg, Alexander. 1998. "The Human Genome Project: Research Tactics and Economic Strategies," in David L. Hull and Michael Ruse (eds.), *The Philosophy of Biology.* Oxford: Oxford University Press.

Rosenberg, N. A., S. Mahajan, S. Ramachandran, C. Zhao, J. K. Pritchard, and M. W. Feldman. 2005. "Clines, Clusters, and the Effect of Study Design on the Inference of Human Population Structure," *PLoS Genetics* 1(6): 660–671. Published online, December.

Rosenberg, N. A., J. K. Pritchard, J. L. Weber, H. M. Cann, K. K. Kidd, L. A. Zhivotovsky, and M. W. Feldman. 2002. "Genetic Structure of Human Populations," *Science* 298: 2381–2385.

Rothenberg, David. 1993. *Hand's End: Technology and the Limits of Nature.* Berkeley: University of California Press.

References

Sahlins, Marshall. 1977. *The Uses and Abuses of Biology: An Anthropological Critique of Sociobiology*. Ann Arbor: The University of Michigan Press.

Said, Edward. 1978. *Orientalism*. New York: Vintage Books.

Santos, Ricardo Ventura and Marcos Chor Maio. 2004. "Race, Genomics, Identities and Politics in Contemporary Brazil," *Critique of Anthropology* 24(4): 347–378.

Sarkar, Sahotra. 2006. "From Genes as Determinants to DNA as Resource: Historical Notes on Development and Genetics," in Eva M. Neumann-Held and Christoph Rehmann-Sutter (eds.), *Genes in Development: Re-reading the Molecular Paradigm*. Durham, NC: Duke University Press.

Scheper-Hughes, Nancy. 2000. "The Global Traffic in Human Organs," *Current Anthropology* 41(2): 191–224.

Schildkrout, Enid. 2004. "Inscribing the Body," *Annual Review of Anthropology* 33: 319–344.

Schindler, Lydia Woods. 1988. *Understanding the Immune System*. Washington, DC: US Department of Health and Human Services.

Schneider, David M. 1980 [1968]. *American Kinship*. Chicago: University of Chicago Press.

Schwartz, Maureen Trudelle. 2001. "Allusions to Ancestral Impropriety: Understandings of Arthritis and Rheumatism in the Contemporary Navajo World," *American Ethnologist* 28(3): 650–678.

Science. 1999. "Sweden Takes Steps to Protect Tissue Banks," 286: 894.

Serre, David and Svante Pääbo. 2004. "Evidence for Gradients of Human Genetic Diversity Within and Among Continents," *Genome Research* 14: 1679–1685.

Sharp, Lesley A. 2000. "The Commodification of the Body and its Parts," *Annual Review of Anthropology* 29: 287–328.

Shaw, Alison. 2003. "Interpreting Images: Diagnostic Skill in the Genetics Clinic," *Journal of the Royal Anthropological Institute (incorporating Man)* 9(1): 39–55.

Shohat, Mordechai. 2000. "The Future of Genetics: Where Are We Going in the Next Forty Years?", *Israel Medical Association Journal* 2: 690–691.

Sholokhov, Mikhail. 1975[1924]. "The Birth-Mark," in Mikhail Sholokhov *Stories*. Moscow: Progress Publishers.

Shreeve, James. 2004. *The Genome War: How Craig Venter Tried to Capture the Code of Life*. New York: Alfred A. Knopf.

Sigurðardóttir, Katrín. 1998. "Stað/setning," in Jón Proppé (ed.), *Flögð og fögur skinn*. Reykjavík: Art.is.

Sigurðardóttir, S., A. Helgasona, J. R. Gulcher, K. Stefánsson, and P. Donnelly. 2000. "The Mutation Rate in the Human mtDNA Control Region," *American Journal of Human Genetics* 66: 1599–1609.

Simpson, Bob. 2000. "Imagined Genetic Communities: Ethnicity and Essentialism in the Twenty-First Century," *Anthropology Today* 16(3): 3–6.

Solway, J. S and R. B. Lee. 1990. "Foragers, Genuine or Spurious? Situating the Kalahari San in History," *Current Anthropology*, 31(2): 109–146.

Soodyall, H. and T. Jenkins. 1992. "Mitochondrial DNA Polymorphisms in Khoisan Populations From Southern Africa," *Annals of Human Genetics* 56: 315–324.

Specter, Michael. 1999. "Decoding Iceland," *The New Yorker*. February 18.

Stacey, Jackie. 1997. *Teratologies: A Cultural Study of Cancer*. London: Routledge.

Starr, D. 1998. *Blood: An Epic History of Medicine and Commerce*. London: Little, Brown and Co.

Stefansson, Hreinn *et al*. 2005. "A Common Inversion under Selection in Europeans," *Nature Genetics* 37(2): 129–137.

Stefánsson, Stefán E. *et al*. 2003. "Genomewide Scan for Hand Osteoarthritis: A Novel Mutation in Matrilin-3," *American Journal of Human Genetics* 72(6): 1448–1459.

Stevenson, Ian. 1997. *Where Reincarnation and Biology Intersect*. Westport, CT: Praeger.

Stix, Gary. 2004. "Geographer of the Male Genome," *Scientific American*. December: 19–20.

Stoler, Ann Laura. 2002. *Carnal Knowledge and Imperial Power: Race and the Intimate in Colonial Rule*. Berkeley: University of California Press.

Stone, Linda and Paul F. Lurquin. 2005. *A Genetic and Cultural Odyssey: The Life and Work of L. Luca Cavalli-Sforza*. New York: Columbia University Press.

Strachan, Tom and Andrew P. Read. 1999. *Molecular Genetics*, 2nd edn. Oxford: BIOS Scientific Publishers.

Strathern, Marilyn. 1992. *After Nature: English Kinship in the Late Twentieth Century*. Cambridge: Cambridge University Press.

1998. "Divisions of Interest and the Languages of Ownership," in C. Hann (ed.), *Property Relations: Renewing the Anthropological Tradition*. Cambridge: Cambridge University Press.

1999. *Property, Substance and Effect: Anthropological Essays on Persons and Things*. London: The Athlone Press.

2004. "The Whole Person and its Artifacts," *Annual Reviews in Anthropology* 33: 1–19.

Sunder Rajan, Kaushik. 2005. "Subjects of Speculation: Emergent Life Sciences and Market Logics in the United States and India," *American Anthropologist* 107(1): 19–30.

Supreme Court of Iceland. 2000. deCODE genetics and Friðrik Skúlason v. Þorsteinn Jónsson and Genealogia Islandorum, no. 292. www.haestirettur.is/domar?nr=877&leit=t. Accessed November 16, 2005.

References

2003. Ragnhildur Guðmundsdóttir *v.* the Icelandic State, no. 151. www.haestirettur. is/domar?nr=2566. Accessed November 16, 2005.

Sykes, Bryan. 2001. *The Seven Daughters of Eve.* London: Transworld Publishers.

Tammpuu, Piia. 2004. "Constructing Public Images of New Genetics and Gene Technology: The Media Discourse on the Estonian Human Genome Project," *TRAMES* 8: 192–216.

Tate, Sarah K. and David B. Goldstein. 2004. "Will Tomorrow's Medicines Work for Everyone?," *Nature Genetics Supplement* 36(11): S34–S42.

Taussig, Karen-Sue. 2005. "The Molecular Revolution in Medicine: Promise, Reality, and Social Organization," in Susan McKinnon and Sydel Silverman (eds.), *Complexities: Beyond Nature & Nurture.* Chicago: University of Chicago Press.

Templeton, Alan R. 1999. "Human Races: A Genetic and Evolutionary Perspective," *American Anthropologist* 100(3): 632–650.

2003. "Human Race in the Context of Recent Human Evolution: A Molecular Genetic Perspective," in S. Lindee, D. Heath, and A. Goodman (eds.), *Genetic Nature/Culture.* Los Angeles: University of California Press.

Thacker, Eugene. 2005. *The Global Genome: Biotechnology, Politics, and Culture.* Cambridge, MA: MIT Press.

Thomas, Nicholas. 1991. *Entangled Objects: Exchange, Material Culture, and Colonialism in the Pacific.* Cambridge, MA: Harvard University Press.

Thorgeirsdóttir, Sigríður. 2004. "Genes of a Nation: The Promotion of Iceland's Genetic Information," *TRAMES* 8(1/2): 178–191.

Thorsteinsdottir, Halla, Uyen Quach, Douglas K. Martin, Abdallah S. Daar, and Peter A. Singer. 2004. "Introduction: Promoting Global Health through Biotechnology," *Nature Biotechnology* 22 Supplement: DC3–DC7.

Tierney, Thomas F. 1999. "The Preservation and Ownership of the Body," in Gail Weiss and Honi Fern Haber (eds.), *Perspectives on Embodiment: The Intersections of Nature and Culture.* New York: Routledge.

Titmuss, R. M. 1997 [1970]. *The Gift Relationship: From Human Blood to Social Policy.* London: LSE Books.

Treichler, Paula. 1987. "AIDS, Homophobia, and Biomedical Discourse: An Epidemic of Signification," *Cultural Studies* 1(3): 262–305.

Tsing, Anna Lowenhaupt. 2005. *Friction: An Ethnography of Global Connection.* Princeton: Princeton University Press.

Turnbull, David. 2004. "Genetic Mapping: Approaches to the Spatial Topography of Genetics," in H.-J. Rheinberger and J.-P. Gaudillière (eds.), *Classical Genetic Research and its Legacy: The Mapping Cultures of Twentieth Century Genetics.* London: Routledge.

References

Turner, Trudy. 2005. *Biological Anthropology and Ethics: From Repatriation to Genetic Identity.* Albany, NY: State University of New York Press.

Turner, Victor W. 1967. *The Forest of Symbols: Aspects of Ndembu Ritual.* Ithaca: Cornell University Press.

Tutton, Richard. 2004a. "'They Want to Know Where They Came From': Population Genetics and Family Genealogy," *New Genetics and Society* 23(1): 105–120.

2004b. "Person, Property and Gift: Exploring Languages of Tissue Donation to Biomedical Research," in R. Tutton and O. Corrigan (eds.), *Genetic Databases: Socio-Ethical Issues in the Collection and Use of DNA.* London: Routledge.

Tutton, Richard and Oonagh Corrigan (eds.). 2004. *Genetic Databases: Socio-Ethical Issues in the Collection and Use of DNA.* London: Routledge.

Twain, Mark. 1997 [1894]. *Pudd'nhead Wilson.* New York: Simon & Schuster.

US GenBank. 2005. www.ncbi.nlm.nih.gov/Genbank/index.html.

Varela, Francisco J. 1999. *Ethical Know-How: Action, Wisdom, and Cognition.* Stanford: Stanford University Press.

Veblen, Thorstein. 1898. "The Beginning of Ownership," *American Journal of Sociology* 4: 252–365.

von Benda-Beckmann, Franz, Keebet von Benda-Beckmann, and Melanie G. Wiber (eds.). 2006. "The Properties of Property," in Franz von Benda-Beckmann, Keebet von Benda-Beckmann, and Melanie G. Wiber (eds.), *Changing Properties of Property.* New York: Berghahn Books.

Wade, Peter. 2002. *Race, Nature and Culture: An Anthropological Perspective.* London: Pluto Press.

Wagner, Roy. 1977. "Scientific and Indigenous Papuan Conceptualizations of the Innate: A Semiotic Critique of the Ecological Perspective," in T. P. Bayliss-Smith and R. G. Fechem (eds.), *Subsistence and Survival: Rural Ecology in the Pacific.* London: Academic Press.

Wahrman, Miryam Z. 2002. *Brave New Judaism: When Science and Scripture Collide.* Hanover, MA: Brandeis University Press.

Wald, Priscilla. 1992. "Future Perfect: Grammar, Genes and Geography," *New Literary History* 31: 681–708.

Waldby, Catherine. 2002. "Biomedicine, Tissue Transfer and Intercorporeality," *Feminist Theory* 3(3): 239–254.

Waldby, Catherine and Robert Mitchell. 2006. *Tissue Economies: Blood, Organs, and Cell Lines in Late Capitalism.* Durham, NC: Duke University Press.

Washburn, S. L. and C. S. Lancaster. 1968. "The Evolution of Hunting," in R. B. Lee and I. deVore (eds.) *Man the Hunter: The First Intensive Survey of a Single, Crucial Stage of Human Development – Man's Once Universal Hunting Way of Life.* Chicago: Aldine Publishing.

References

Watson, James D. 2004. *DNA: The Secret of Life.* New York: Alfred A. Knopf.

Weiss, Brad. 1996. *The Making and Unmaking of the Haya Lived World: Consumption, Commoditization, and Everyday Practice.* Durham, NC: Duke University Press.

Weiss, Gail. 1999. *Body Images: Embodiment as Intercorporeality.* London: Routledge.

Weiss, Kenneth M. 1998. "Coming to Terms with Human Variation," *Annual Review of Anthropology* 27: 273–300.

Weldon, Sue. 2004. "'Public Consent' or 'Scientific Citizenship'?," in Richard Tutton and Oonagh Corrigan (eds.), *Genetic Databases: Socio-Ethical Issues in the Collection and Use of DNA.* London: Routledge.

Weston, K. 2001. "Kinship, Controversy, and the Sharing of Substance: The Race/Class Politics of Blood Transfusion," in S. Franklin and S. McKinnon (eds.), *Relative Values: Reconfiguring Kinship Studies.* Durham, NC: Duke University Press.

Wikler, D. 1999. "Can We Learn From Eugenics?," in A. K. Thompson and R. F. Chadwick (eds.), *Genetic Information: Acquisition, Access, and Control.* New York: Kluwer Academic/Plenum Publishers.

Wilford, J. N. 2000. *The Mapmakers.* Revised edition. New York: Vintage Books.

Williams, Vanessa. 2000. http://dailynews.yahoo.com/h/nm/20001122/sc/genes_tonga_dc_1.html.

Winickoff, David E. 2006. "Genome and Nation: Iceland's Health Sector Database and its Legacy," *Innovations: Technology, Governance, Globalization* 1(2): 80–105.

Woese, Carl R. 2000. "Interpreting the Universal Phylogenetic Tree," *Proceedings of the National Academy of Sciences of the United States of America* 97(15): 8392–8396.

Wright, Sewall. 1969. *Evolution and the Genetics of Populations, Vol. II: The Theory of Gene Frequencies.* Chicago: University of Chicago Press.

Zelizer, Viviana A. 1992. "Human Values and the Market," in M. Granovetter and R. Swedberg (eds.), *The Sociology of Economic Life.* Boulder: Westview Press.

Zola, Irving Kenneth. 1972. "Medicine as an Institution of Social Control," *Sociological Review* 20: 487–504.

Index

Index

Index

Index

Index

Index

Index

Index